PAPYRUS

PAPYRUS

The Plant that Changed the World—
From Ancient Egypt to Today's Water Wars

JOHN GAUDET

PEGASUS BOOKS
NEW YORK LONDON

PAPYRUS

Pegasus Books LLC
80 Broad Street, 5th Floor
New York, NY 10004

First Pegasus Books cloth edition June 2014

Interior design by Maria Fernandez

Frontispiece: *Stone Age marsh men hunting in an ancient papyrus swamp in the Nile Valley, 5000 B.C.*

Library of Congress Cataloging-in-Publication Data is available.

ISBN: 978-1-60598-566-4

10 9 8 7 6 5 4 3 2 1

Printed in the United States of America
Distributed by W. W. Norton & Company

To the millions of young people who will lead the way to the new world,
a place where I hope swamps and marshes will flourish
and peace and harmony will prevail.

CONTENTS

MAPS

PAPYRUS

Prologue

Ancient Egypt and Papyrus, the Eternal Marriage

Where the Eastern waves strike the shore . . . or where the seven-mouthed Nile colors the waters, . . . whatever the will of the heavens brings, ready now for anything . . .

—Catullus, 61–54 B.C.

A resource treasured by the kings of Egypt, a prince among plants, a giant among sedges, and a gift of the Gods, the papyrus plant has been with us since the dawn of civilization. It allowed Egypt to be papermaker to the world for thousands of years and in doing so ruled the world in the same fashion that King Cotton ruled the South, the demand being met exclusively by the papyrus swamps of Egypt where it grew at a phenomenal rate.

Where did papyrus come from? To an early Egyptian this question was so obvious he need not say a word; he could simply point to a relief or a statue of Hapi, the god of the Nile inundation. This shows a seated, blue-colored, chubby man with pendulous breasts, a Pharaoh's fake beard, and a belly hanging over his girdle. Bizarre, yes, but in a way not entirely foreign to some of us who are entranced by that most impressive Hindu god, Krishna, who was blue-skinned, said to be the maximum color in nature as in blue skies, oceans, lakes, and rivers, thus an appropriate color for special people.

Hapi, the god of the inundation (after Budge).

What I really find striking about him is his crown, which looks like a large clump of papyrus growing from his head.

The popular notion was that the plant was a sacred gift, much like the Tree of Knowledge in the Garden of Eden. In reality, papyrus came to us, as did many flowering plants, after a long stage of evolution from primeval Jurassic ancestors. It had already been established in the Nile Valley and elsewhere in Africa for thousands of years before the early settlers arrived. The important thing was that these settlers (see frontispiece) recognized papyrus as a good thing and fell in love the minute they saw it. They had come to the Valley because of the river, and they stayed on because they wanted no more to do with the Sahelian droughts of 6000–5000 B.C.

In the Nile River Valley they found a permanent sustainable existence, a part of which was the swampy terrain, a water world made up of quiet pockets of water and patches of waterlogged soil scattered throughout Egypt. And there, growing in the flooded areas, was Egypt's new partner, papyrus, a viable hunting preserve, a source of reed for boats, housing, rope, and crafts, and above all an eye-catching part of the landscape.

After having evolved over millions of years, papyrus could be counted on to produce a swamp community that was in equilibrium with itself and a species that was perhaps more extensive, more useful, more efficient, and more luxuriant than anything seen today, because at that time the air, soil, and water quality were almost untouched, unspoiled. Thousands of years in the future, the ancient Egyptian would disappear and the eternal marriage would be dissolved against all reason, and afterwards, like some brave widow, papyrus would carry on, serving different masters through the years—Persians, Macedonians, Greeks, Romans, and finally Arabs, all of whom would use her in turn. Yet despite everything, she stayed green, lush, fragrant, and self-contained until the very end.

As Herodotus once famously noted, "Egypt is a gift of the Nile," and so also were the swamps and marshes that formed in the backwaters of the early river, swamps which served as a natural larder with fish thriving in swamp pools year round and birdlife for the taking. These swamps developed in the floodplains (or "upper Nile"), then as soon as the river deposits changed from sand to silt they spread downstream into the delta (or "lower Nile").

That change in the delta coincided with the migration of people from the Sinai who, like those of the Sahara, were also escaping droughts.

The water of the main river and floodplain averaged about 2 miles in width and was hundreds of miles in length (570 miles from Thebes to the sea) and provided a mighty internal highway to allow the development of Egyptian civilization. This could not have been possible, according to Fekri Hassan, Petrie Professor of Archaeology at the University College, London, without riverine navigation, which requires a boat. Yet forest trees and wood being in short supply, and carpentry skills lacking, they turned to papyrus. As Steve Vinson, an expert on Egyptian boats, pointed out: "It is difficult to believe that there was ever a time when humans failed to take advantage of the ubiquitous papyrus to build rafts or floats." Thus evolved, in those early days from 6000 B.C. onward, the reed boat, which must have been a godsend to a hunter-fisher-gatherer.

The Egyptian wasn't alone in this discovery. In those days, throughout several river deltas in the arid world, and the lake cultures in treeless high altitudes, reeds were used to build boats, houses, and everything that made life easier while the early families established themselves in these regions.

With time it became difficult to give up life on the Nile because here they found whatever they needed, and they grew accustomed to the lack of rain and the constant presence of water in the river. They also liked the twelve hours of bright sunshine every day and the regularity of the annual flood.

And soon it was 3100 B.C.—the point, we are told, when civilized history begins. Now improvements in agriculture and irrigation follow, wooden boats under sail are seen on the Nile, bountiful harvests are common, papyrus paper shows up, kings and pharaohs ascend thrones in succession, and immortality is now felt to be a certainty and yours for the asking. If you hankered after enduring fame, civilization was just the thing, and it had arrived to stay. Is it any wonder that the Egyptians looked for ways to live securely and forever in this paradise?

Their largest concern was inundation. To the believer, Pharaoh guaranteed it. After all, wasn't he a god on earth? The annual flood was as certain as the daily miracle of sunrise that followed his morning invocation. To the more skeptical residents of the valley, heartaches, headaches, and sweaty palms developed each year at springtime when they wondered what was to prevent the inundation from being a bit too much or a bit too little.

If it was too low, a drought developed that hammered them for the rest of the year. If it came in excess, the flooding would wash out dikes, retaining walls, berms, mud-brick houses, and anything not nailed down. Years of back-breaking work would disappear in moments.

"Please, Hapi, just 15 cubits (25ft), that's all we need" became a most important plea as the years went by, and in that way the overweight, blue-colored, effeminate, easy to laugh at, solo god came into his own.

The Pyramid Texts suggested that his wife, Wadjet, had given birth in the delta to the first papyrus plants and presumably Hapi was the father. This was an appropriate beginning because with time the major papyrus swamps came to be synonymous with the delta. One of several deities associated with that part of Egypt, Wadjet's name was written using the heraldic plant, which became the hieroglyph for Lower Egypt (so named because it was downstream).

Hapi had a second form that represented southern or Upper Egypt (upstream) and for that reason he had a second wife. The two forms of Hapi commonly used on tomb paintings or on monuments proclaimed the fact that the pharaoh of the moment controlled both parts of the country.

Wadjet means "the papyrus-colored (or green) one," which was also the general name for the cobra, appropriate for a pre-dynastic snake goddess, though the reference to green is not clear. The only green snake in Egypt would be the asp, a lime-green snake of Cleopatra fame but a snake that was imported; the native cobra is mottled gray-brown or black.

Thus, Hapi was an ancient and powerful deity who drew even more power through wives like Wadjet who in turn was connected to the forces of growth. It was later revealed that Hapi was a son of Horus and therefore a grandson of Osiris. But such lofty connections seem not to have helped much, as he had no temple and was set apart from the other gods. Though worshipped separately, he remained one of the most powerful because he controlled the lifeblood of the country. And you can see him on almost any night in the constellation Aquarius, visible in autumn in the Northern Hemisphere and during spring in the Southern Hemisphere. When the sun passes through Aquarius, or Hapi, or "Waterman," the wet season begins. He is thus the harbinger of floods and spring rains. In ancient Egypt his constellation was pictured as himself pouring water from two jugs, symbolizing the start of the inundation. In the zodiac of the famous ceiling relief in Dendera, he is shown in two forms: one with a standard crown, and the other with a dense mass of papyrus, almost a small swamp, on his head.

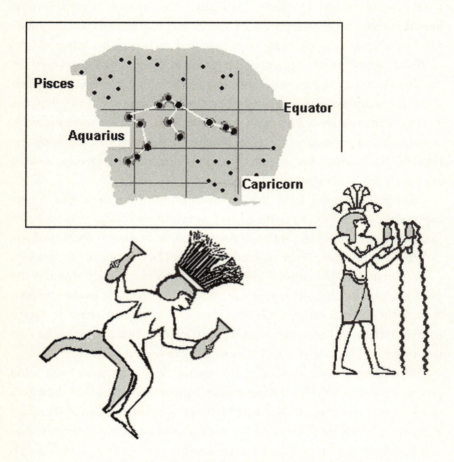

Several forms of Hapi as Aquarius in the zodiac at Dendera.

True to the concept of immortality, Hapi popped up in the international news a few years back when a major exhibit of sunken Egyptian treasure went on the road. The exhibit contained spectacular artifacts unearthed by Franck Goddio, the undersea archaeologist and founder of the Institut Européen d'Archéologie Sous-Marine (IEASM), taken from the waters of Alexandria and other ancient city ports. The exhibit drew a crowd of 450,000 in Berlin.

The show went on to a bigger and better reception at the Grand Palais in Paris and was the subject of several feature stories in the leading French newspapers and *Paris Match*. Next stop was Bonn for more attention and a feature in *Der Spiegel*, following which it closed in January 2008, when the pieces were scheduled to be brought back to Egypt to make up a permanent exhibit in Alexandria.

One of the leading items of this collection is a 16.5ft statue of Hapi, the largest free-standing sculpture of an Egyptian god in existence, now the object of attention by millions of people; and on his head, still proclaiming to everyone his magnificent gift to the world, are three stems of papyrus.

Part I

Ancient Heritage

1

First Encounter

Any visitor to Uganda landing at Entebbe airport on the northern shore of Lake Victoria will see papyrus swamps stretching out on both sides of the runway as their plane bounces, shimmies, and roars along the tarmac. It is hard to miss; after all, it is an extraordinary plant. Among the sedge plant family, to which papyrus belongs, we are talking about a giant, and in a quiet tropical swamp on the Equator, its stems easily achieve a height of 15ft or more.

At Entebbe the tall bright-green stems wave in the rush of air from any passing jet, but even more obvious is the fluttering of the bushy umbels, the feathery plume at the top of each stem which produces small papery seeds.

My first trip into a papyrus swamp took place in Uganda in 1971. In that country there is never a problem finding a swamp, since freshwater habitats, lakes, ponds, swamps, and rivers make up almost a quarter of Uganda. Everywhere you look, there is some sort of wet terrain. The closest swamp in the vicinity of Makerere University was a large one on the southern edge of Kampala city that borders an area called Nakivubu, on the shores of Lake Victoria. This swamp lies between the city and the lake and is reached by a narrow dirt road that passes through one of the largest slums in this part of Africa.

"What's that smell?" I remember asking.

"Ah, you've noticed," said the driver, smiling.

"It's the sewage from the town," I was told by Keith Thompson, a former expatriate lecturer in plant ecology. A reserved Brit and a fair-skinned pipe smoker, he is still very keen on wetland ecology. Eventually he settled in Waikato, New Zealand, where wetlands also abound, and where he is now much involved with the National Wetland Trust.

In a papyrus swamp in Africa (Denny, 1985).

He pointed to a large open canal that ran alongside one part of the road and carried the effluent from the main sewage works. With us in the vehicle was Anthony Katende, a taxonomist from the herbarium at Makerere University who, along with Keith and the driver, was ready to help introduce me to the ecosystem that was to become the main focus of my life for the next eight years.

"When the rainy season begins," I was told, "the canal overflows and this whole area is flooded. If you come here a few weeks from now it will be impossible to drive in."

The houses became shabbier and smaller, then disappeared as the road petered out and we came to a halt in front of a green wall. Papyrus at last.

Once out of the vehicle, we unloaded collecting bags, machetes, cameras, notebooks, binoculars, and sampling bottles to collect swamp water. The air was so humid that every surface was damp. The close sulfurous air, black cloying organic mud, and clouds of mosquitoes and lake flies hinted at much discomfort to come. My hat, long-sleeved shirt, heavy trousers, and canvas-topped waist-high waders ending in heavy boots set me apart from the other three, who were all dressed in short-sleeved light clothing and canvas shoes. My wardrobe was designed to protect me from the snakes and waterborne diseases that I had been warned about. I had become especially concerned about contracting bilharzia, which I had been told caused blood in the urine. This was a condition I felt I could do without.

Was I right to be so concerned, I wondered, as I slathered insect repellent on the few exposed parts of my body. The other three simply stared at me in a bemused fashion as I prepared to meet my fate. They waited until I nodded a sign that I was finally ready; not much was said from then on as we marched forward into the swamp.

Not long after entering the swamp I had the feeling of being boiled alive. The early afternoon African sun reaches down and is totally absorbed by dark clothing and canvas, such as the waders were made of. The whole lower part of my body heated up; sweat drenched my thighs and poured down my legs into the boots, where it squelched between my toes. Another problem was that I could hardly see; my sunglasses had fogged over as I staggered forward, plopping one booted foot after another into the morass and stumbling from one papyrus rhizome to another. Rhizomes are stems that grow out on top of the peat and form the matrix that allows papyrus to thrive in the swamp. My future as an expert in this ecosystem seemed doomed from the start, but what else could I do? Tony, who was by then quite famous for his knowledge of the local flora, at that point decided to teach me how to walk in the swamp.

First he made me sit down on a clump of papyrus that had been cut by Keith and piled up by the driver. Then he helped me climb out of the waders, which we left in a heap to be picked up on our way back. In their place I put on my sneakers, which I had carried with the laces tied around my neck. I rolled up my trouser legs and shirtsleeves, opened my shirt-front, took off my hat and glasses, and at once felt relieved and much cooler as we moved forward into this new green world.

"Step from rhizome to rhizome," Tony explained, showing me how to avoid the water in between. I soon understood that the matrix of horizontal stems served as a thick platform that grew out from the shore. From this matrix the upright tall green stems grew up, each topped by a feathery umbel. The matrix became a thick, free-floating raft as it grew out over deeper water. To traverse it we simply hopped from rhizome to rhizome, remaining dry-shoed in the process, yet looking back we could see the whole swamp undulate as we went along.

The upright green stems (also called culms) parted easily, and before long there was no need to hack at or cut the stems; we just pushed them aside and walked between them. As we went further into the swamp, I noticed something else: the mosquitoes and lake flies vanished, though ants and crawling insects were still present on the tussocks and rhizomes. It seems the mosquitoes breed mostly at the land edge, in cattle tracks and muddy places where the soil is disturbed by man. In the swamp, though water permeates the whole system, there are so many water-dwelling predators that mosquito larvae are eaten immediately. Lake flies avoid the swamps because they prefer open water habitats where they can lay their eggs.

In addition to relief from insects, the odor of the sewage was replaced by fragrant air. I learned later that papyrus has a natural compound in the rhizome, something akin to incense—Pliny referred to it as "the aromatic weed." The rhizome is especially potent in this way; in Ethiopia today, papyrus rhizomes are dried, cut into fragments, and incorporated into the incense mixture used in Orthodox Church services. Thus in a papyrus swamp there is always a slight pleasant essence in the air.

And it was quiet. Other than the sounds we made stepping from rhizome to rhizome, it was very quiet. The absence of buzzing and chirping insects, few if any frogs, and the restriction of wading birds and ducks to the edges, all contributed to an unusually calm, noise-less ecosystem. It was different from anything I had yet experienced—except perhaps a walk inside a large church during the middle of the week.

ᔕ

Swamps, remote unexplored regions, by tradition are the domain of deformed, mutilated, scary monsters and legendary creatures that rise from misty depths. Farmers avoid swamps, as their farm machinery and cows are apt to sink in the morass; hunters are careful to sit in blinds at their edges while trained retriever dogs leap into water full of poisonous snakes and snapping, mean, long-toothed demons to fetch their shoot; and humans young and old are warned of the dangers lying in wait for anyone venturing inside.

So it happens that a wall of fear and superstition is built up around swamps. In the early days in the USA, with the exception of the Cajun bayou dwellers, people stayed away. Swamps and wetlands of all sorts were protected by these myths and warnings, or they used to be. Now, in their search for exotic birdlife, birdwatchers flock to such places, farmers pressed for arable land clear and drain them to raise food or run cattle on them, airboats bring trappers and hunters right up to and on top of the elusive game, developers build houses and towns on them, and, once assimilated into something called "tropical river basin development," swamps disappear.

Among the swamps of Africa, papyrus swamps are a distinctive type, a wetland that is easy to spot from air, land, or water. This is because wherever it grows, papyrus (*Cyperus papyrus*) develops into a monoculture with a light green canopy that looks like a fluffy blanket from above. Among other things, the papyrus swamps in the middle of Africa are now considered to be among the most productive plant communities on earth because papyrus has one of the highest growth rates in the world.[1]

Papyrus is thus unique. It is also an excellent indicator species: wherever it grows, there is a 99% chance that you will find permanent swamps and standing water in the vicinity. Migrant wading birds depend on freshwater animals that live in these swamps for food, and these birds, riding the thermals on their way south to Africa for the winter, soaring along the migration flyways at 9–12,000ft in the air, can spot papyrus literally a mile away, papyrus which yields a bounty beneath.

Yet from the 1970s on it became all too apparent that the geographic isolation of papyrus swamps, a factor that protected them in earlier times, was no longer working. All over Africa, in deltas, valleys, and along interior waterways and lake edges, papyrus is disappearing.

The question is asked: Would we miss it?

In order to answer that question it would be interesting to know what the world would have done without it. What would have happened if it had never existed at all? Specifically, what would have happened in Egypt if papyrus never was?

If there was ever a place where the effect of its absence would be felt, it would be in Egypt because it was there, in ancient times, that papyrus was so intimately entwined with the development of the people and their civilization. Its absence from the ancient Nile Valley would be inconceivable.

Consider the fact that papyrus affected every aspect of the typical ancient Egyptian's life. The earliest boats, houses, and temples were made from the stems of papyrus; papyrus rope was used to move monuments, build pyramids, and craft items around the house. The fish they ate were nursed by the swamps; the wild birds they captured wintered in the swamps. If all else failed, they could use papyrus as fuel to cook with, and if they were hungry they could eat it, and when they died they went by papyrus boat to their heaven: the greatest papyrus swamp of all, the Field of Reeds. To get there they used a map and set of directions: a scroll containing the *Book of the Dead*—made of papyrus.

More deeply embedded in their culture, especially in their art and architecture, was the concept of the temple as a papyrus swamp. The 80-foot-tall columns of Karnak based on papyrus stems or bundles of stems, and a temple plan that mimicked the reed shrines of old, revealed how close papyrus was to their souls. Papyrus motifs adorned their paintings, temples, and tombs; it graced the designs of their amulets and mirrors and jewelry; and most outstanding of all, after 3000 B.C. papyrus paper and papyrus rope became major export items, with papyrus paper providing significant export earnings for thousands of years after that.

It is impossible to know how the absence of papyrus would have affected their lives, but we can guess.

2

Nature's Bounty

On the wall of a tomb in Egypt, I saw a painting which I remember thinking at the time was unusual. I had seen others similar to it in the British Museum, the Metropolitan Museum in New York, and in books on Egyptian art, but none were quite like this. The painting shows an Egyptian man drawn twice as large as the papyrus skiff in which he is standing. The hunter is tall, confident, and balanced in a way that says he knows exactly what he is doing. There are others with him: his wife, children, and perhaps other household members, drawn much smaller and looking quite vulnerable. A small girl clutches at his manly legs while he appears twice in the painting, simultaneously on both sides of the swamp, ready for anything.

This was several years after my introduction to papyrus swamps, and I could now appreciate the detail and accuracy of the ancient artist who had captured this scene. As someone in the crowd of tourists clustered around the painting remarked, "It looks almost like it's frozen."

Hunting in a papyrus swamp (Egyptian tomb painting).

In the air above the hunter are throw-sticks caught at the moment when everything is happening. A dense flock of birds has just been flushed out of the papyrus umbels by beaters; some are still hesitantly perched, trying to decide whether to take flight or not. A few butterflies flit about as the undecided birds stare at their fallen colleagues, whacked by the throw-sticks. In the water are all manner of fish. A wily crocodile clamps its jaws tightly around one, while the mirror image of the hunter spears a world-class tilapia on the other side of the swamp.

Everyone in the picture has something to show for this man's effort. Ducks, cranes, and other stunned birds are being taken up, while the women gather papyrus umbels and water lilies, perhaps for decoration at home or for wreaths or temple offerings. Papyrus was a favorite for all of that. If you look closely you can even see bird eggs ready to be plucked from nests perched on the papyrus umbels. But the hunter better be quick, because there is also a wild cat and a large rodent with eyes focused on those same eggs.

The tall stems of papyrus lean out toward this lithe, graceful hunter as if bowing in adoration, a reflection perhaps of the intimate knowledge that ancient Egyptians had of the habits and properties of plants and animals, the same organisms to which they paid homage in the temples, yet took their lives without regard in the swamps.

The ancient hunter reminded me of a young Louisiana swamp ecologist I'd met at a seminar on wetlands in the southern USA. He said he loved paddling his pirogue into a backwater region not far from home, where he never went without a light rifle, some tackle, and his dog. I imagine his boat was not all that different from the papyrus skiff shown. He would only have to slip on a fancy Egyptian necklace and a wig and he'd be a dead ringer for that 4,000-year-old high-born swamp crawler.

In all this, I saw again how papyrus creates its own unique and interesting habitat. In ancient days in the Nile Valley, aquatic birds swam or waded along the edges in search of the plentiful aquatic life, water insects, amphibians, aquatic weeds, plankton, and small fish that thrived there. Land birds perched in the umbels while others settled on stems gracefully leaning out over the water; some even wove nests there. Papyrus swamps, in ancient days as well as today, provide refuge for twenty-two species of Palaearctic and Afro-tropical migrant birds. They are also the preferred breeding grounds and habitat for the Papyrus Gonolek and Papyrus Yellow Warbler, and the feeding grounds for wading birds, including the globally vulnerable shoebill known in scientific circles as *Balaeniceps rex*.

The shoebill is an extraordinary bird; it is above all things a throwback in history. A massive creature about 3–4ft tall with bluish-gray plumage, it is a shock to see one for the first time. Watching one wading at the edge of a papyrus swamp gives the impression that nothing has changed in the intervening millennia. In fact, the shoebill has been with us for the last 30 million years. When the bird guidebooks say "it looks prehistoric," they are certainly telling the truth.

The most obvious feature of this bird, which lives almost exclusively in papyrus swamps, is of course its distinctive broad bill which does resemble a shoe, in particular a greenish-brown size-ten slogger, of which I own a pair. Those now sit in my study, reminding me of the first time I ever saw one of these birds. Its bill ends in a formidable hook, which it uses to pull apart the unlucky lungfish on which it feeds. Once seen, the shoebill is never to be forgotten, and it continues to baffle. Although it was formerly called a "whale-headed stork" (hence the Latin name), taxonomists are still undecided if it is a stork, pelican, or heron. Unfortunately this bird is now rare. Like papyrus, it has survived only by inhabiting regions that were left behind by history but are now being developed, and it is running out of places to hide.

The shoebill, formerly the whale-headed stork (after Brehm).

Of the few mammals found in a papyrus swamp, the most unusual, outside of man, is the sitatunga, a small, shy antelope (*Tragelaphus spekii*). It has an obvious adaptation to papyrus swamps in that its splayed hooves are extremely narrow and long, up to four inches in length, with extended false hooves. It is well and truly adapted to this environment because with its mini-ski type feet it can walk from rhizome to rhizome, just as I did. Perhaps they were the means by which early African people happened onto this trick. Another useful habit of the sitatunga is that it is an excellent swimmer, even in deep water where they have been known to submerge themselves completely, and occasionally even sleep, with only their nostrils above the waterline.

The sitatunga, African swamp antelope with splayed hooves (after Haeckel).

Along the edges of the ancient and modern papyrus swamp, and also in the small ponds inside, we find fish that are attracted to the swamps because of the refuge provided from predators. Nowadays that would be the Nile Perch, which has driven many fish species to extinction in lakes such as Lake Victoria. Among these fish are the snake-like lungfish (*Protopterus annectens*), which is the most unusual of the lot as it is a faculative air breather that can live out of water for many months. It does this by using a pocket in its gut that is lined with thin-walled blood vessels which serves as a lung. The lungfish also possesses gill arches with gills; thus it can breathe in either air or water, which is a useful adaptation for marshes and swamps (which dry occasionally) and illustrates a transition in the evolution of creatures breathing water to creatures breathing air.

The lungfish is normally preyed upon by the shoebill and other wading birds that spot it swimming in the water just above the mud. It is vulnerable even when it is at rest inside its mud burrow, as Africans on occasion dig up the fish, along with the whole burrow. They store it intact in a corner of their hut until they feel the need for fresh fish—a useful practice in remote areas where refrigerators are still rare.

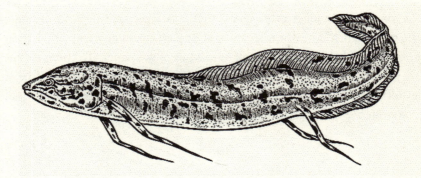

Air-breathing African lungfish (after Govt. Queensland).

The ancient Egyptians knew all about these strange creatures and the unique qualities of the papyrus ecosystem. They were enchanted by it, and they worshipped many of the animals and plants that were found there, unlike the Greeks and Romans who conquered Egypt in the last days of its majesty, when it had grown weak and tired of its own inept dynasties. The new rulers were interlopers on the world stage of ancient civilizations and not familiar with the exotic ecosystems they found in Africa. They thought the beatified organisms of the Egyptians peculiar, or most strange to say the least. Plato swore by "the Egyptian dog" or "the barker" (Anubis, the jackal-headed Egyptian god of the afterlife) in place of proper Greek gods. The Greeks were more circumspect than the Romans, who were outright scornful and thought the Egyptian practice of mummification of thousands of ibises, crocodiles, cats, bulls, and dogs was bizarre. Imagine the repugnance of the cultured men of Rome when they saw the paintings and statues of the crocodile-headed Sobek, patron god of the army, and Ta-Urt, the goddess of fertility with her crocodile tail, pregnant-looking hippopotamus body, and hippo head.

Who does not know, Volusius, what monsters are revered by demented Egyptians? One lot worships the crocodile; another goes in awe of the

*ibis that feeds on serpents. Elsewhere there shines the golden effigy of
the sacred long-tailed monkey. (Juvenal. 100–127 A.D. Satires XV)*

As for the sacredness of papyrus, that was a concept beyond the pale
of the conquerors. They hardly thought of papyrus in any way other than
as a commercial enterprise: the plant used to make paper. To them Egypt
was a granary, a plantation with little to offer the civilization they knew.
They left records of their disdain on bits of papyrus paper in the personal
correspondence collections found at Oxyrhynchos in the 1800s.

∽

Botanists today are no strangers to tropical vegetation; little surprises
them among the exotic plant types found in tropical locales. But newly
arrived visitors in the tropics are often dismayed to find the local plant
life vaguely familiar. They are dismayed because on closer inspection they
see that many are simply overgrown houseplants! The potted plants they
took for granted back home—the philodendron, dieffenbachia, croton,
oleander, and euphorbia—are all here, growing unfettered, almost scary
in their untamed luxuriance.

And papyrus? Well, it's no different. In the '70s, as I looked out over
swamps that extended for miles and miles across meandering valleys and
covering whole sections of lakes and banks of rivers, I had to remind myself
and others that it was a *sedge*. What does that mean? To most gardeners,
sedges are lawn weeds. Every time you cut your lawn, depending on its
condition, you could be mowing down hundreds of sedges! But in Africa,
papyrus is a tall, robust, overpowering sedge, a 15–20ft giant that is almost
as absurd to Western eyes as the other overgrown houseplants.

Papyrus reaches its maximum growth potential in the equatorial regions
of the Great Lakes of Central and Eastern Africa. It grows in standing
water over vast expanses of the Southern Sudan and along the rivers of
this region (Map 1, p. 17). Riverine papyrus swamps are found on the
Victoria Nile, the Nile that flows from Lake Victoria through the Lake
Kyoga swamps and into Lake Albert in northwestern Uganda. All along

this part of the Nile one can see lush growths of papyrus on both banks of the river, with tall plants producing enormous umbels that wave gently in the breeze like small green clouds. An impressive sight when seen from a small boat, and familiar perhaps to viewers of the movie *The African Queen*, part of which was filmed in this region.

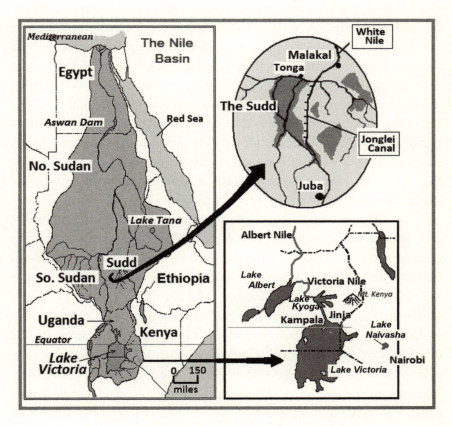

MAP 1: *Nile catchment, Sudd area, and Lake Victoria.*

My favorite line in that movie is spoken to Hepburn by Bogart from the top of the mast: "Nothing but grass and papyrus as far as you can see!"

These riverine papyrus swamps lie for the most part inside national parks and are therefore protected. As the river traffic is light and the population dispersed in these regions, the swamps will probably not change much in the future. From the air they resemble light green bands that run along both banks of the river for miles. Inside such swamps we find that the leading edge is a floating matrix or mat of papyrus that grows out onto the river. It is anchored to the shore by plants growing on wet mud along the flooded shoreline, and the rhizomes are interconnected in the matrix. If the river were to slow down or become silted up, papyrus would in fact grow right over it from bank to bank, as it does in river valleys and swampy ravines in many places in Uganda. Under those conditions it is capable of extending over a large region, since papyrus is capable of growing up to two inches a day. It reaches an annual growth rate of thirty to fifty tons dry weight per acre per year, a rate that puts papyrus in the same class as bamboo and other fast-growing grasses and ecosystems, such as the tropical rainforest. The secret behind its impressive growth is its C_4 plant status which, in botanical terms, means that it falls among the elite in terms of its photosynthetic pathway. Only about 7,600 species of plants—about 3% of the 250,000 known species of plants—use C_4 carbon fixation, the pathway allowing the fastest growth rate among vascular plants.[1]

In addition to fast growth, it does not seem to be much affected by disease, and it is seldom eaten by animals, other than the sitatunga or starving cattle or goats. Its protection from disease and the parasites that carry it derives from the fact that the upright stems have a tough green skin, a skin that as we will see serves admirably for making rope.

The morphology of papyrus is straightforward and typical for a sedge; each upright stem, or culm, appears and grows upward from the tip of a horizontal stem, or rhizome. The upright stem expands at its top and spreads out into a large tuft of slim, flowering branches, or umbel. The base of the stem is closely sheathed in scale leaves, and the umbel at the top of the stem is enclosed in scale-like bracts prior to opening. The stem is triangular in cross-section, a distinctive feature that sets the sedges apart from grasses. Collectively, swamp grasses, grass-like plants, sedges, and rushes are all called "reeds."

Papyrus grows on wet mud at the water's edge, where young rhizomes tend to grow over older ones; the whole mass so created, along with a layer of peat, then spreads out over the water as a floating mat. This is possible because the plant is equipped with many air spaces in the stems that provide the necessary buoyancy. On large African lakes or deep rivers, it will form a substantial floating swamp, with stems so tall that it is difficult to look over them unless you are on the deck of a steamer. That was the only way that Harold Hurst, a British scientist, could see elephants moving about in the shallow end of a swamp on the White Nile in 1952.

With such amazing growth potential, the question arises: Why then hasn't it covered the globe? The fact is that it is susceptible to changes in water level, salinity, or rough wave action. Thus on wide rivers, such as the Congo, and lakes, such as Lake Victoria, large segments break off and float away from the swamp. Such islands can be a hazard to inland water shipping and the fishing industry. Papyrus also does not do well if the water level drops during drought conditions. The swamps are then stranded on dry land, at which point they dry out and die, making them very susceptible to burning and clear-cutting, a factor that has led to the demise of papyrus in farmed areas throughout Africa.

❦

In the time of the Victorian explorers like Sir Samuel Baker, who passed through Cairo and Luxor on his way to Uganda in search of the source of the White Nile, the papyrus swamps of Egypt had been cleared for agriculture, and much of the original vegetation on the river had been replaced by a cultivated landscape. But the Nubian swamps, or "Sudd" (Map 1, p. 17), well south of Egypt, had escaped a similar fate because of their isolation. It was here that the same explorers found papyrus growing luxuriantly, and, unluckily, it was through this part of Sudan that they had to hack a path for their steamer.

The Sudd is an enormous complex of wetlands and aquatic ecosystems, ponds, rivers, lakes, swamps, and seasonally inundated grasslands on black soils. Recently surveyed with remote sensing, the Sudd was found to cover 2.3 million acres during the dry season. That would be a good measure of the extent of permanent swamp and would include ca. 1 million acres of papyrus swamp, which dominates the permanent wetlands. When flooded, the Sudd expands to a whopping 10 million acres—the size of the Netherlands.[2]

It is in this terrain that we find the ideal habitat of the Nile Lechwe (*Kobus megaceros*), an antelope with elongated splayed hooves as in the case of the sitatunga, but less extreme. This adaptation distributes the weight of the animal and allows it to spring from tussock to tussock and easily race through shallow water. But the lechwe doesn't do so well on dry land. The total population has been recently estimated at only 30,000. That low a population number, and its restricted distribution, suggests it could easily be threatened by extinction if the swamps were to be drained.

The Nile Lechwe, along with two other antelope, the Tiang (*Damaliscus korrigum lunatus*) and White-eared Kob (*Kobus kob lucotis*), were featured in the Sierra Club video film *Mysterious Herds of the Sudan: Migration of the White-eared Kob*, and in the November 2010 edition of *National Geographic* that featured "Great Migrations." This collection of antelopes forms the second largest group of free-ranging large mammals in Africa, second only to the wildebeest of the East African plains.[3]

The swamps are not easy places for large animals to get in and out of. The most common large animals in African swamps are the amphibians, such as crocodiles and hippos, but even they are relegated to the swamp edges. They are seldom seen inside the actual swamps because hippos are too large, and crocs, being cold-blooded reptiles, prefer rocky outcroppings or mud banks out in the open sun, where they can prowl the mucky shallows in search of fish among the aquatic weeds and still stay warm.

Elephants occasionally take refuge in swamps, especially in the dry season when they are attracted to the water found in the swamps of the White Nile and the Okavango in Botswana. These were the animals seen by Hurst from the top deck of a steamer, with white egrets perched upon their backs. This fondness for swamps may run in the family, as the *Moeritherium*, a prehistoric elephant with a flexible upper lip and snout, spent most of its time half-submerged in the primeval swamps. Modern elephants use the swamps as a refuge while they feed on seasonal grasslands nearby. The remoteness of the Sudd swamps provided protection for thousands of elephants during the last Civil War in the Sudan.

☙

From its present pattern of growth, and considering local topography and hydrography, it is possible to paint a general picture of what papyrus swamps must have looked like in ancient days. The Nile Valley in both ancient and modern times was a free-draining region, unlike the weed-choked swampy southern region, the Sudd. The ancient Nile River channel allowed an amazing quantity of water to pass through; under such conditions it would be difficult for permanent swamps to become established except in the backwaters.

During this time, savannas were a feature of the valley. Grass-dominated, they greened up with the spring rains to provide a pasture and grain-growing soil (Map 2). Widely dispersed farming and ranching communities sprang up with lifestyles tuned to the annual savanna cycle. Towns like Hierakonpolis in the south and el-Omari in the north became regional centers where grain was harvested and traded in quantity.

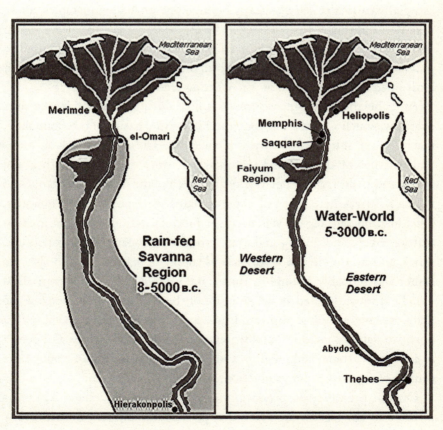

MAP 2: *Rain-fed savanna of archaic Egypt and the water-world.*

Closer to the river, a water-based culture or "water-world" developed within the Nile floodplain. This part of the floodplain was at least half-covered by vegetation and thickets, interspersed with 3,000 sq. miles of agricultural land irrigated by the flood from annual inundations.[4] And so it continued for centuries, until the summer rains began to fail. By then the rain-fed areas had begun to contract and the savannas disappeared. Now the eastern and western deserts came into being, and seemingly the good days of free range and waving fields of grain were over. During all this, the water-world acted as a natural buffer. It became a sustainable reserve as the savannas died out and aquatic resources were increasingly exploited. During the climate change toward the end of the Palaeolithic (25,000–7000 B.C.), large mammals were still part of the diet, but fish, especially catfish (*Clarias*), clearly became one of the main staples, along with wetland tubers.[5]

With time, the water-world itself was cleared, developed, and used to provide the basis for the irrigated world of pharaonic times, a period that blossomed with the arrival of water-lifting techniques.

At its height, the water-world was united during the flood by the river overflow, which spread out among the 130 natural basins of the floodplain, reaching well into the waterways of the delta.[6] Unlike the brackish wadis and marshes of the rain-fed sector, which were overgrown with grass, reeds, and rushes, the water-world supported many freshwater plants and animals. It was here that tall papyrus stems were produced in quantity. This lush bucolic region was used for food collection, seasonal grazing (cattle, sheep, and goats), and craft production (boats, mats, paper, and rope), and it also yielded a year-round supply of water fowl and fish. Its center was probably Memphis, the capital established by Menes in 3000 B.C. That town, located at the juncture of the Nile and at the apex of the delta, was in a strategic position. It was a place of feverish activity, with a port, workshops, factories, and warehouses. Memphis thrived as a center of commerce, trade, and religion, and in later years also became one of the centers of papyrus paper production.

Outside the valley proper, swamps flourished in the delta and in parts of the Faiyum region. At that time, papyrus swampland ranked below irrigated agricultural land as a major feature of the landscape, but still the swamps were considered prime property and were well protected because they increasingly provided the paper and rope needed as export money-spinners that helped Egypt rule the East. On one of the few historical records of that time, the Narmer Palette, papyrus was featured over a dozen times.[7] The palette, thought to be the first document in the history of the world, dates from around 3000 B.C. and commemorates Narmer (also called Menes). The earliest Egyptian king known to rule the swampy region of the delta was closely associated with Horus, who is often depicted as a falcon. On the palette, Horus is shown with a rope in his claw. He has tied up and contained the enemies of the land, typified by the head of a bearded Assyrian, ready to be delivered to the victorious ruler. Significantly, Horus is perched on a clump of papyrus umbels that represents the extensive delta swamps, which were later placed under royal mandate and considered the property of Pharaoh. Like other valuable commodities in Egypt, they became jewels in the royal crown.

Pictogram of falcon perched on top of six papyrus plants (Narmer Palette).

❧

How extensive were the swamps of ancient Egypt? Early writers, knowing the importance the ancients attached to papyrus swamps, thought of the pre-historic Nile as just a large swamp, perhaps something like the large papyrus swamplands of the Sudan. They wanted the Egyptian Nile to match their idea of a wall-to-wall wetland. But as Dr. Karl Butzer, Professor of Geography and Environment at the University of Texas and author of the famous book *Early Hydraulic Civilization in Egypt*, has pointed out, unlike the Sudd, which is a permanently flooded flatland, the Nile in Egypt was only seasonally flooded; otherwise it had a deep main channel with a strong flow. Any permanent swamp would have to be located off the main channel in the areas he called "papyrus land" or expanses ". . . amid the papyrus, reeds, and lotus pads of the cutoff meanders, backswamps, or deltaic lagoons."

Danielle Bonneau, an Egyptologist and specialist in water use in ancient times, reckoned that there were at least 49 sq. miles of papyrus swamps in the Faiyum basin, the region in which Crocodilopolis stood, one of the most fertile areas in Egypt. Bonneau based her estimate on information from ancient legal cases that were set out in old papyrus documents. She used estimates of damages and settlements made because of breaches in dikes to estimate the size of the swamps or croplands. According to another authority, Prof. Naphtali Lewis, the Faiyum region was the site of the "Great Swamp." Lewis also noted that hardly any village in Egypt could exist without a neighborhood swamp—the plant was that important.[8]

Within the main river valley, two large swamp regions were located on the western bank by the Egyptologist Michael Herb. The water in these swamps must have been replenished each year when the Nile overflowed. Both regions are now filled with silt, but can be roughly estimated on maps of the floodplain. They comprised about 636 sq. miles.[9]

Papyrus also grew extensively within the delta, where several major centers of papermaking were located. Prof. Lewis indicated one center at Sais, and another on a spit or "tongue" of land not far from Alexandria and referred to as *taenea*. Throughout the eastern delta, other centers were located at Mendes, Tanis, and the ancient city of Memphis just south of the apex of the delta (Map 3, p. 25).

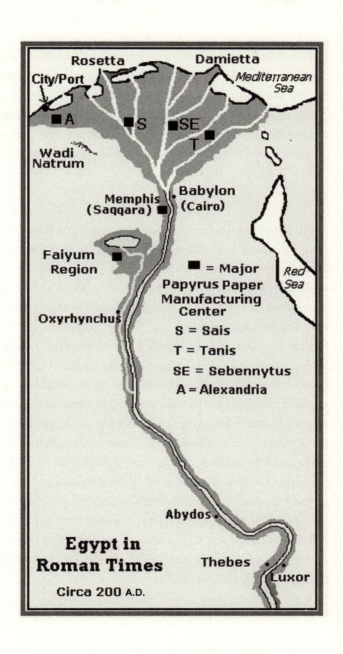

MAP 3: *Major papyrus paper centers in ancient Egypt.*

In the early days, according to Butzer, the delta region including Alexandria was sparsely populated. Swamps located there would have been very little disturbed. If papyrus swamps made up 22% of the area (the same proportion of papyrus swamps in the Faiyum region), a conservative guess within the delta would mean 1,855 sq. miles were taken up by papyrus. This suggests that the total area of papyrus from before the Ptolemys until late into the Roman Empire would be roughly 2,500 sq. miles, an area slightly larger than the state of Delaware, and an area that was the sole source of paper for the entire world for four thousand years.

◯

Unlike food, papyrus paper was a non-agricultural product that could be exported year in and year out without regard to famine conditions. Political disturbances did take their toll and there were times of disruption in paper exports because of riots in Egypt, but the increased production in paper in the heyday of ancient Egyptian civilization was mostly due to the overseas market.

To the average Egyptian all this would be of little interest, as few in the general population could read or write. Reading and writing was the sole job and skill of scribes, who were high up in the social hierarchy. The most useful thing about the plant was not the making of paper or the importance of papyrus paper to the world, but the multitude of things that could be made from it at no cost for use around the house. Though halfa grass and palm leaf were used extensively for basketry, these had to be bought or traded for in some fashion. For the swamp dweller and people living on or near the water in need of a quickly built boat, a mat, a length of cheap rope, or even a house, it must have been a comfort to have papyrus close by, which could be used to fashion all of those things simply by harvesting the reed. It was indispensable. Truly a gift of the gods, and a plant on which an entire civilization arguably rested.

3

Papyrus Boats, the Pride of Ancient Egypt

The history of Egypt boggles the mind. By any standard the scale of achievement was enormous, but through it all it seems clear that the economy remained rooted in agriculture. It was the everyday business of the ancient Egyptians to produce food. This they did using a system that was the envy of all. Sandra Postel, Director of the Global Water Policy Project, said that overall, Egypt's system of basin irrigation proved inherently more stable from an ecological, political, social, and institutional perspective than that of any other irrigation-based society in human history, including the Fertile Crescent of Mesopotamia where a fallow year had to be interposed to rest the land between harvests on land that was also subject to salinization, something that did not happen along the Nile. "Fundamentally . . . the system sustained an advanced civilization through numerous political upheavals and other destabilizing events over some 5,000 years. No other place on Earth has been in continuous cultivation for so long."

According to Dr. Butzer, during late Paleolithic times the great bulk of early settlements were concentrated in the floodplains on the levees and the immediate riverbanks of the Nile. From 5000 B.C., well before the first wooden boats, it probably occurred to most Egyptians that travel by water was a must. Today from satellite images, arable land in the Nile Valley is seen as a long green swath running the length of Egypt, with a bright blue river running down its center reminding everyone that if they intended to travel from one end of the country to the other, the message was clear: use a boat. Since boats made of wood were costly, everyday vessels—the thousands, even millions of small craft that were the work boats of ordinary souls—had to be made of cheap, reliable stuff. And that was as true in prehistoric times as it is in the 21st century.

Today it is plastic and fiberglass. Then, it was papyrus.

In building a reed boat, the trick is to tie the bundles in several places in order to trap air inside the reeds. The tighter the binding, the better the buoyancy, much like the effect created by flotation tanks of modern times, another innovation that made for greater safety on the water.

Reed boats sit high in the water and will not sink unless they are broken apart or become waterlogged, which happens if they are left for a year or two in water without being periodically dried out. These early vessels could not support a stepped mast typically made from a single heavy pole because with time it would work its way through the reed bundles. Thus, many reed boats were probably equipped with an A-frame, a light frame made of wooden poles that had two feet held in place by a complicated set of lines called "serial stays."

These consisted of a parallel series of six lines on either side of the bipod or A-frame mast, with all twelve lines (i.e., stays) anchored to the gunwales aft of midships.[1] This arrangement provided flexibility to the stern section of a reed boat and allowed the hull to follow the motion of the sea. If they had used a single stay, as in modern sailboats, the mast would have snapped or the stern of these ancient reed craft would have worked loose from the rest of the boat. On a modern sailboat, the fore and aft stays are important: they keep the mast centered. On a reed boat, the stays serve a different purpose. Since reed boats have no keel, the long bundles of reeds would buckle unless kept under compression by the serial stays, so the stays served in place of a keel.

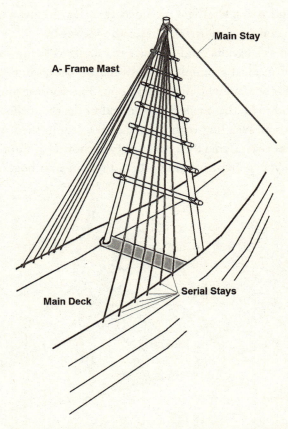

Serial stays—rope lines used to steady the mast on a reed boat.

All of this meant that boatbuilding required a great deal of rope, which in turn drove the need for rope production made from papyrus.

◎

It is not surprising that papyrus boats go so far back in history; models of papyrus boats from 5400–4000 B.C. are among the earliest datable evidence of boats themselves. This dependency on boats persisted throughout all of recorded history. Boats were equated with life, an attitude that must be expected when one lives in a floodplain that is inundated for almost a third of the year. From before 7000 B.C. until the First Millennium, for at least eight thousand years, the Nile provided the great highway and papyrus provided the common material, one of the means by which the country could develop as a nation. And let's face it, as long as the raw material was growing wild in local swamps, boats would be cheap and easy to build, and God help the man who didn't have one. The poorest soul in the next world was said to be the one left on shore after death, at the mercy of the elements, his soul pleading with someone for a seat in their papyrus boat. Of course, that also offered the opportunity to show Osiris and others what a fine person you were by offering others a seat in your boat.

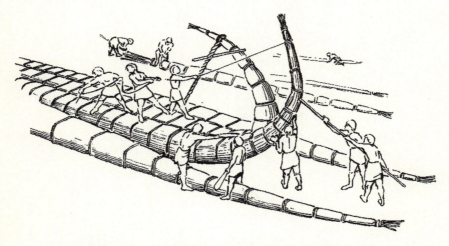

Boatbuilders at work along the ancient Nile forming the distinctive upturned prow of a papyrus boat. Note the tightly tied bundles of dry papyrus stems (© S. Manning, 1973 with permission).

Throughout Egyptian history, the tradition persists that any boat made of papyrus would repel crocodiles. I had only one opportunity to test this out. It happened on Lake Tana in Ethiopia, one of the many lakes in Africa where papyrus grows in abundance. It was from this lake that in 1969 Thor Heyerdahl shipped tons of papyrus to build his ships, *Ra I* and *Ra II*. The lake is also famous as the source of the Blue Nile. I was there to collect samples of papyrus for analysis. I intended to take them back to Kampala, where I was comparing papyrus plants collected from other places to see if there were any regional differences.

I landed at a small airstrip near the lake and checked in to the government hotel, where I explained my intentions to the manager. He told me he would help me locate the owner of a *tanqwa*, a canoe made of papyrus. The next morning, a fisherman was waiting to show me a proper tanqwa made of papyrus stems sewn together and fitted with a bundle of stems as ballast in the center, a method not changed for thousands of years. He offered to help me collect the samples of papyrus that I needed and, once we agreed on a price, we set off from the hotel landing. He poled us out along a channel close to shore, a channel that ran some distance before we reached the open lake, a body of water 1,350 sq. miles in area.

That day the surface was calm and we made good progress, but not far from the hotel I spotted a large specimen of *Crocodylus niloticus*. I say "large" because this beast was at least 16ft long. When the Greeks first saw one in Egypt they called it a *krokodilos*, after their old word for a lizard, or "stone worm." To them, this "stone worm" was so called because of its habit of basking in the sun on rocky areas near riverbanks. True to their ancient observation, this specimen was basking on a stony outcrop close to shore, so close that we would have to pass under its snout if we held our course. We were still in the channel and hemmed in by papyrus on one side and the shore on the other side, on which lay this man-killer with jaws now wide open, glaring at us.

I turned to the fisherman and indicated excitedly that he should back-paddle—and fast. He had the only paddle and I could do nothing, as I was balanced precariously on top of the bundle of papyrus stems used for ballast. The least movement seemed to tip the boat, but he only smiled and said in accented English, "No worry, crocodile is afraid."

Was I having a bad dream, I wondered? Here we were, aimed straight at an animal that was about 2 or 3ft longer than our canoe and at least three times as heavy, and, to make matters worse, if we continued in this direction the prow would poke him right in the nose.

Perhaps reading my mind, the crocodile made a loud noise halfway between a bellow and a hiss. Frantically I again turned and motioned to the fisherman, who smiled as usual and said, "See," and with several strokes propelled us straight at the animal.

The next few minutes seemed an eternity. I was reconciled to a savage, watery death—but suddenly the crocodile got up on its four legs and, as the animal behaviorists say, "high walked" off the stony ledge into the muddy water. Once there, with several powerful lashes of its tail it quickly swam away from us. As it disappeared down the channel I turned and looked at the fisherman, who smiled a third time and shrugged his shoulders. "They are much afraid of papyrus boat!" he said. And I thought, though Isis may have established this with her canoes, I don't think I'll ever have the guts to try it again.

When is a boat more than a boat? Alexander Badawy, late Professor Emeritus of Art History at UCLA, suggested that in the early days quite a few people made their homes and lived their entire lives on papyrus boats or large rafts. And why not? Such a home built floating in a backwater swamp would rise and fall with the water and would be mobile and quite handy to have during inundations. As the flood decreased, the reed boat would be stranded on the mud, where it would continue serving as a house while it dried during the remainder of the year. When the sun passed through Aquarius, or Hapi, it would be ready to float again the minute the first trickle of water reached the hull.

Many of Badawy's pre-dynastic papyrus boats had elaborate structures with decks, flags, and awnings as well as cabins. Some looked astonishingly like modern houseboats. Their cousins, I'm sure, can be found today in the backwaters of Louisiana or even moored along the Thames in London's posh Chelsea district.

According to Prof. Vinson, the first wooden boats were built only after the woodworking skills and tools were available, perhaps from the Fourth Millennium. Until then, from about 8000 B.C. onward, not having papyrus would have meant looking for alternatives, more experimentation, and less foreign exchange from exports.

During a long period of prehistoric time, papyrus was essential in order for people to make use of the river. As Fekri Hassan said, "The development of Egyptian civilization would not have been possible without riverine navigation." We can conclude, then, that for thousands of years Egyptians were very lucky to have papyrus at hand.

The sleek models drawn by antique ship and boat designer Börn Landström, the late Swedish-speaking Finnish writer, illustrator, artist, and yachtsman, are examples of the early papyrus craft in use by the dwellers of the water-world. Landström was the man who designed Thor Heyerdahl's *Ra* boats. His boats followed the lines of several drawings of Egyptian sailing vessels taken from vases dating back to 3200–3100 B.C. He pointed out that these drawings were the earliest known pictures of boats under sail.

At that time and until many years later, sails were made of the skins of papyrus stems woven into a mat; the same skins could also be twisted and braided into rope for the lines. Being so equipped, the first sailing boat was papyrus from stem to stern; the only things not made from papyrus were the stone anchor, the light wooden mast (light enough to be carried on a reed hull), and the steering oars and paddles.

Papyrus boat in pre-dynastic times. Paddles were necessary on the voyage downstream to guide the craft, which rode high in the water. The sail helped going upriver— prevailing winds were from the north (© S. Manning, 1973 with permission).

But what if papyrus had not been there? Reed boats were in common use in other river valleys of the ancient world where civilizations were also evolving, as in Mesopotamia and the Indus Valley. In those cases the people used cane grass, a tall reed called phragmites. Phragmites also grows on the Nile; might that be used in place of papyrus?

Not at the time. In the modern era, after the Aswan High Dam was built, when the salinity of the Nile increased and the flooding cycle was modulated, phragmites made great strides. It grows today along both riverbanks all the way from the delta to the dam. Often mistakenly called "papyrus" by the unwitting tourist, it is a grass, not a sedge, and in pre-dynastic days it would not have fared as well. The flow and flood regimes outlined by Prof. Butzer would have been too much for it to thrive at a high enough level to be of use on so pervasive a scale and in large enough quantities.

The Cairo University pioneer ecobotanist Prof. Migahid grouped phragmites with the bulrush Typha in the low-flood species category, which means that both plants have to be rooted in mud and will only tolerate flooding to a limited level.[2] Stable mud and low water would be rare in the path of a raging watercourse. Papyrus on the other hand is a high-flood species that does not have to be rooted; even though it has stems that grow to 15–20ft tall, they are light enough so that the plant floats and accommodates itself to the water level.

In other words, in prehistoric days on the Nile there would have been no substitute for papyrus. But times change; the wealth and stability of the governments that evolved demanded stonger, roomier cargo vessels. This meant a shift from the light paddled reed boats to heavier wood plank boats powered by oars and sail.

The Arrival of the Wooden Boat

According to Prof. Ward, maritime archaeologist at Coastal Carolina University and an expert on the subject, the first proper wooden boats were built in carvel fashion, that is, from planks that were laid edge to edge to form a smooth outer surface, rather than overlapping as in the form of a lapstrake boat. The planks could then be braced and strengthened inside. In this manner of early shipmaking, the planks were simply stitched together with rope, so even after the Egyptians turned to wooden boats, the demand for cheap and abundant papyrus rope never slackened, as this rope was still a vital part of the building and rigging of wooden vessels.

Herodotus mentioned that the typical plank used in these boats was made of acacia wood and was about 3ft long. In practice, the planks could also be of tamarisk or sycamore fig and they came in all shapes and sizes, which probably allowed for a greater efficiency in the use of the wood. Was this perhaps a sign of conservation of a scarce resource?

With careful fitting and "joggling" (cuts made to prevent slippage along the edges), every piece of planking available could be used. One sketch by Dr. Ward shows a series of planks that were cut in so many ways, they resembled a large jigsaw puzzle.

On the wooden boats, cloth sails gradually replaced papyrus sails, though papyrus was still used for caulking (fresh stems pounded into the spaces between the planks once they were fitted and tied together). The lashed-together Egyptian wooden hulls had the advantage on inland waters in that they could easily be partially or completely disassembled for repair, cleaning, or portage. So, when they were confronted with the cataracts of the lower Nile near Aswan, they simply took the boat apart and reassembled it after carrying it around the obstacle.

Easy enough to think about boats and building them out of wood, but unlike papyrus, wood was never a commodity one could lay hands on without paying through the nose. Two famous experts on ancient Egyptian boats, Börn Landström and Prof. Ward, felt that in ancient Egypt wood for building early boats was available from local trees. But once these virgin forests were cut, regeneration of the trees would be quite slow since the climate had become much drier—a situation perhaps made worse by the intensive cutting of trees. As a result, wood for boat-building would become even scarcer. Thorben Larsen, a Danish economist and ecologist, said, "As far back as 4,500 years ago we hear complaints that acacia wood for boatbuilding had to be brought in from deepest Nubia, on the present Sudanese-Egyptian border." And by the reign of Sneferu (2550 B.C.), a fleet of *more than forty ships* was commissioned to bring cedarwood logs from the Levant into Egypt.[3]

Vivi Täckholm, co-author of the book *Flora of Egypt*, who devoted most of her life to studying the flora of Egypt and inspired botanists in Egypt for some fifty years, noted that flagpoles were also in great demand as well as masts, and since Egypt lacked conifers such as pine or hemlock, they all had to be imported. Add to this the early requirements of large-diameter wooden posts for early temples,[4] and wood for furniture manufacture and house-building, and we can see why Phoenician traders found the profits so worthwhile. So good, in fact, that the famous Lebanese cedar forests were devastated to meet Egypt's demand.

Thus the changeover from the reed boats of the early water-world to the wooden boats of pharaonic times had a negative effect on the forest resources of neighboring countries. It is worth noting also that at this point in history the race had begun to provide boat timber for the burgeoning navies of the world, a race that extended later throughout Europe and Britain and did not abate until the Bessemer process cheapened the cost of steel in 1855. From then on, wooden hulls and sailing masts became things of the past, but by then the damage to the Old World forests had been done.

ॐ

The development of river transport and the papyrus boat industry in Egypt ranked as one of the most important industries, alongside paper-making and agricultural production. Boats also came to play a large part in myths, legends, religious ceremonies, and pageants, as expected from people whose passage into the next world would be accomplished by boat, virtual or real. Accordingly, much importance was assigned to keeping boats close at hand, especially as one approached the end of this life. And of course the ideal boat to own was one made of the sacred sedge—a condition that was true even after wooden boats became *de rigueur* for the powers that be. There was always a soft spot for papyrus boats throughout the population, and especially among those people who couldn't afford wooden boats.

Papyrus was used as a motif in countless designs and featured often in ancient Egyptian art, but most famously it was mentioned on the Narmer Palette, the siltstone slab that dates from 3000 B.C. One of the more cryptic symbols on the palette is an A-shaped object, which caused consternation when it was interpreted as evidence of a pyramid thousands of years before the pyramids were built in Giza. It turns out to be simply the hieroglyph for "be prepared," a glyph based on the papyrus flotation devices worn by hunters when harpooning hippos. A more common version without the cross brace was used by boatmen as an item required of every small-boat owner in the U.S. by the Coast Guard: the PFD, or personal flotation device.

The papyrus float on the Narmer Palette, the hieroglyph, and the first lifesaver in action.

As usual, we can look to the Egyptians for the first of its kind, and not surprisingly these first life preservers were made out of papyrus. The green stems bent into a loop and tied behind, leaving a head and shoulder hole, became the simplest and most effective kind of buoyancy device. Presumably, a good bow-man never manned the prow without one of these lifesavers. Appropriately, both papyrus boats of Thor Heyerdahl, the *Ra I* and *II*, were equipped with them.

Thus the water-world of ancient Egypt was a great place and time for invention and innovation, and it excelled as a showplace for skills, crafts, and the ingenuity of early man. By far the most ingenious item that emerged from that period was rope, without which building boats and houses would have been more difficult, not to mention the erection of monuments for which Egypt is remembered in later times.

4

Rope, the Workhorse of Ancient Egypt

In 482 B.C., just two years after the Persian king Xerxes had put down a rebellion and appointed his brother ruler of Egypt, he assembled the largest army ever: almost a half million men on the southern side of the Hellespont. The Persian Empire controlled Egypt, northern India, Asia Minor, and southern Europe, but Greece had yet to be subjugated. To achieve this and begin his invasion of Greece, Xerxes called on his generals to build two bridges across the Hellespont.

Herodotus tells us that in carrying out his order the Phoenicians made one bridge using flaxen cables, while the Egyptians made a second from cables of papyrus. Essentially, each of the two bridges would require the use of three hundred wooden ships acting as pontoons that would be anchored and kept in line by the cables—an enormous undertaking as the strait is 0.75–4 miles wide and at times can be quite turbulent.

The famous Ancient Greece scholar Nicholas Hammond demonstrated that in modern engineering terms the bridges could be reconstructed in theory and would work in practice.

Imagine then the competition as the two bridgemasters, Phoenician and Egyptian, vied for a place in history and the heart of this vengeful king. The cables would have to be almost a mile long and each would weigh hundreds of tons! Some authors suggest that the cables were made on site, in which case the Egyptian engineers would have to ship large quantities of papyrus rope to Abydos, the Persian town on the Hellespont where the bridges would begin, and here it would be twisted into cable form. The rope used for the Egyptian cables would be of the standard three-strand variety of papyrus rope, which was then still in fashion among shipbuilders on the Nile. But the quantities required by Xerxes stretch the imagination.

A modern natural-fiber hawser cable would be *two feet in diameter*; for the Egyptian engineers to deliver enough rope to twist into four papyrus cables of that size would mean that about 675 miles of three-strand papyrus rope would be needed, and would have to be produced under pain of being beheaded.

Could they do it? Thousands of years before this, the typical wooden ship of the Nile required about 1,000 feet of papyrus rope in her rigging. A papyrus reed ship would need even more because the reed bundles had to be bound up. Xerxes' order would amount to rope enough to rig about 2,000 ships, a tall order but not impossible because the ropemakers of Egypt had been in the business a long time, and they were the first in history to come up with the techniques to make rope on a mass-production basis. One good example of them at work is shown on the wall of a tomb in Saqqara on the west side of the river close to Memphis, the ancient capital (both were south of Cairo, the modern capital).

It is no ordinary tomb; it belonged to Khaemwaset, son of Rameses III, and dates from around 1100 B.C. It clearly shows ropemakers hard at work in—of all places—a papyrus swamp.

The puzzle to some people is: Why make rope from papyrus, let alone in a swamp? Also, what's so special about papyrus with regard to rope-making in particular? There were many other fibers that could be used to make rope in those days. High-quality rope was made from the fibers of flax, leather, animal hair, or the fibrous leaf base and leaflets of palm leaves. In fact, palm leaves are still used today to make traditional rope in Egypt and elsewhere by shredding the leaflets into strips of about an eighth of an inch wide, soaking them in water, and twisting them by rolling between the palms of the hands. These are then twisted into a cord and further into a two- or three-strand rope of about half to three-quarters-inch thickness.

Although antique hemp rope has never been found in Egypt, there were other excellent fibers available from grasses found in semi-arid areas, such as halfa grasses (*Desmostachya bipinnata* and *Imperata cylindrica*). Ropes made from such material were much in demand, but often the rope that came to hand was the cheapest available: that made of papyrus. It was even used to move large blocks of stone. Dramatic proof of this came in 1942 when British soldiers digging in a quarry not far from Cairo found a block of identical size and shape to those used in the building of the pyramids. "Around this block was a length of rope, the free end of which was evidently handled by a team of men whose skeletons were also found. Under the block were traces of wooden rollers used to ease its movement to the mouth of the cave. It is thought the Nile was wider in those days, so that rafts could be brought up to the entrances of some of the caves and the stones were then loaded and floated downstream, for landing on the West bank near the pyramid building sites. In this instance, however, the cave must have fallen in, burying the occupants alive before their task was completed."[1]

The rope wrapped around the block was 168ft long and made from papyrus twisted into three strands. It dates from 300–50 B.C., and a small piece taken as a souvenir by the soldiers was recently sold at auction by Bonhams for $1,000.

It came as no surprise to me to hear that the oldest intact coils of rope and the largest, longest ropes from ancient days were made of papyrus—a finding made recently by Dr. Ksenija Borojevic, Professor of Archeology at Boston University, during her study of a large cache of rope found in caves in the ancient Egyptian harbor on the Red Sea, the pharaonic port of Mersa Gawasis that dates from 1800 B.C.[2]

She agreed with me that in ancient Egypt, papyrus was likely the plant of choice for making thick rope in large quantity. The question remains as to whether the rope found in the cache was used by the shipwrights or whether it was awaiting export.

Although papyrus rope is not a slim, high-tensile performer, it is still quite strong and it had its uses, and because it was so cheap to make, it could be doubled up to make it as strong as linen or grass rope. That there was a market for it is illustrated by mention of it on account sheets of the day, and it had great advertisement. Theophrastus, for example, reported that Antigonus Gonatas (c. 320–239 B.C.) during the Second Syrian War won a great naval victory against Ptolemy II, and it happened that Antigonus had recently equipped his fleet with papyrus rope. Papyrus was still being used in Sicily to make rope as reported in 972 A.D., during the Muslim occupation. Ibn Hawqal, a merchant from Baghdad on a visit to the island, described a marshy area near Palermo where ". . . there are swamps full of papyrus. . . . Most . . . is twisted into ropes for ships . . ."[3] and it is still used today to make rope on the shores of Lake Victoria in Kenya by Luo fishermen.

It was made close to the swamp for several reasons, one being that the swamps provided fresh raw material for free. Papyrus rope can be made from crushed stems twisted together or from the skin. Each stem has a thin tough rind, or skin, that is easily peeled from the triangular stem. These green strips of skin can be further split lengthwise into even thinner strips while they are still fresh, so they can be twisted into twine, cord, rope, or even lamp wicks.[4]

Stems or skins of papyrus have a big advantage over the smaller segments of grass and palm because they can be up to 15–20ft long, ideal for making a fast, cheap rope. Often the green skins were available from the papermakers who were working in the same swamp.[5] Since papermakers were only interested in the inner white pith that is revealed once the stems are peeled, the green skins went begging. And since millions of sheets and rolls of papyrus paper were produced every year, and every stem produced three strips of skin, it was natural for the Egyptians to use these for something. Why not rope?

With one blow they would solve two problems: how to make money off a waste by-product of papermaking, and how to produce cordage that allowed small craft and larger vessels to be built, since the rope produced in the swamp could be used directly in making the boats as well as rigging larger boats.

So all along the edges of the extensive swamps in the floodplain and the delta of the Nile, workers were hard at it. When the Egyptian engineers stood there on the shores of the Hellespont, they could be confident that they could produce, and they were certain that their product would stand up.

Papyrus skiff being built by tying papyrus bundles together tightly. Relief in the tomb of Ti 3360 B.C. (after Jones).

But not long after the bridges had been put in place, a great storm blew up and the pontoons pulled loose from their anchorage. When the bridges came apart, Herodotus tells us that Xerxes became very angry. He flew into a rage and decided to punish the culprits. He perceived these as being both the bridge builders and the sea. The former were beheaded and the latter, the Hellespont, for its role in thwarting the king, received three hundred strokes of the whip administered by royal whippers. They literally waded into the miscreant, fulfilled the king's orders, and for good measure threw a pair of foot-chains into the sea.

Herodotus commented that this was a highly presumptuous way to address the noble Hellespont, but it was typical of the king's attitude. A new set of engineers set about repairing the bridges. They put the cables back in place, which allowed Xerxes' army to cross from Persia into Greece. Though their advance was famously blocked at Thermopylae, all of Boeotia and Attica fell as the Persian army laid waste to the region. In the process,

Athens and the temples and buildings of the Acropolis were plundered and burned.

Who ever thought rope could be so important?

Rope was to evolve also as a factor in building the first houses in early Egypt, where it was used to bind papyrus reeds to the light frames even as it had been used to create the early boats on the Nile.

For the pharaoh, only the best quality rope was used, since the royal boats were the height of sophistication. In the Cheops Solar Boat discovered near the pyramids in 1954, halfa grass rope was used to tie the planks.[6] Likewise, when rope was presented to a temple such as that of Amun-Re in Karnak, it had to be the best rope made of grass or palm fiber. But the workhorse of the nation was the everyday production from the papyrus swamps, which found uses throughout the history of ancient Egypt. Papyrus rope, twine, and cord were handy, cheap, and made money. So it is no wonder that some of the first pictures of ropemaking in the history of the world were set in papyrus swamps.

5

Papyrus Paper, in All the Offices of the World

. . . A wonderful product in truth is this wherewith ingenious Memphis has supplied all the offices in the world . . .
—Cassiodorus, 540 A.D.,
Letter in Praise of Papyrus, Variae

If one serious misapprehension has colored our thinking about Egypt for thousands of years, it is this: Most modern Egyptians, tourists, and students of Egyptian history as far back as the end of the First Millennium have no idea what the ancient Egyptians meant when they talked, wrote, or dreamed about papyrus or papyrus swamps, or pointed to their Paradise, their Heaven, the great papyrus swamp of the afterlife called *Sekhet-Aanru*—the Field of Reeds. This comes about because the Egypt of our times was—and still is—a land without papyrus.

To correct that image will require a walk on the wild side. Literally, we'd have to go and take a stroll inside a modern papyrus swamp, and therein lies part of the problem. Most of the papyrus swamps of significance today are located in areas that are under fire, or remote and difficult or costly to get to. And when you finally arrive at the side of a papyrus swamp in Africa, it presents itself as a 15–20ft solid wall of green that may be floating on 6ft of water, guarded by a crocodile or two, with a hippo or elephant thrashing around and possibly a python lurking close by.

If you hesitated before going any further, you wouldn't be alone. But there were some—the early Victorian explorers—who were forced to enter. They were driven by greed, ambition, or curiosity to go into such places and beyond, often cutting their way through miles of such swamps in order to reach their goal, the source of Africa's great rivers. Of these men there were quite a few who never returned.

How do we know the papyrus swamps of ancient Egypt were like these rather formidable and dangerous ecosystems of today? How do we know they were even as tall?

As Helene Kantor, late Professor of Archeology at the University of Chicago, pointed out in her thesis, the paintings of papyrus in Old Kingdom tombs formed a centerpiece for fishing and fowling scenes that towered high above the human figures. In later times the tendency was to diminish the size and rigidity of the swamp landscape until it became nothing more than a graceful clump, despite the fact that the papyrus plants of ancient Egypt remained tall and robust during all that time. This is evident from the writings of Pliny the Elder, the Roman naturalist and polymath, who in 23–29 A.D. wrote that he had seen papyrus plants, growing in marshes and sluggish waters along the Nile, that were 15ft in height.

We can also infer the robustness of the plants in ancient days from the width of the dried slices of pith used for making paper in the early days in Egypt. Surviving samples indicate that at least some of the plants were of hefty size.

The best example of this comes from Sir Wallis Budge, the Egyptologist who acquired one of the most extraordinary copies of the *Book of the Dead* by Scribe Ani yet discovered. Budge was the first to analyze it. He found that some of the plants used in the manufacture of this 78ft papyrus scroll had to be at least 4½ inches in diameter.[1] Though unusually large compared to the papyrus plants cultivated in Cairo today, it is a size easily reached by plants found in equatorial Africa.

It is difficult now for tourists and students of Egyptology to conjure up that vision, but for the ancient citizen it was daily association with this unusual plant that made the intimate connection so easy. This vigorous picture of the plant they knew probably explains why it was so much a part of everyday life in Egypt in ancient times. And also why it pops up as one of the most common symbols associated with lush places and abundant growth, such as the hieroglyph for Lower Egypt, the name for the wife of the Nile god Hapi (Wadjet, the mother of papyrus), and as the hieroglyph for the word "green" and thus "to flourish" or be "eternally renewed."

The Egyptians used papyrus for thousands of years to build millions of boats, houses, and craft items, and millions of miles of rope that allowed them to keep pace with other river cultures. And, luckily, they were also blessed with a resource that was unique to them, a resource that allowed them to forge ahead of other civilizations and to make the West dependent on Egypt for the next four thousand years—papyrus paper. From 3000 B.C. until 900 A.D., Egyptians made papyrus paper and went on to supply the whole of the Roman Empire with millions of scrolls and sheets.

The early Christian scholar, statesman, and writer Cassiodorus did not know how the civilized Western world had gotten along without it, since by then it was used for books, records of business, correspondence, orders of the day for the Roman army, even the first newspaper: the *Acta Diurna*, carved originally on metal or stone, was later recorded on papyrus which was, after all, a lot easier to carry around.

Pliny tells us that in 44 B.C., "(Papyrus) paper tends to be in short supply, and as early as in the time of Tiberius a shortage led to the appointment of commissioners from the Senate to oversee its distribution; otherwise daily life would have been in chaos." Here was the one plant in the history of the world powerful enough to stop the Roman Senate in its tracks. In this way it ruled the world in the same fashion that King Cotton ruled the South, the demand being met exclusively by the papyrus swamps of Egypt. Whoever controlled Egypt controlled the medium of choice. And it was big business, employing thousands of people, some highly specialized for the different branches of the industry: cultivating and harvesting the plant, transporting the raw material to the factory, fabrication, sale, and shipment of the finished product.

Even Shirley Hazzard, the bestselling novelist and writer, found this key role played by papyrus in ancient times extraordinary. In Naples in May 1983, she covered the 17th International Congress of Papyrology as a "Far-Flung Correspondent" for the *New Yorker*. Here she tells us that "Failure of the Egyptian papyrus crop could mean to the Roman world a paralysis of commerce and affairs of state, and suspension of work for innumerable scribes who carried on the enormous labor of transcription."

Where would the world be without papyrus paper? Like an early Egyptian without a papyrus boat—up the creek without a paddle.

"Parchment," someone says. Possibly.

In ancient days, parchment was associated with Pergamum, a city in Anatolia that was fast becoming a center of Greek learning and stood in direct competition with Alexandria in Egypt. On one occasion Ptolemy II is said to have stopped the export of papyrus paper in an attempt to stifle book acquisition at Pergamum; thereafter they used parchment for all their books. This story is an oft-quoted example of cutting off your nose to spite your face; according to Pliny, who had it from Varro, as a result of the papyrus paper embargo, parchment—which was made from animal skin (particularly goat, sheep, or cow) that has been scraped or dried under tension, or vellum made of calfskin—was invented in Pergamum in about 250 B.C. This seems to be another one of those stories that were designed to keep historians busy for years, as we learned that parchment was already known to exist well before that time.

The reality is that parchment-making is definitely an art rather than a science. Although it was invented, according to Herodotus, in the 5th century B.C., it would have required great skill to come up with a consistently high-grade product. The classical scholars Colin Roberts and T. C. Skeat thought a parchment industry on a scale adequate to serve the needs of the ancient world would have required many years, perhaps even centuries, to work out the details by trial and error. To build up and train a sufficient labor force spread over the length and breadth of the world, and eventually the Roman Empire, would have cost much time and money.

Also, parchment may not have arrived in time to record the early works of Homer's *Iliad* and *Odyssey*, Sappho's poetry, the *Song of Songs* and early books of the Old Testament, Hesiod's *Work and Days*, with its early discussion of the work ethic and justice, and his *Theogony*, from which we get the descent of the gods and the genesis of Greek mythology.

Missing also, perhaps, would be the works of Pythagoras, and philosopher-poets such as Xenophanes, and Aesop, and many others such as the New Testament and the Koran, which were all written originally on papyrus and then passed on by others to be copied or paraphrased, while the originals vanished.

Meanwhile, desperate humans over the years would and did try virtually anything that came to hand—pieces of stone, bone, cloth, tablets of clay, wax, or wood, palm leaves, pottery shards, sheets of lead, and even tree bark as media of record—but papyrus paper was still the primary choice. And it could be made simply, and quickly, by laying strips of papyrus pith in sequence and then pressing and drying, as shown below. It requires no skill, only a sharp knife, some water, and the stems of papyrus plants. Simple, efficient, and cheap to produce, until Chinese "laid" paper appeared on the market at the end of the First Millennium, it was indispensable.

So a world without papyrus would have been inconceivable, until laid (also called "rag" or "linen") paper appeared and made its way to Egypt, where it was even manufactured alongside papyrus paper. By 1035 A.D. in the markets of Cairo, vegetables, spices, and hardware were being wrapped in laid paper, which was cheaper and more pliable. This pretty much spelled the end for papyrus. Shortly after this, papyrus plants went missing from Egypt while the swampland where it grew was converted to agriculture. Papyrus plants did show up again in 1969 when cuttings were brought back and it was cultivated as a novelty. Today it grows on the Egyptian Nile in Cairo, where it is used to make papyrus paper for tourists.

❧

Although it is simple enough to make, papyrus paper requires some attention to basics. For example, the stems have to be peeled. It is not possible to just smash them flat and by chance produce a sheet of paper, let alone a roll of a dozen or more sheets joined together in such a way that the joins are as smooth as the made paper. Thus the question arises: How was papyrus paper made?

In my reading, I came across a term often used in error; it was used by the unwary in describing papyrus paper as a "weave." Even when looking at finished papyrus paper lit from behind, it does look like a "weave," but clearly the strips of papyrus pith that are used to make paper are laid overlapping (as explained below) and are *not* woven.

Naphtali Lewis, the ultimate expert on papyrus, once pointed out that the term "weave" (used even by Pliny) in descriptions of how to make papyrus paper is clearly figurative. It is faster and more efficient to simply lay the strips rather than weave them, but I think that the first paper produced was just that—a woven product. Which brings up the next question: Knowing that the tough skin of a papyrus stem has to be peeled away before anything else can be done, how did the first papermaker acquire strips of the inner pulp of the papyrus stem to try weaving it into paper in the first place?

The story probably starts in Memphis, a city that in pre-dynastic days and during the first dynasties was everything that an ancient Egyptian could want. Located in a strategic position between Upper and Lower Egypt, close to the great burial grounds of Saqqara, it is a likely candidate because it was close to the swamps of the surrounding floodplain, and it later became a papermaking center in its own right. It is also likely that in early Memphis, in pre-dynastic times, weavers were a common sight, peeling stems for baskets, sails, or mats. It was and still is common practice in Africa to use the long tough strips of fresh papyrus skin for weaving mats; they have to be used fresh because that's the moment when they are still supple, pliable, and useful in weaving.

The soft pith of the stem is left over from this process and it would certainly attract the attention of any children sitting there as their mothers weave away. The children could easily have been playing with the inner pith that had been left in long strips. Possibly, as kids do, they began copying their elders and wove some primitive mats of their own out of the pith. Even more fun would be squashing them, and after that, if they were left to dry, humankind would have an early form of paper.

Further refined, the pith sliced into thin slices and laid rather than woven, then pressed rather than squashed, becomes a process that might have produced the first pieces of papyrus paper.

Born around 3000 B.C. during pre-dynastic times, it would catch on quickly. Perhaps this evolution was helped when the child's father came home. He is a potter and decorates his work in dark red with pictures of animals, people, and boats. Not much of a job, but he is a curious young man and interested in life about him and in things like this dry, white, featherlight mat that his child has left behind on the floor of their simple mud-brick house or papyrus-reed hut. This is the day after his wife finished weaving some window mats made from papyrus skins, just in time for the rainy season. He turns this product of his child's work over in his hands. His child wakes from her nap, comes to him, and he shows her how to decorate the mat using the tools of his trade, a reed brush and colored inks. He is also a recorder for the village chief and must tally the grain that is stored in the village granary, and he comes to realize that using this simple mat of papyrus pith is much easier than spending his time scouring the neighborhood for flat bones and rocks, or collecting pieces of pottery from his workplace.

Now the idea catches on. Well aware of what he has, and given the inks and pens at his disposal, and the obsession of priests for temple documents and records, and the village chiefs for accounts, he improves on it. His career goes forward. He is soon known as a scribe in the region, things begin to look up markedly, and he gives thanks to the gods for his family, his kids, and this new medium.

❧

No matter when or how all this happened, paper so invented would require years to evolve into the mass commodity it was for 4,000 years. It was perhaps improved on with every generation until after some years the refined method became the standard that is still in use today in producing papyrus-paper souvenirs.

Interestingly, as shown below, it doesn't require much skill to make papyrus paper. The better forms and higher grades employ sizing and polishing, and joining the sheets into rolls. Perhaps at that stage some expertise is needed, but basically the making of the paper itself is a simple process, and fortunately Pliny preserved the description for the historical record. Using Pliny's account, and after a great deal of research, Hassan Ragab, the late founder of the Papyrus Institute in Cairo, was able to re-create the process. In 1979 he earned a Ph.D. from Grenoble in the art and science of making papyrus paper. During this time he brought cuttings of plants from Sudan to Egypt and started cultivating papyrus in shallow, protected areas of the Nile River not far from the old Sheraton Hotel.

His method of making paper was as close as possible to the original method, and has given rise to many papermaking centers in Cairo and Luxor where scenes are daily repeated of what might have taken place in ancient times. Standing in such a site near Memphis or in the delta or Faiyum (Map 2, p. 21) we would have seen workers hauling in armfuls of green stems freshly cut from a nearby marsh exactly as they do in Cairo today.

One famous tomb drawing showed papyrus collectors assembling bundles destined for the boat, rope, mat, or paper makers. In the drawing, one stem is being peeled; perhaps, as suggested by Prof. Quirke at the Petrie Museum in London, the skin would provide ties for the bundles. The pith so revealed could be sliced lengthwise and used for paper.

In this tomb drawing, the ancient artist also used the scene to show us the Ages of Man, from a lad on the left pulling papyrus stems into a papyrus skiff, to a gray-haired, paunchy fellow carrying a bundle of stems.

Making Papyrus Paper

1. Green stems are trimmed into pieces about 12 inches long. These are soaked in river water until they are peeled.
2. The tough skin peels easily, exposing the white pith of the inner stem. This pith is then sliced thin with a razor blade.
3. The slices are squeezed to remove excess water.
4. The strips are laid parallel, slightly overlapping, to form a sheet. More strips are laid on top, at right angles to the first layer.
5. The two layers are then squeezed between blotters and held under pressure until the papyrus is dry and the strips have fused into a sheet.
6. The sheet is burnished with a fine clay powder until the surface is smooth and ready to write on.

Making papyrus paper: slicing the pith; rolling pith slices; laying out the slices; and pressing the sheets made from the slices.

At this point it is useful to note that if you are making papyrus paper at home in small quantities, it is no longer necessary to have access to fresh stems or a papyrus swamp. Thin dry strips of papyrus pith are readily available on the Internet from suppliers in Egypt. In the case where you are using dry strips bought from such a supplier, simply skip the first few steps and soak the thin dry slices overnight, then use them as if they were the fresh-cut slices called for in the process.

The thin slices, after being squeezed and pressed to remove excess water, are laid out parallel, slightly overlapping, to form a sheet. More strips are then laid on top of that sheet at right angles, and the two layers are rolled with a rolling pin or hammered with wooden mallets to flatten the sheets. This squeezing or hammering forces water out of the sheets and allows them to dry faster.

The wet sheets are then laid out on linen and compressed between boards. Bound tightly and set aside to dry, preferably stacked against some sunny wall, they are opened later and the dry sheets taken out. These are now sheets that are tough enough to be burnished with fine clay powder until the surface is smooth. At this point also the paper can be tested. According to Dr. Ragab, "Good papyrus paper is quite flexible." In addition to feeling smooth to the touch, high quality papyrus paper should be easy to bend and must remain flexible. This is an indication that the natural juices that bind the sheet and help keep it intact have been properly distributed throughout, a condition that comes only if pressure is used while the sheet is fresh and still wet.[2]

If there is any secret in the manufacture of this paper, it is that sufficient hammering with a wooden mallet or rolling or pressing during the early stage is essential if the strips are to adhere to one another. This allows the sheet to stand up to everyday wear and tear. Smoothing of the surface with a pumice or polishing stone makes for a better surface, but is not an absolute necessity, as you can write perfectly well on a freshly made sheet as soon as it has dried.

After the sheets are removed from the presses, they can be joined together to form scrolls of twenty sheets (later referred to by the Romans as a *scapus*), a process done using starch paste rather than glue in order to preserve the flexibility of the roll. In the final stages of the assembly line in an Egyptian paper factory, large rolls 60–100ft long were sometimes made up on special order.

The Early Use of Papyrus Paper

The very first production of papyrus paper in Egypt must have been before 3100 B.C., since by then a tied roll of papyrus—the hieroglyphic sign signifying the process of writing—was already in use. The oldest papyrus paper ever found was a pair of blank rolls found in 1936 by a young Egyptologist, Walter Emery. The rolls were in an inlaid box in the burial place of Hemaka (ca. 2850 B.C.), chancellor and royal seal-bearer of Pharaoh Den in the First Dynasty. More recently, the Cambridge Egyptologist Toby Wilkinson concluded that the two rolls, though uninscribed, not only were proof that papyrus paper existed 5,000 years ago, but also that Egyptian writing already existed in the First Dynasty (a span of eight kings from Narmer to Qa'a over the period 2950–2750 B.C.). He based his conclusion on the fact that a cursive form of writing called hieratic was tied to papyrus, which lent itself to this speedier form of writing. Thus if the paper existed, then writing must already have been in use, which is a double first for papyrus: not only was it the first paper but it was proof of the first cursive writing by man.

The earliest literary use of papyrus is the Prisse Papyrus, known from the name of its former owner, a French Egyptologist who called the text "The Maxims of Ptah-Hotep." It is a copy of a work written earlier by the Grand Vizier Ptahhotep, an administrator and first minister during the reign of King Djedkare Isesi (2475–2455 B.C.).

The earliest Greek papyrus is believed to be a papyrus excavated near Saqqara on which was written the poem "The Persians" by Timotheus, poet and musician of Miletus, 450–357 B.C.

The most famous of all papyrus scrolls is the Papyrus of Scribe Ani found at Thebes, and purchased by the Trustees of the British Museum in 1888. It is an extensive account of *The Book of the Dead* as recorded by Ani, who was more than a scribe, being ". . . accountant of all the gods . . . governor of the granary of the lords of Abydos . . . and . . . scribe of the sacred property of the lords of Thebes." It measures 78ft and is the longest known papyrus of the Theban period. Other long papyri are: the Papyrus of Nebseni (18th Dyn) 76ft; the Papyrus of Hunefer (19th Dyn) 18ft; the Leyden Papyrus of Qenna (18th Dyn) 50ft; and the Dublin Papyrus (18th Dyn) 24ft. Many of these early rolls were cut into smaller sections for ease of handling. One of the longest papyri still virtually intact and on display is the 63ft Book of the Dead of the Priest of Horus, Imouthes (Imhotep) at the Metropolitan Museum in New York.

All of these are memorials to the skills, patience, and dedication of artisans who knew the value of good papyrus paper when they saw it. The fact that the papyri survived means that papyrus paper, whether freshly made or centuries old, is quite durable if kept under the right conditions.[3] One roll over 3,000 years old in the Egyptian Museum in Berlin could still be rolled and unrolled by the curator without the slightest danger to the material.[4]

If kept under reasonably dry conditions, it lasts for a very long time; but once exposed to humidity, papyrus paper becomes perishable and a great deal of effort must then be made to preserve it from destruction by insects, fungi, bacteria, light, and air.[5]

❧

In making Egypt a province of their Empire, the Romans were simply formalizing a longstanding arrangement with a major trading partner. In ancient Egypt, in exchange for luxury imports and raw materials such as gold coins, glassware, olive oil, wool, purple fabric, and metal weapons and tools, Egypt exported grain, gold, linen, glass, painted pottery, and papyrus paper and rope.[6] For years Egyptian grain exports had fed the ports, cities, and populace of Italy. Grain imports would rise to more than 100,000 metric tons per year under Augustus.[7] But this was a two-way street; Egyptian exporters saw it as an opportunity in their race to export value-added items, a challenge that has still not abated (even after thousands of years, it is still with us in the modern day).

The first instance I saw of the value-added principle in action was in Ghana when I was consulting on the environmental impact of a new and very expensive dam. Aluminum ore was locally available in quantity, and the new hydroelectric facility near Accra was destined to be used to provide the power to smelt the ore. But to make exports competitive and profitable, economists on the project suggested it would be better to export improved or finished products. They suggested that instead of exporting ingots, Ghana would be better off exporting aluminum pots and pans.

When Egypt came under Roman administration, Egyptian paper-makers were under pressure, since they were now subjected to strict quality controls in terms of grading and standardizing sheets. But they rose to the occasion by producing finished high-quality paper and were also still able to keep the consumer price for papyrus paper high. Prof. Lewis tells us that the paper factories were able to operate twelve months a year, since papyrus was harvested year round. It also helped that a cartel existed among the plantation owners.[8] As a result, when the rolls left Egypt bound for the Roman markets, they represented a marvelous example of the value-added principle, unlike grain which was sent raw to be ground into flour by the Roman mills, or glass and linen that required much work, and gold that needed to be refined. In the case of glass, pottery, and refined gold, fuel was needed in a country where wood was scarce. The kilns and furnaces in Egypt often used chaff (waste from grain milling), dried papyrus stems, and, reluctantly, "chaparral wood"— local bushes and stunted trees from the arid regions.

So the Roman Empire stood to make a great deal of money because Egyptian papyrus paper was a model in the world of value-added. Back in Egypt, the papermakers furthered their cause by keeping the process of making the paper secret, until Pliny spilled the beans. Until then, the papyrus cartel was able to keep the price of paper high for hundreds of years. And over many centuries the paper trade also provided steady, reliable work for thousands.

Although most ancient Egyptians were illiterate, many benefited from the manufacture of papyrus paper during the time when Egypt was paper-maker to the world.

Part II

*When Swamps Are More
than Just Wet Places*

6

The Floating World

Herodotus in 440 B.C. called them "the marsh men" and tells us "Those who inhabit the marshes have the same habits as the rest of Egyptians . . . but they practice certain peculiar customs." Well, that does sound like swamp dwellers of every generation, including the Cajuns of modern times and how they "carry on" in their beloved bayous. Swamp dwellers are often thought of as people who would rather cope with an isolated, exotic, or dangerous environment than rub shoulders with the Establishment; but years ago, the marsh man was often there for a higher purpose and with distinctly positive goals, important ones at that.

Take the ancestors of the Cajuns and my own family: the Acadians of 18th-century Canada. They chose to live in the marshes of Nova Scotia because they knew everything about swamps and marshes, including how to put them to productive use. In the region of France where they came from, they were experienced in draining and cultivating such land. They were the ideal pioneers for the low regions of the Maritime Provinces in the

New World. To the Acadians, the reed-filled marshlands of Canada in the 1600s were a paradise, whereas they would have been seen as a virtual hell-hole for those not experienced with living in a wetland environment. Not only could they move in and settle in coastal marshes (places shunned by other settlers), but, over a period of time, they were able to convert those marshes into the best agricultural land in the country. They also set aside marshes for salt hay to provide winter feed for their cattle, and as fish and wildfowl refuges to supplement their diet. They were so successful that they were envied, and at the height of Acadian culture in the 1750s they were driven off their land by British and American Loyalist troops and settlers, who forced the Acadians onto boats while they redistributed the land for their own benefit and ownership, land that had been vastly improved by drainage and careful sustainable management.

So began the tragic exodus made famous by Wordsworth's epic poem *Evangeline*, an exodus that took them down the coast to Louisiana and elsewhere in the world. When they landed in Louisiana, the three million acres of lakes, ponds, bayous, marshes, bogs, and swamps provided an ideal environment for their new life, and the basis for a world of culture that was eventually passed on to their descendants, the modern Cajun.

Swamp dwellers and marsh people from other parts of the world, such as the Aymara Indians of Lake Titicaca in Bolivia and Peru, and the Marsh Arabs, or *Ma'dan*, of the Tigris-Euphrates river valley, have preserved to some extent the way of life of earlier generations. The Marsh Arabs established themselves on the fringes of Mesopotamian swamps—on the whole, swampland that was generally seen as undesirable by the rest of the world, and so their way of life remained unchanged for five thousand years.

The men who worked the papyrus swamps of ancient Egypt were the ancient watermen who knew the swamps like the backs of their hands. Like the swamp Cajun, they lived and stayed close to water because their work took them there, and so that was where they made their homes. It remained a natural world, preserved by their efforts and the will of Pharaoh, who for a long time to come would use the papyrus swamps as a hunting reserve and for papermaking. There was no immediate need to modify or clear the swamps because, according to Prof. Hassan, until the time of the New Kingdom there was no lack of arable land.[1] Then by the time of the New Kingdom, the value of the swamps was such that they were probably worth as much as, if not more than, agriculturally productive land.[2]

Though ecologically sustainable, like other models from early cultures, the Egyptian method of agriculture differed in that farmers raised food in excess. It was this potential to generate much more food than was needed for their subsistence that, Prof. Hassan tells us, "enabled the emergence of full-time managers and craft specialists who could devote their time and energy not only to assisting in minimizing agricultural failures and keeping settled, large groups together, but also to exploring in depth the intellectual and artistic domains of the human mind."

Thus, each year it was the peasant farmer who was the miracle worker, the driving force behind the evolution of civilization; but as he spent more and more time working on community projects, water control, and Pharaoh's monuments, he required more and more assistance. Hence the specialists, the harvesters, the threshing crew, the animal keepers who drove their charges into the fields to trample the seed or provided pack animals to carry his surplus to market, or herdsmen who would round up his cattle and set out with them on the long trail north into the delta where dry-season forage was to be had. Lastly, he was dependent on the marsh men who provided him with skiffs, baskets, rope, fish, wildfowl and other food products from the swamp, the same people who harvested papyrus for Pharaoh's paper industry, or to fuel the Roman baths in Alexandria.

For this last, according to an edict of the Roman Emperor Caracalla, papyrus reed collectors were to receive special protection. Following his visit to Egypt in 215 A.D., he ordered all Egyptians removed from Alexandria because ". . . they disturb the city by their number without being useful," with the exception of pig merchants, boatmen, and ". . . those who bring down reeds to fire the baths . . ." (*Edicts of Caracalla, On Expulsion from Alexandria*, 212–215 A.D.). This meant that enormous amounts of papyrus were required daily to be dried for fuel. Papyrus for this purpose came from the delta swamps surrounding Alexandria and other large city centers where baths were in use.

While they went about their business, the ancient marsh men were like rural people elsewhere in time and place, able to enjoy life and take pleasure in what was going on around them. As Jon Manchip White, the

Welsh-American author and anthropologist, put it: "The old notion that the Egyptians were a prim, solemn, and joyless set of people, frozen like the figures on their monuments into cramped attitudes, is quite false and unjustified. . . . A closer look at them will reveal that they almost always possess a host of sly details betraying an irresistible sense of fun. . . . For the ordinary Egyptian, the good moments of life outnumbered the bad." And at the end of their work day we know from wall paintings that the boat people now and then faced off in light-hearted jousting contests with long poles on light papyrus skiffs. The winners must have been treated to barley beer, the brew of choice for thousands of years along the Nile.

Marsh men on papyrus skiffs jousting in water near a hippo (after Herb).

The marsh men also seemed much like those Cajun ancestors, the men and women of Acadia, who worked hard for half the year until the dikes were repaired, the crops harvested, the cod caught and dried, and the apples pressed. That left the other half of the year for leisure, parties, weddings, festivals, and music. Yet the Acadians remained God-fearing, morally pure individuals with large families in which illegitimate children were scarce. Outsiders found them generally free of malice and vengeance; they were, like the marsh people in Egypt, cheerful, light-hearted, and good.

When the ancient marsh men had free time at night in their reed huts in the papyrus swamps, or when relaxing in the evening on their reed boats or floating homes, someone would be bound to pick up a lute, flute, or drum, and as Herodotus noted of a party of Egyptian pilgrims on the water, ". . . men and women together, and a great multitude of each sex in every boat; and some of the women have rattles and rattle with them, while some of the men play the flute during the whole time of the voyage, and the rest, both women and men, sing and clap their hands . . . some dance, and some stand up and pull up their garments." Does that sound familiar? It should, if you've ever been to New Orleans during Mardi Gras!

The Egyptologist Greg Reeder also gets close to the character of the marsh people in his comments on *muu* dancers, said to be cosmic dancers, part of the funeral processions that accompany the dead as they begin their journeys into the unknown. "The *muu*'s affinity with boat people can hardly be doubted. . . . Clearly they were characters patterned after the common folk on the Nile Delta, people who lived along and worked on the canals of the north, surrounded by lush flora and diverse fauna. . . ."[3]

Two muu *dancers with papyrus hats (after Reeder).*

The striking thing about the muu dancers are their hats: made of papyrus stems, they look very much like wastepaper baskets upturned, and fun to wear—that is, if you are the type of person who likes to try on a lampshade or two at parties. *Laissez les bons temps rouler!*

The famous Egyptologist Adolf Erman, in his 1885 classic treatise *Life in Ancient Egypt*, described the marsh men as swamp dwellers who had no settled home; "their reed huts could be moved from place to place when needful. The Greek description of them in late times corresponds very nearly with the representations on the monuments of the Old Empire more than two thousand years earlier."

Reed huts were in common use perhaps from before 7000 B.C., and they were not exclusive to the marsh men. Prof. Badawy believed that most people in those days used papyrus reed houses and huts, and that they were built on land or on papyrus rafts or large boats. "Settlers on both sides of the Nile erected their shelters and huts in the style of the (boat) cabins. . . ." This meant that for thousands of years, before permanent housing became the rage, the Floating World was close at hand and a vibrant way of life. How do we know? Badawy bases his conclusion on two points: first, the fact that the typical Egyptian of the Old Kingdom always had in him "something of the propensity of his Neolithic ancestor for fowling and gaming and sailing boats." An aquatic lifestyle was in his blood; this was attested to by the numerous paintings, decorations, and carvings that depicted water scenes in this world and the aquatic paradise of the next.

Second, there is a persistent recurrence of boats with cabins in predynastic decoration, pottery of the Naqada period, and numerous mural scenes in dynastic tombs and temples. This indicated to Badawy that many of the boats involved were not simply taking part in some funereal custom. He also concluded that "at a certain stage in cultural development the Egyptian must have dwelt in boats."

A Floating World composed of papyrus? The culture of the Marsh Arab shows us it can be done. Wilfred Thesiger, in his famous study of the Marsh Arab in 1964, described his impressions of his first visit to the marshes: "Firelight on a half-turned face, the crying of geese, duck flying in to feed, a boy's voice singing somewhere in the dark, canoes moving in procession down a waterway, the setting sun seen crimson through the smoke of burning reed beds, narrow waterways that wound still deeper into the marshes. . . ." This could well serve as a description of the floating water-world in Egypt during prehistoric times.

Eventually the aquatic lifestyle had to give way to the solid ground of pharaonic Egypt, but that was later. Until then, in prehistoric Egypt, papyrus was a plant of consequence. It ruled like a king, with no usurpers in sight.

One problem with building a world out of such ephemeral material is that very little would be left, which perhaps accounts for the great lack of evidence today, outside of drawings and written testimony. No permanent housing structures have survived from pre-pharaonic times, though traces of housing exist in places like Merimda. Here, postholes dated from 4700–3000 B.C. indicate that the huts were oval in shape and, according to Badawy, were made from poles overlain with papyrus woven into the framework.[4] In the evolution of houses, this must have been an improvement on the simple papyrus huts built on vessels.

After that came housing made of mud brick. According to Maria Correas, a graduate student in Archeology at Durham University in England, the transition between reed houses and mud brick probably began very early, at least before 3200 B.C. After that, mud-brick buildings were found in agricultural settlements and in the special towns set up to shelter the thousands of workers in areas where monumental projects were under construction. Sun-dried mud brick continued to be used during the New Kingdom (1500 B.C.) and onwards. An interesting fact is that the better-built mud-brick houses incorporated wooden beams tied together with papyrus rope—which reminds us that papyrus was still useful many years after the papyrus hut period.

But even with mud brick there were problems, especially in low-lying areas where houses were liable to be dissolved or washed away during the inundation. Residents in those areas had to rebuild on top of old houses. In the process they built up a mound, and eventually provided a more secure environment, but it must have been discouraging each year to start from scratch, unlike the old days when you and your family floated high and dry in your papyrus craft as the life-giving water spread throughout the land and rocked you to sleep every night.

❧

Setting aside the question of where they came from, we can at least guess at the date marsh men arrived in Egypt. According to Egyptologist Mike

Brass, the date of arrival would follow the catastrophic flooding experienced in 10,500 B.C. The receding floods 11,000 years ago allowed fishing and aquatic plant exploitation to become a viable means of subsistence. Later, between 6000 and 5000 B.C. the mid-Holocene droughts brought the fusion of the Saharan Neolithic economy of herding and cultivation with the Nilotic fishing strategy, and also with the first proto-agricultural communities along the floodplain edge. These last were the semi-nomadic, sparsely populated tribal societies described by Toby Wilkinson, the people who grazed their cattle on the pastures of the savanna until they dried up. The disappearance of the grass forced them to drive their cattle north through the valley to graze in the delta.

At this point the marsh man and the herdsman familiar with marshy terrain came into their own, as from then on the water-world became a focus of life, until it too began to diminish and fade as the population increased and the landscape changed again.

This period was also a time of change in the diet of the ancient Egyptian. In earlier days, birds, wildlife, and fish made up a large part of the Egyptian diet, which required the services of the marsh men to provide (see frontispiece). This diet was being replaced by a more vegetarian diet that included beer, bread, and vegetables such as leeks and onions, a diet that would be well entrenched by the time of the building of the pyramids. All of which spelled trouble for the swamp people, since their living depended a great deal on hunting and fishing.

Herodotus mentioned seven classes of people who were distinct from the rest of the Egyptian population because they came from certain districts and observed the laws of their own castes.

The classes, in order of importance, were: priests, soldiers, scribes, shopkeepers, boatmen, cowherds, and swineherds. The swineherds could perhaps be equated with the lowest castes of other societies. Wilkinson narrowed the classes further to just four and included huntsmen and boatmen with the military, but assigned bird hunters and fishermen to a class that included various herders and common people in general.[5] The marsh men did not constitute a class of their own. They probably worked closely with the boatmen and even more closely with the herdsmen, the cowboys of old Egypt. Erman describes the herdsmen as simple, unkempt swamp people with clothing made of rush-mats. The way they wore their hair and their beards made them appear barbaric. They were the fellows who drove the cattle to the grasslands of the delta, the lush places near papyrus plantations where the cattle grazed during the dry season.

This annual trek took them and their animals across canals, branch rivers, and swamps. Once arrived in the delta, they lived with their cattle. But unlike the marsh men, Erman felt that the Egyptian herdsmen seemed to have had no delight in the romance of "this life in the marshes." Erman draws a picture for us of their life, one that matched an Old Kingdom illustration (2600 B.C.): "It is evening and the work is at an end; some of the men are squatting round the low hearth roasting their geese on wooden spits at the fire; one has not got so far and is only plucking his goose. Others are occupying themselves either with plaiting papyrus reeds or cooking dough for the cattle. Another man is comfortably asleep. A large jug, a basket with some small vessels, and a few papyrus mats are all the goods required for our herdsman's housekeeping."

Doubtless, the herdsmen longed for the trek back and the comforts of home. For the marsh men, however, there was never any homeward trek for the simple reason that once they reached a swamp they *were* home.

Erman found signs and allusions that glorified "the pleasures of life to be enjoyed in the marshes. From the days of the Old Empire down to the Roman time, the Egyptians thoroughly enjoyed this life." But for many, reality set in during pharaonic times when taxes were levied on crops and arable land, taxes that were based on the height of the inundation. This meant that good times brought higher taxes and more community responsibility, as well as more social and political control. Egypt was becoming a different place, no longer the wild, wet country that encouraged marsh men, swamp dwellers, and the floating life of the water-world. Civilization advanced and different values were set in place; the work ethic was encouraged and daydreamers were discouraged. Gradually the splendor of the upper class, the largesse of military officers, and the contented wealthy life of the temple priest became the goal. Aspirations in these directions meant there was less room in the future for the Noble Savage of the swamps.

As history marched on, marsh men were still to be found, though in the minority. They still brought in the wild birds and fish to the markets, and delivered that rough yet ubiquitous floor covering, the papyrus mat, used also as room dividers in newly acquired mud-brick houses. As the world changed, leather, wood, and cloth became more fashionable and durable, replacing the old-fashioned papyrus sandals, mats, boats, and baskets. The mud-brick house on dry land, away from the mosquito-ridden swamp margins, became more attractive to younger generations than the cabin of a floating skiff.

In our world today, the most soul-satisfied Cajun seems to be the one who makes a living by a mix of traditional craft, small industry, and part-time jobs. Horsehair rope-making, sport fish guiding, handicrafts, black-smithing, alligator farming, boatbuilding—you name it. Fishing, hunting, and agriculture, previously done for sustenance, now seem to be pursued for pleasure. In Egypt the marsh men took on day jobs in order to keep up, just like watermen of the Chesapeake Bay or swamp men of Louisiana who have to find part- or full-time work, sometimes with oil companies—the same companies that inexorably wear down the environment they love. The watermen of old Egypt, perhaps hired out as reed cutters or as laborers draining swamps for cultivation, were unavoidably destroying the ecosystem that supported them for so long.

The gap between the marsh man and the Establishment widened as the marsh man saw his world disappearing. His middle-class boss, the man who leased the swamp or managed the paper-producing business, or the head of the prosperous family that he supplied with fish and game, was more and more concerned about climbing the social ladder. From the time of the Greek occupation onward, we hear of Egyptians changing their names or pleading with influential officials to certify that their relatives were born of Greek or Roman parents. Naphtali Lewis summarized the times: "For the mass of Egyptians under Roman rule, the touchstone of status was Hellenism." They applied to have their children enter the "right" schools, institutions that would guarantee their futures by association with the "right" people. Not much different from today.

We can rest assured that in the early days the swamp people would not be considered the "right" sort. And their reputation did not improve with the publication of the first full-length work of fiction in the history of the world, the novel *Aethiopica*. Written around 300 A.D. by Heliodorus, it is a tale of adventure in which the young, beautiful heroine Chariklea and her handsome lover Theagenes are stranded on a beach in the delta in Egypt. Taken prisoner by a band of thieves, they are whisked off to a camp in, of all places, a papyrus swamp. Here they are witnesses to a small part of the floating life of the water-world.

> . . . there is but little land above the water, some live in small cottages . . . which were made only of the slender reeds that grew on the marsh banks . . . others in boats, which they use as well for their house as for passage over the pool. In these do their women serve them and, if need require, be also brought to bed. When a child is born, they let him suck his mother's milk a while; but afterwards they feed him with fishes taken in the lake and roasted in the hot sun. And when they perceive that he begins to go, they tie a cord about his ankles and suffer him only to crawl the length of the boat or the cottage. . . . (Heliodorus, 300 A.D. *Aethiopica*. Trans. T. Underdowne, Anno 1587)

Heliodorus refers to the thieves using the Greek word *boukoloi*, or "herdsmen," and informs us that they are brigands. So much for the colleagues of the marsh men! But it gets worse, as the author goes on to explain that the swamps of the Nile Delta attracted men of that class—that is, bandits. No matter that these settlements in the delta might be honest places started by marsh men, and that bandits and rebels later found refuge in the labyrinthine network of lakes, channels, and reeds; the inference is that they did so with the help and complicity of the local inhabitants. In this way Heliodorus wipes out the image of the honest, happy-go-lucky, devil-may-care marsh man, who in real life was perhaps no better or worse than most in Egyptian society at that time.

Not only is this ancient swamp dweller branded forever as a brigand, within a few hundred years he is to lose his livelihood when papyrus swamps disappear as Egypt has less and less need for them and him.

Heliodorus's novel foreshadows the future. Throughout the book, Greek gods and goddesses show up, sacrifices and oracles play their parts, and the pagan way of life plays a large role. Not too far into the future, from

313 A.D. when Constantine announced toleration of Christianity, books began to feature Christians, and the most popular book of all would be the Christian Bible. Written on papyrus paper, it gradually shifted from scrolls to the early book form, or codex, which was essentially a scroll cut into papyrus-paper pages and sewn together. Christians seemed to prefer this compact form over the scroll, since the papyrus codex was cheaper and more compact. Also, you could write on both sides of the page, and it was easier to bookmark a page in a codex than on a scroll. Still, papyrus paper was being used in quantity, so the market must have continued strong in Egypt, until the 4th century when the Bible would be written more and more often on parchment.[6] With the Arab takeover in Egypt in the 6th century until the time of Gutenberg in the 1400s, parchment was popular and remained so until it also was displaced, by rag paper.

The changeover from papyrus paper to parchment did not happen overnight, perhaps because many copyists, writers, and librarians may have found it difficult, first to change from a scroll to a book, or codex form, then to develop a reliable source of parchment. The fact that it took 400–500 years indicates a degree of resistance. Also, although a parchment Bible at the "high end" cost little more than a papyrus Bible, at the "low end" (i.e., low-quality scribal work) it made a difference.[7] Thus, "pulp" Bibles made of papyrus probably kept the Egyptian market going, but over time the market sank and the swamps were converted to agriculture, at which point the marsh man was out of a job.

❧

Where would it end? Evolution of the land was bound to happen. Like the Wild West that gradually turned into a place of shopping malls, housing developments, and urban centers, so the swamps were drained for farmland and papyrus was relegated to antiquity. What would happen if a marsh man went looking for work in Egypt today? He wouldn't have an easy time of it. Bird hunting might be a possibility in the delta, which lies on the migratory flyway from the Levant. Millions of birds pass through the region seasonally, but since most of the land is now farmed or built up, the birds roost, nest, or pass through the four northern lakes of the delta,

Lakes Mariut, Edku, Burullos, and Manzala. Called the "Four Sisters," the four lakes are spread out along the coast from Alexandria like the webs of a fan (Maps 2 and 3, pp. 21 and 25).

Here our marsh man would find an active community of bird hunters, especially around Lake Manzala. Wim Mullié and Peter Meininger, experts in African bird ecology, calculated in the late '70s and early '80s that 98,000–162,000 water birds were killed annually on the lake. The number of people practicing these activities was estimated to be less than 2,000 in a population of about 40,000 fishermen. However, the majority of the birds were taken by less than 100 men.

Since then, the number of birds and hunters rose to a peak until 2009, when the government canceled the annual bird hunt. They did this in order to minimize contact between people and migrant birds. They also banned the import of live birds and tightened quarantine controls at airports to keep out Asian bird flu. But with civil unrest, bird hunting has come back with a vengeance. A recent report in *National Geographic* by the novelist Jonathan Franzen (*Last Song*, July 2013) reveals that bird nets in Egypt cover entire areas on the coast, with hunting concentrated near oases. It is obvious now that hunting pressures are affecting bird population in the region.

Where else in the modern delta could an ancient marsh man look? Reed cutting would be out, as the papyrus had disappeared. Phragmites, the reed grass that had taken its place, is still used for mats and windbreaks, but the marshes have been much reduced as farm and community development has increased at a rapid rate.

Perhaps fishing in the Four Sisters would be the best opportunity, as they are still productive sites. Mean annual catch figures from the National Institute of Oceanography and Fisheries in Egypt show Lake Manzala first in production at 60,000 tons, Burullos second with 48,000 tons, followed by Edku at 9,000 tons, and Mariut near Alexandria at 5,000 tons. We are also told that 56% of the fish consumed in Egypt comes from fish aquaculture (of which 75% comes from fish farms in the delta lakes); 23% are wild caught from the Four Sisters; 12% comes from the Nile River; and 9% are marine.

But the future doesn't look good for our marsh man if he were to go in for fishing in the Four Sisters, since all have become highly polluted.

In Lake Mariut alone the sewage load has doubled within the last ten years. All four lakes receive huge inputs of industrial effluents as well as phosphorus and nitrogen from domestic sewage that sparks the growth of algae.

The reaction of the government to this problem seems mixed. Some official reports note that the incoming sewage is simply replacing, even exceeding, the original nutrients in the river that were lost when the High Dam at Aswan was closed. Following that event, fishery on the Nile took a nosedive; but now with pollution, the fish are coming back in response to the bloom of algae.

But is it safe to eat the fish? Malcolm Beveridge of the Malaysia-based World Fish Centre says, "With human waste, the principal concern is parasite and disease cycles, but I don't think there's much evidence to show that fish feeding (on sewage) pose a risk to human health, particularly if the fish are cooked properly before they are eaten. A bigger concern might be contamination by industrial and agricultural wastes, especially by heavy metals and toxic pesticides." Still, according to Cam McGrath reporting in the Inter Press Service News Agency in 2009 ("Egypt: Fishing in the sewer"), many Egyptians are concerned about the effects of contaminants on the Nile fish. "The river is basically Egypt's sewer and I wouldn't eat anything living in it," says Mona Radwan, a marketing agent who lives in an upscale Cairo neighborhood. "Many Egyptians eat fish from the Nile because they are too poor to afford meat or chicken."

The degree of pollution in the Four Sisters is such that no one can doubt there is a danger to humans. The UNDP confirms that the incoming sewage and industrial waste is so oxygen-poor (i.e., septic) that when it meets the water of Lake Manzala, the iron in the water is oxidized immediately. Rust forms, and this is precipitated onto fish gills, causing tissue damage and mortality. As a result, only the hardiest organisms can tolerate Lake Manzala near the entrance of the drains. A UNDP report confirms that "Among these species, malformations, discoloration, and stunted growth are common. Near the Bahr El Baqar drain, which is the most productive fishing area, only tilapia and catfish survive, and the tilapia show a high frequency (85%) of organ malformation and discoloration, caused by environmental and contaminant stress."

According to Ray Bush from the University of Leeds, and Amal Sabri, Director of AHED, an Egyptian environmental organization, over 60% of fish sampled in the four delta lakes contained DDT and benzene chloride. "Numerous other investigations in the four lakes have shown high levels of heavy metals, pesticides, and PCBs in fish. Fishers themselves are usually the highest consumers of fish, and they are the most exposed to the health hazards posed by fish contaminated by heavy metals, pesticides, and sewage. Large numbers of Manzala fishers and their families have worm infestations and high incidences of salmonella, shigella, and viral hepatitis."

The people who live around the lake are now afraid to eat the fish from a lake that once provided 30% of all Egypt's fish. Fish farming is thought to be a solution, and there has been a steep rise in aquaculture, with an annual harvest of 300 tons in 1972–1973, reaching to as much as 136,500 tons in 1998—a figure exceeding 25% of Egypt's domestic fish harvest. The problem, however, is not resolved by farming fish, because the fish are often raised in enclosures on Lake Manzala, which means they are still growing in polluted water.

Our ancient marsh man would be better advised to look elsewhere, perhaps in Lake Nasser above the High Dam, where the water is less polluted, or in the rehabilitation schemes that are now being started in the delta under pressure from the fishers who have voiced their complaints. One solution to the pollution problem is a UNDP project that led to the establishment of a filter swamp in 2002.

Presumably in the twilight period of Ancient Egypt, the marsh men stuck it out through thick and thin, hoping papyrus would someday come back to the Nile. As pointed out by Mike Tidwell in his book *Bayou Farewell*, Cajuns of today have a similar hope. After being beaten down by Katrina, land subsidence, the diversion of the life-giving silt, and the BP oil spill, they are hanging on with the hope that once the oil is gone, rejuvenation of the land will bring back old times.

Of course it's a dream; but in that dream, Tidwell says, the Mississippi River comes to the rescue, and ". . . Louisianans return the favor, for themselves and a grateful nation, using gentle hands to restore a natural place until, at long last, the old debts are repaid. And the cycle is complete."

Like the Cajuns, the ancient marsh man held on in the hope that the tide would turn. And their White Knight would be papyrus, a plant that is now known to take up toxic material and sewage at a phenomenal rate. It also acts as a filter to stop the erosion of soil, conserve groundwater, and finally act as a preserve for the conservation of fish, birds, animals, and ultimately man.

Now maybe after thousands of years it would come back and save Egypt.

Small patches of papyrus have been discovered growing wild in the delta, indicating that it was never completely eradicated. It could be that, in combination with salt-tolerant wetland species, papyrus might someday help to restore the delta. It may not be over yet.

7

The Other Marsh Men,
an African Perspective

During his twenty-five years in Africa the Rev. John Roscoe, a missionary in Uganda from the Church Missionary Society, had acquired a vast knowledge of the continent and its people. In 1908, shortly before he was due to return to England, he had much on his mind. In his role as "Local Correspondent of the Royal Anthropological Institute," he was always on the prowl for oddities, strange and grim ceremonies, evidence of cannibalism, and such. Now he had received a plea from the authorities at home to put aside his missionary duties and concentrate his remaining time on the anthropology of Ugandan tribes. He was very good at that.

Anthropologists back home, especially Sir James Frazer, the renowned author of *The Golden Bough*, whom Roscoe counted as a friend, wanted more from him and, God willing, he would provide for Sir James's needs. Left to his own resources, he decided to take one last tour before heading home. He climbed into a canoe for a tour of the swamps of Lake Kyoga. This is a watercourse that is more like a broad, shallow swamp than a lake. It is formed by a vast widening of the Nile north of Jinja (Map 1, p. 17).

This was a new experience, and he remarked that in these swamps ". . . the eye rests upon a sea of green with feathery tufts . . . pretty to look upon . . . where numbers of busy people live." The busy people he referred to were from the Bakene tribe, who lived out their entire lives in papyrus swamps and had done so for generations. Their houses were a long way from shore, but Roscoe had the advantage of a Bugandan boatman who knew the shallow water. The boatman punted them along in the fashion of a gondolier on a canal in Venice, and that was exactly the scene that came to mind as Roscoe skimmed by an ancient green wall as noble and venerable as any of the ancient stone walls in the city of the Doges. In place of palazzos, he saw here the simple papyrus houses of the inhabitants, the "busy people."

The waterway he traversed was about a quarter mile long, and an old chief welcomed him, telling Roscoe that the Bakene had come there years ago to escape Arab slavers and rival tribes that robbed and laid waste to their huts on land.

"We decided to build our houses in the papyrus swamps and for many generations we have lived here permanently."

"How do you cook?"

The chief showed Roscoe a mud mound in the center of his house, and above it Roscoe was astonished to see a round hole in the ceiling. He had traveled many places in Africa, had seen many things, but this was the first time he had ever seen an outlet for smoke in a hut.

He also noted that in the houses of the Bakene the floor consisted of stems of papyrus laid crosswise until a firm base was set that was several feet thick. Then a bed made of a wood frame was positioned and covered with dry papyrus stems. The chief felt it was important to raise the bed frame 4–5ft above the floor because a heavy rainfall in the hills might cause the water to rise several feet overnight. The water would soon subside and the island or swamp would slowly rise, but, according to the chief, it was best to be on the safe side.

After the bed had been put in place, a frame of light branches was raised over it and tied in the fashion of a large upside-down wicker basket. This served as the frame of the house, which was then covered with a thatch of papyrus stems.

"And in the night, what if the water rises above the door?"

"We cut a hole in the roof above the bed," said the chief. "We then climb out, get into our canoes, which we always keep close by, then we go fishing until the water subsides. At which point we can go back to bed."

He took Roscoe on a tour of the main canal, about 10–12ft wide, with lanes leading off to the houses of his wives and families, each lane accommodating one family and ending in a cul-de-sac. The chief's home at the top of the lane was marked by an arch close to the landing made of papyrus reed and decorated with fetishes. He told Roscoe that some of the Bakene built houses on small islands that floated about; these were people who were not bothered by the fact that they might wind up each night in a different place—the forerunners, perhaps, of the modern mobile home owners roaming the byways of America.

Other people from his tribe built their houses on the main floating swamp in order to be near the chief. Like him, they preferred to live in an area that rose and fell with the water level, which normally happened so slowly that they were hardly aware. Others preferred to build closer to shore, where the papyrus was rooted and where there was less need to wait for the water level to adjust after a heavy rain. In those areas one simply raised up the hut, added more stems to the floor, and then settled down to continue life in this field of reeds.

"What do you eat?"

"Fish, much fish. And we trade fish for millet from the traders who come by canoe. Each day we have porridge."

Roscoe noted that some of the families kept goats, which provided milk and, occasionally, roasted meat. The animals had to be taken to graze daily on land, but otherwise the Bakene kept to themselves. This was a life chosen to provide a place apart and secure from hostile tribes; they wanted to keep it that way.

To Roscoe, the Bakene were "simple" because there was nothing unusual about their lives other than the fact that they lived on water. Basically they were "busy" inside their tall papyrus, which provided ". . . perfect shelter for their floating homes . . ." and fish to eat. He also thought the young children ". . . a pretty sight . . . as happy on the water as other children are on land. A child learns to love its watery surroundings, and seems to become amphibious. . . ."

One hundred years later, David Kaiza, a journalist and health-and-environment writer for several East African newspapers, visited the same swamps. Kaiza's first impression of the people of Lake Kyoga was just the opposite of Roscoe's rosy picture.

Kaiza saw it as a grim existence. After landing on one of the islands inhabited by people who had lived there for generations, he remarked that "The islands are a strange, paper-thin world. The landing site is a filthy jumble of rotting plants, paper, fish gills and scales. Like Alice in Wonderland, the people lead a topsy-turvy existence. When you disembark, the ground (if layers of plant and mud floating on water can be called ground) sags under your feet. A high wave sends the whole thing rippling. It is as if the whole village were built on a sponge mattress."[1]

Today the older tribal regime of the Bakene discovered by Roscoe is gone. In its place Kaiza found about 6,000 people, mostly fishermen, from a number of different ethnic groups who live there for a variety of reasons. Some are there because they escaped from Idi Amin's tyrannical regime earlier and now have no other place to go; some are said to be smugglers and pirates. No matter what the reason, according to Kaiza they all may soon have to go. The provincial authorities don't think of the swamp dwellers as very productive citizens; they suspect them of tax evasion and they wouldn't mind seeing them gone tomorrow. But it's difficult to evict a moving target. The floating islands drift about, and the lake jurisdiction falls within thirteen districts. A family will go to sleep in one district and wake up in another.

Kaiza asked one of the residents, Mr. Philip Onyango, an 80-year-old senior citizen, about what attracted him here. Taking his time answering, Onyango sighed and said under his breath, "This place is very beautiful." And, not surprisingly, in Uganda the swamps are still peaceful and relatively safe places. Away from the landings they are not necessarily a floating "slum." Though, as pointed out below, papyrus swamp dwellers will always have to cope with malaria, which is still common at the swamp margin.

Regardless of the problems of living in a papyrus swamp, Kaiza himself could not help coming under its spell: ". . . there is a kind of beauty to the place . . . there is an almost absolute silence, broken only by the birds chirping and the lapping of the water."

8

Sacred Swamps and Temples of Immortality

In September 1911, Count Eric von Rosen rowed out to the floating edge of a papyrus swamp on Lake Bangweulu. This lake lies inside the basin of the Zambezi River in south central Africa, close to the place where Dr. Livingstone died 40 years earlier. A landing place had been cleared and cut stems laid down in a crisscross pattern to make a platform. In the near distance were a few simple huts made of papyrus. It was clear that the swamp people who lived there, the Batwa, had disappeared just moments before his arrival. The count stepped out of his boat and walked forward cautiously. At the moment the Batwa were in hiding, but he assumed they were watching him, a typical reaction of those who live in swamps worldwide. They are notoriously suspicious. The problem he faced was that if the Batwa didn't like what they saw, they had a reputation for swift and final retribution.

He had trouble keeping his balance walking on this floating, swaying mat. It was like walking on a waterbed, and he had little time to think because he was worried about the kind of reception that might be in store for him. He tells us that ". . . at every step the ground shakes and water and mire often rise above the ankles." It required all his attention to keep his balance. In this environment everything was in motion. He and his caravan staff complained of dizziness and the feeling that they no longer had control.

He managed to get as far as the cluster of papyrus huts when the Batwa appeared. They reluctantly welcomed him and he stayed on, living with them and studying them for some time. But once he had described their strange and watery world in his reports, he put them out of his mind.

Years later, in the spring of 1927 while he and his wife Mary, Countess von Rosen, were visiting Egypt, they were given a guided tour of the Step Pyramids in Saqqara. The site was being excavated by Cecil Firth, Chief Inspector of Antiquities. As von Rosen toured the place, he saw what many tourists have seen over the years: an extraordinary temple complex dating from 2630–2611 B.C. that is said to be the first major architectural enterprise executed in dressed stone, and the first formal architectural representations in the Western world.

Located on a wall in the House of the North are three columns, thin graceful papyrus stems made of stone, referred to as "engaged" because they are in relief, not free-standing. Nearby are other columns, also engaged, but these are fluted to resemble bundles of reeds.

Later in the tour, the count was shown a blue-glazed wall covered with faience tiles. He was astonished. The wall looked identical to the papyrus reed panels used by the Batwa to seal the front entrances of their huts. Firth then showed him a display of faience *djed* columns along the upper part of the wall, that mysterious Egyptian cult symbol said to represent a tree, or a god's backbone, or a complex column, or a pole around which were tied sheaves of grain. Later on they saw a façade in the House of the South, a *khaker* frieze that resembled the djed decorations.

To von Rosen, all of these looked like papyrus reeds lashed into bundles of one sort or another. When he turned to Firth for an explanation, Firth confirmed what he already suspected, that papyrus reeds tied into bundles must have been used in the past for all sorts of construction, including what could be construed as the first arches, balustrades, and curtain walls, as well as the first paneled doors!

The count was beginning to see papyrus reflected in almost everything that he looked at, and in his mind he saw the Batwa building their houses using techniques for bundling or weaving papyrus stems similar to that of the ancient Egyptians.

If he had known about them, he would have been further intrigued by swamp dwellers from other parts of the world, especially the Marsh Arabs, who live along the Tigris and Euphrates rivers and build houses and mosques using bundles of reeds on floating islands in the same fashion as the Batwa. A major difference is that Marsh Arabs use the grass reed, phragmites, and their buildings are larger, sturdier, and more decorative than the Batwa's papyrus huts, but the concept is the same.

In modern times, because of the war in Iraq, the lifestyle of the Marsh Arabs has changed and the area of the Iraqi marshes has been considerably reduced, but they still practice the same techniques of house and mosque construction with reeds as their forebears did thousands of years ago.

The count happened to be one of the few anthropologists of his day who had ever been inside a papyrus swamp, and the experience impressed him so greatly that a year after his visit to Egypt, he wrote a paper called "Did prehistoric Egyptian culture spring from a marsh-dwelling people?" His thesis was that one branch of the prehistoric culture of Egypt "germinated" from among a primitive people of hunters and fishermen who dwelt in the swamps of Lower Egypt. "Early Egyptian life was guided by swamp people. . . ."

As he wrote that, von Rosen could have had no idea that his theory of the origin of early ancient Egyptian life from swamp people, a culture represented by the world of the Batwa, would be dear to the hearts of many of today's Afrocentrists, those who hold a view that emphasizes the importance of African people in the evolution of world history and civilization.

Though he never specifically says so, von Rosen's paper suggests that he wouldn't be at all surprised if someday someone found progenitors in Egypt who had come originally from Africa via papyrus rafts.

That there may be some basis for this theory comes from a story released in 2009 by a BBC news team. After examining the remains of Cleopatra's sister Princess Arsinoe, found in Ephesus, Turkey, Hilke Thuer of the Austrian Academy of Sciences concluded that the evidence indicated that the mother of the two women had African facial features.[1]

The count was overwhelmed by the idea that ancient Egyptians, like the Batwa in modern times, made use of local materials to create a basic architecture that was carried forward into the annals of history. But in a way, it was just common sense. Papyrus played a large part in the construction of the early buildings in the Egyptian water-world because it was available everywhere, easy to work, and sacred.

Later, as settlements grew into towns, these archaic reed houses and rustic temples were replaced by mud-brick structures and stone constructions. The exceptions were in the small villages, where reed shrines probably persisted as the one and only choice.[2]

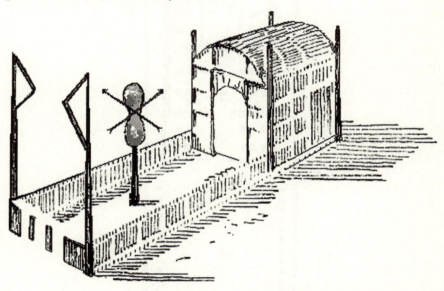

Archaic temple to Neith with a shield and arrow emblem of that god, built of light materials ca. 3000 B.C. (after Badawy).

It is worthwhile to note that the temple builders of later times preserved the simple floor plan of the reed temple with a forecourt and main rectangular building, inside of which was the sanctuary. The two sacred flag-like structures at the entrance of the early reed temples were later replaced by pylons, often massive structures with flags on top, while the forecourts displayed elaborately painted masonry and spectacular columns that were incorporated into hypostyles, peristyles, etc. But the essence remained that of a reed or papyrus hut on a mound—an environment which from then on evoked the concept of the peace, quiet, and reverential space found inside a papyrus swamp. In these early buildings, bundles of reeds, a carryover from the days of the papyrus house, became a major feature, eventually morphing into the columns and open capitals of later years.

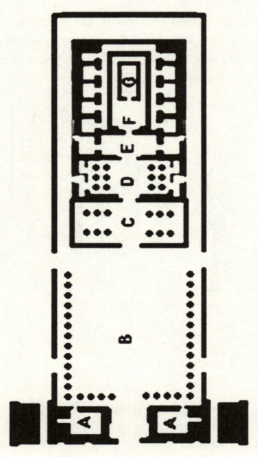

Outline of the floor plan of New Kingdom temples (1575–1085 B.C.).

In Egypt the temple was the cosmos in microcosm. Enclosed as it was by the outer walls and accompanied by a temple lake, it resembled the sacred primeval lake of Nun, the god of the waters of chaos and the father of Ra. The hypostyle hall in front of the sanctuary and its papyriform columns recalled a papyrus swamp not only because of their form but also because they were often provided in excess (that is, there were more columns than needed to support the roof).[3]

Further proof that these sophisticated temples emulated a natural setting were: the ceilings of the halls decorated to represent the sky; basal walls fashioned to represent the swamp that surrounded the whole; and the mound on which the sanctuary stood representing the place of First Creation. "Situated in sacred space and time, the temple was a divine domain on earth."[4]

Reed temples built on mounds above high water had allowances made in order to have access to the river during the inundation. We see this feature in the later temples where an avenue was made, flanked by sphinxes, or a canal was dug to provide a connection to the water. It was assumed that the temple gods would need access to the river, as did everyone else, so a papyriform temple boat was provided. This was a boat fashioned after a papyrus skiff, or more often it was a replica of one that could be carried by the priests during festival processions as they transported sacred images to the water's edge. In drier regions the boat or replica was even mounted on wheels.

The transition from reed or papyrus huts to some of the most impressive monuments ever built among temple architecture, and the role played by papyrus in this transition, is striking. In many ways, world architecture begins at Saqqara and Luxor, where the sacred towering plant was a major symbol and inspiration.

❧

Traveling to Luxor, as with all sailing on the Nile, was at most times an easy task because little effort was involved either way. The prevailing wind is from the north, thus boats can sail upstream and then drift down with the river current on their return journey. Easy to remember when you think of the hieroglyph for the expression "travel up the river, or south" which is a papyriform boat with sail set. The same glyph with sail furled is used to mean "travel down the river, or north."

On arrival at the modern town of Luxor, which is the southern part of what was once Thebes (the northern part on the river's eastern bank is known as Karnak), we find many religious buildings that include some of the largest temples ever built. Especially interesting is the Temple of Amon-Re, which despite thousands of years of architectural evolution still has the familiar rectangular ground plan. Passing through the temple, we see papyrus reflected in the motifs and symbolic carvings, even in the pylons, of which there are no fewer than ten. These large rectangular towers with slightly sloping faces are separated by courts and halls, but along their edges we see an edge molding carved to represent bundles of reeds, a concept that takes us back once again to the original reed temple huts and their gated enclosures.

Similarly, the overhanging fringe, or cornice, that runs along the upper edge of the pylons is said to represent the drooping heads of the plants.

Once inside the temple compound, the most striking feature is the vast Hypostyle Hall commissioned by Seti I and finished by his son, Rameses II. Within an area of some 54,000 sq. ft. we find twelve enormous columns, some 80ft high, that once supported the roofing slabs of the central aisle to produce a clerestory. Today they are clearly seen as symbols of papyrus and are referred to as "papyriform," with open capitals resembling the umbels of the sacred plant. At night the columns are illuminated, glorifying papyrus as never before. These columns are certainly large enough to make a lasting impression on even the most jaded of all ancient or modern tourists, and this fluted papyrus column form has influenced architecture throughout history, from classical Greek and Roman architecture even to the columns in the Washington, DC Metro system.

Progressing through this temple compound, we come upon one of the most common forms in Egyptian temple architecture: the bundled column. It resembles a bundle of reeds bound together to provide strength. These bundled columns in later years were refined and simplified, and appear again in a more streamlined form in the fluted columns of Greek and Roman times. Other plants were also models for columns and other structures in the Egyptian temples, especially the lotus, acanthus, and palm tree, but there is a primacy to the role of papyrus, in that the swamps dominated by this plant were the settings for some of the most important of the ancient religious legends of the Egyptians.

Tall, open papyriform column, 1400 B.C. Insert shows a bundled papyriform column, 2600 B.C.

Horus, falcon-headed god of all Egypt, patron lord of the kings and son of Osiris, King of the Blessed Dead, was born and lived his early life in the papyrus swamp at Chemmis in the Nile Delta. And Anubis, jackal-headed god of the dead, stood guard over the entrance to papyrus swamps at the northern part of the underworld, through which no soul could pass until judged. But above all else, papyrus played an elemental part in the lives of Osiris and Isis.

Osiris reigned as king of the earth and not without reason; he had civilized the archaic inhabitants of the Nile Valley by giving them laws, teaching them what to eat and how to grow and cultivate crops, as well as how to worship the gods. His jealous brother, Seth, killed him, then, blinded by rage, ripped him into fourteen pieces and scattered them throughout Egypt. For many years Osiris's wife, the goddess Isis, sailed up and down the Nile swamps in a papyrus skiff, looking for the pieces; and that is why when people sail in boats made of papyrus, it is said that crocodiles do not hurt them for fear and respect of the goddess. And that is the reason, too, why there are so many graves of Osiris in Egypt, for she buried each limb or portion as she found it, where she found it.

In a larger sense, the swamps have an additional importance in that when the dead arrived at their final resting place, the followers of Osiris believed they would live forever in a celestial marsh similar to the papyrus swamps here on Earth.

> *Sekhet–Aanru, or Field of the Reeds, was a name originally given to the islands in the Delta, or to the Oases, where the souls of the dead were supposed to live. Here was the abode of the god Osiris, who bestowed estates in it upon those who had been his followers, and here the beatified dead led a new existence and regaled themselves upon food of every kind, which was given to them in abundance. According to . . . the Book of the Dead, the Sekhet–Aanru is the third division of the Sekhet–hetepu, or "Fields of Peace," which have been compared with the Elysian Fields of the Greeks. (E. A. Wallis Budge,* The Book of the Dead, *1895)*

The temples then were representations of the sacred papyrus swamps, houses of the immortals, and also the universe at the moment of creation;

above all, they were timeless havens under the protection of the spreading umbels. Like the mounds first built by Egyptians to provide escape from the inundation of the river, the temples became in the Egyptian mind a mound of survival, and each day at dawn the doors of the sanctuary were opened by the priests, and the world was recreated as they brought forth a new day out of the waters of chaos. It was the focus of cosmic order, "the radiant place."

Standing inside the Amun-Re Temple is akin to standing in any other large columned space. You could as well be in one of the large cathedrals of the west or the major temples of the east. What sound there is diminishes quickly from an echo to a whispering sound as the tourist crowd passes through and the space takes over your mind. Deep into a natural swamp the only noise will be the umbels above you waving gently as a breeze passes overhead. That creates the whispering, soft sighing that is as unworldly as any sound in nature, but very much like the sound that you hear inside the temple in Luxor.

Von Rosen, unusual in that he could appreciate what it meant to be a swamp dweller, was amazed at the fact that so few scholars before him had commented on the importance of papyrus swamps to the ancient Egyptians. His enchantment with the notion of the swamp as a place to live joined him philosophically with another radical, the 19th-century thinker and naturalist Henry Thoreau.

Dr. Rod Giblett, a writer, lecturer, and conservationist at the Edith Cowan University in Australia, called Thoreau the "Patron Saint of Swamps" because he enjoyed being in them and writing about them. For Thoreau, "my temple is the swamp. . . . When I would recreate myself, I seek the darkest wood, the thickest and most impenetrable and to the citizen, most dismal, swamp. I enter a swamp as a sacred place, a *sanctum sanctorum* . . . I seemed to have reached a new world, so wild a place . . . far away from human society. What's the need of visiting far-off mountains and bogs, if a half-hour's walk will carry me into such wildness and novelty."[5]

Who would have thought a New England Yankee could have put the case so well? This sums up not only Count von Rosen's feelings—but that of the ancient Egyptians.

No permanent housing structures have survived from pre-pharaonic times in Egypt, but some evidence exists suggesting that, in addition to mud-brick buildings, reed huts were also in use in the Faiyum and Merimda region. Postholes dated ca. 4700 B.C. suggest that if such structures existed, they were oval in shape with poles overlain with mats or reeds.[6] In the early days, also, small reed houses and reed temples built on mounds probably came to be as much of what Lewis calls "the Egyptian style of architecture" as the monumental constructions of pharaohs and cities of innumerable mud-brick buildings. Badawy's reconstruction of these ancient huts looked a great deal like those of the Batwa.

Batwa papyrus hut, Lake Bangweulu, 20th century

Merimda, Egypt, papyrus and wood post huts, 4000 B.C.

door

Batwa papyrus hut under construction compared to ancient Egyptian papyrus huts
(after von Rosen and Badawy).

One view of what an early Egyptian papyrus hut on a floating mat might look like is shown in a famous mosaic that dates from 100 B.C. A vestige of Sulla's sanctuary in Palestrina, Italy—a sacred place dedicated to Fortune that was at the time the largest sanctuary in Italy—the mosaic depicts the inundation of the Nile in Roman times. It may have no basis in fact, since it was fashioned from the impressions of ancient travelers, but the house in the mosaic looks very much like the houses of the Marsh Arabs. This leaves open a number of interesting possibilities, especially when we look at ancient reed structures that were reconstructed by the architect Badawy from very old clay tablets, seals, implements, and temple drawings.

A reed house in ancient Egypt during inundation in Roman times (Palestrina mosaic, Italy).

Some of his drawings are uncanny in their resemblance to the reed houses and mosques of the modern-day Marsh Arabs in Iraq. Their distinctive type of construction is still in use after 3,000 years, though it may be older still, as the same communal buildings seen in contemporary marsh culture were found on Sumerian seals from 5,000 years ago. The anthropologist Paula Nielson points out that the agricultural and irrigation practices were similar between the ancient Sumerians and the Marsh Arab. Like Marsh Arabs still do today, the Sumerians traveled in slender reed boats, caught fish and birds with long spears, lived on marsh islands in reed houses, and herded water buffalo, sheep, and cattle.[7]

The type of construction used involves the bundling and binding of reeds to form "posts." The butt ends of these posts are sunk into the substratum, where they can then be left upright to support a standing wall or bent over to be interwoven and joined with opposing members to form an arch. Once covered with reed mats, the result is an astonishingly strong vaulted building similar to a Quonset hut. This kind of house is much more versatile than mud brick, as it can be built on dry land or inside a marsh or swamp or on a mound of reeds. In Iraq today, the whole mound on which the houses are built rises and falls with local water levels. It is doubtful that the whole mass of a papyrus swamp would so react, as it is much too heavy to easily raise or lower with sudden changes in water level. A more fascinating possibility is that suggested by Badawy, that huts woven from papyrus were simply mounted directly on boats, which would be very light in comparison to the whole swamp. In the early days, he says, "It may be surmised that settlers on both sides of the Nile erected their shelters and huts in the style of the (boat) cabins. . . ."

Building a Marsh Arab house (after Ochsenschlager).

Herodotus is silent about any housing used by these people; we have to assume that if they were using a particularly distinctive type of housing by then (440 B.C.), we would have heard about it or seen traces in paintings or reliefs. If the ancient Egyptian marsh men did build houses inside papyrus swamps, they would have had an advantage over the Marsh Arab since, as Thor Heyerdahl found, the Marsh Arabs' floating mounds on which they build their houses—simple platforms made of reeds laid down over many years—are soft, almost unsteady. In a papyrus swamp the interlocking matrix of the rhizomes, though it also undulates, provides a much stronger foundation than that of the floating reed islands in Iraq.

Without papyrus, hundreds of thousands of settlers in prehistoric and pre-dynastic Egypt would have had to survive the inundation with houses built of alternate materials, a process that would require thousands of years to evolve. Such housing would also have to wait until mounds were built above the flood. All indications are that, as with boats on the early Nile, a shortage of housing during the period 7000 B.C. to 3500 B.C. would mean a slower rate of development, less production, and a slower advance of civilization. A world without papyrus could only have been seen as a great setback.

In addition to the habitations of marsh men in ancient Egypt, it is also interesting to speculate on what the Egyptian terrain would have looked like during inundation. Herodotus tells us that, in the time of the first human king of Egypt, ". . . all of Egypt except the Thebaic district was a marsh: all the country that we now see was then covered by water, north of Lake Moeris, which is seven days' journey up the river from the sea. . . . And I think that their account of the country was true. For even if a man has not heard it before, he can readily see, if he has sense, that that Egypt to which the Greeks sail is land deposited for the Egyptians, the river's gift—not only the lower country, but even the land as far as three days' voyage above the lake. . . . Inland from the sea as far as Heliopolis, Egypt is a wide land, all flat and watery and marshy."

The agricultural year did not begin until the inundation subsided in autumn, leaving the earth of the floodplain soaked and overlaid with a fresh layer of black silt. The impression one gets is that the floodplain was emptied of vegetation, domestic animals, and people during the floods of summer and early autumn.

"When the Nile overflows the land, only the towns are seen high and dry above the water, very like the islands in the Aegean sea. These alone stand out, the rest of Egypt being a sheet of water. . . ."

In later times, mud-brick houses predominated in and around Egyptian cities and towns, and also in agricultural settlements on dry land; but a substantial number of people, fishermen, boat builders, papermakers, craftsmen, and their families still lived closer to their work in or near swamps. The Floating World in ancient Egypt thus provided an opportunity for early architects and craftspeople to create what Prof. Badawy called "prototypes," compact bundles of papyrus reeds that served as corner posts and arch supports. First made by simply tying dried papyrus stems together with rope and twine (also made from papyrus), the bundles could then be shaped and fashioned into all sorts of designs. These were the forerunners of the fluted columns and scalloped parapets, as well as vaults and domes that were later copied in brick and stone to become the architecture of the Western world.

9

The Field of Reeds as a Way of Life

On Lake Chad on the other side of Africa, another larger group of swamp dwellers, the Yedina tribe (earlier called the Buduma, meaning "people of the reeds"), inhabits papyrus islands and swamps. Like many other African tribes, they enjoy a cattle-based lifestyle with a diet of cow's milk, fish, and occasional grain products. Early visitors to the region, such as Olive Macleod, the travel writer who came through there in 1912, were amazed to see the distinctive curved-horned cattle being herded into the water and made to swim to nearby islands, or small herds loaded onto large papyrus boats called *kadays* for transport on long journeys across the lake. If Egyptologists had seen this, they would have been quick to draw a parallel to the herdsmen of old Egypt, who drove cattle across branch rivers in exactly the same way, including the use of papyrus skiffs.

During the dry season, Yedina men move out to floating papyrus islands where they have fishing camps. At other times they live on the larger, more stable islands and make their huts from papyrus reeds in the same way that

Roscoe found among the Bakene on Lake Kyoga and von Rosen found among the Batwa on Lake Bangweulu.

As in the fashion of the Bakene, the huts on Lake Chad can be lifted up and moved to higher or lower ground if there is a change in water level. But now they face a crisis. Lake Chad is drying up and the Yedina are very close to being forced to give up their aquatic lifestyle. Lake Chad was featured in Al Gore's documentary, *An Inconvenient Truth*, as one of the extreme examples of a disappearing ecosystem. Not mentioned in the film were the papyrus swamps, the habitat in which these people live, nor the people themselves, who are suffering as the lake and swamps dry out.

As Gore pointed out, "Once one of the largest lakes in the world, it has dried up over the last few decades to almost nothing, vastly complicating the other problems." It has gone from 10,000 square miles down to about five hundred or less in a period of just ten years.

For the 88,000 Yedina, this is devastating. The drying up of the lake is due to a number of causes, including global warming and water extraction from the river that feeds the lake. The water that was taken from the river was used for irrigation and domestic use, but in any event it "starved" the lake. According to Sylvia Sikes, a naturalist who explored the lake by sailboat in 1969–1970, a large factor is the general drying of the region due to weather and man's activities, or desertification caused by cutting and clearing vegetation in the basin.

In October 2013, NASA astronaut Karen Nyberg snapped a photograph from the International Space Station that shows what's left of the lake: a small patch of water illuminated by sunlight. Around it, and to the northwest, are ripples indicative of sand dunes in places that were once water. In one area smoke plumes, perhaps from fires set by farmers, drift over a former swamp region.[1] It is now a desolate sight. If the lake does dry completely, all of the Yedina will be forced to take up dry-land farming or herding, a drastic change from their present lifestyle.

☙

As the Bakene, the Batwa, and even the Yedina were well aware, papyrus swamps are great hiding places in times of trouble, provided that one can stay healthy. The first recorded use of papyrus swamps as hideaways comes from Egypt in the time of the Persian occupation (525–404 B.C.). Libyans and Greeks who served together as mercenaries in the Egyptian army rebelled at the harsh taxation leveled by the Persians. In defiance of the government, they settled in the delta and built several fortified towns in the papyrus swamps, one of which, Papremis, was the site of a famous battle won by the Libyan Inaros in 460 B.C. In the process, Inaros killed the Persian satrap (governor) of Egypt, Achaemenes; but after fighting for another year and a half in the papyrus swamps, Inaros was taken captive and later put to a barbarous death, a combination of impaling and flaying alive.

This swamp action lived on in Egyptian history until 206 B.C., when another rebellion arose that became one of the first historically documented guerrilla wars.[2] Egyptians under the leadership of the last of the pharaohs revolted against the government in Alexandria. The rebels in Lower Egypt, in defiance of the Ptolemys, hid in the papyrus swamps of the delta for *twenty-one years!* Finally coaxed out with an offer of peace, the leaders were killed and the revolt halted; interestingly, the terms of the treaty that settled this rebellion make up part of the text on the Rosetta Stone.

Incredible as it may seem, it is possible to live for generations on floating reed rafts or artificial reed islands. Good examples are the boats and islands on which Marsh Arabs in Iraq and the Aymara Indians on Lake Titicaca currently live, which last for many years, provided that the substrate is replenished with dry reed over time. Potentially, the islands they live on could last forever if properly maintained, and papyrus islands are stable to the point that Chadians kept cattle on some of them. The marsh men of ancient Egypt may have found homes on man-made islands or large papyrus boats or rafts that acted as living platforms. Even if they gradually became waterlogged, new layers of dry papyrus stems could simply be piled on top of the old during the inundation, which lasted from late July to late October; after that, there was adequate time for the island or platform or boat to dry out before the next flood.

In modern times, the people living in papyrus swamps are there for a reason. When Livingstone was descending the Shiré River, a river that flows south from Lake Malawi into the Zambezi, he found a number of families of the Manganja tribe hidden in the broad belt of papyrus. They had been driven from their homes by the raids of a rival tribe. "So thickly did the papyrus grow, that when beat down it supported their small temporary huts, though when they walked from one hut to another, it heaved and bent beneath their feet as thin ice does at home. A dense and impenetrable forest of papyrus was left standing between them and the land, and no one passing by on the same side would ever have suspected that human beings lived there. They came to this spot from the south by means of their canoes, which enabled them to obtain a living from the fine fish which abound."

Life in the swamps in von Rosen's day was thought by some to be a unique and bizarre experience. The count's adventures were felt to be so unusual that they starred briefly in the Tarzan series of Edgar Rice Burroughs. Burroughs used a Batwa-type village in his 1928 story *Tarzan and the Lost Empire*. One of his characters, a European archeologist called Erich von Harben, bore a remarkable resemblance to von Rosen. In the story, the young Erich and his trusty African helper, Gabula, are captured by Africans, allies of a tribe descended from ancient Romans, and taken to a lost outpost in a secret valley in Africa where "A half hour of steady paddling along winding water-lanes brought them to a collection of beehive huts built upon the floating roots of the papyrus, from which the tall plants had been cleared just sufficiently to make room for the half dozen huts that constituted the village. Here von Harben and Gabula became the center of a curious and excited company of men, women, and children . . . [and later were] conducted into one of the small huts of the village . . . [where] they were brought a supper of fish and snails and a dish concocted of the cooked pith of papyrus."

The reference to eating the plant comes directly from Herodotus. In ancient times the rhizome was dried and ground into flour that was used to "stretch" local bread flour. Most experimenters (including myself) after eating it conclude that the plant might do as a side dish, but not as a main course. Quite often ancient and modern people living in or near papyrus swamps chewed on the green stem, which has a thin sweet sap like a diluted form of sugarcane juice.

One thing to note is that sugarcane was unknown to the ancient Egyptian. It may have arrived in Egypt with Alexander, or after, but the main sweeteners in the old days were figs and honey. In comparison, then, chewing on a fresh young papyrus stem might actually be considered different, almost a treat, and was made even more attractive because it was readily available at any time of the day or night, and it was free.

"Erich von Harben" is not far from Eric von Rosen. Did Burroughs ever read about any of von Rosen's exploits in Africa? Before and after WWI, the count published scientific papers in English, German, and Swedish, as well as several books that became best sellers of their day in Europe. Burroughs appears to have sought them out.

○

The protection offered by papyrus swamps has been a blessing for desperate people many times in history. In its northern extension from the Nile swampland, papyrus is found in the Jordan Valley where the Bedouin sought refuge years ago. Papyrus swamps were also once found along the coastal road north of Jerusalem. These swamps were famously used by Richard I, the Lionhearted, to protect his troops during the Third Crusade.

During Richard's march toward Jerusalem along the coast of Palestine in September 1191, he was pursued by Saladin, the Sultan of Egypt and Syria, whose strong force hid in a forest overlooking the shore road. Saladin harassed the Crusaders mercilessly and was intent on ambush, but cautious Richard used the papyrus swamp that lay between him and the enemy to protect his troops for one evening, allowing them to rest through the night. The next day, the swamp also served to guard his rear flank while the king withstood the attack.[3]

Saladin was repelled, and Richard went on to capture Arsuf and later Jaffa. Seven hundred and twenty-seven years later, almost to the day, British troops again made use of the same swamp to drive Turkish troops away from Jerusalem in the First World War. This time going in the opposite direction, Gen. Allenby's forces used the same swamp to protect their right flank. The swamp served them well, as in September 1918 they attacked the area north of Arsuf on their way to Damascus and victory.

This impassable ground was called Birket El-Ramadan and consisted of a papyrus swamp that was then six square miles in area. Later reduced by half by encroachment in the years following WWI, it was finally drained for agriculture by the British administration in Palestine in the late 1930s.

Perhaps the thought that papyrus swamps offered ideal cover for undercover operations led to the most novel use yet proposed for any papyrus swamp. This came about in June 1976, while the Israeli secret service was finalizing plans to recapture an Air France jetliner hijacked to Uganda, the famous "Raid on Entebbe," an event made into a TV movie starring Charles Bronson in 1977. The Israelis proposed to parachute twelve fighters into Lake Victoria who would splash down, get into inflatable dinghies, paddle to the swamp edge, creep through the papyrus swamps (the same swamp that tourists see today on arriving by air in Uganda) to reach the terminal, and kill the terrorists.[4]

At the time, it seemed so very appropriate as a form of retribution against the tyrannical and murderous Idi Amin. Like Isis and her son Horus emerging from the papyrus swamps of old to wreak revenge on the evil uncle Seth, so it would have been with Amin. Somehow, someday, vengeance would emerge from papyrus and perhaps be his undoing.

Problems with the plan arose immediately when they considered what would happen if all twelve got stuck in the swamp, and how the evacuation of more than a hundred hostages would be carried out by this intrepid dozen. The plan was abandoned, and the rescue of the hostages went forward without the trek through the swamp. Instead, it was carried out at night by a specially trained assault team using transport planes that landed directly at the airport.

Unfortunately, the body of Dora Bloch, the only hostage to die in the attack, was found later in a papyrus swamp north of Kampala, a cruel irony considering how the rescue was originally intended to be staged. But the swamp would still have a role to play in expelling Amin from Uganda. Ten years later, in 1986, Yoweri Museveni, now the President of Uganda, led a successful overthrow of Amin and his government by launching what the BBC in 2001 called ". . . a guerrilla struggle based in the swamps of central Uganda." The papyrus swamps of Lake Victoria would have a role to play after all in finally avenging the havoc wreaked by the murderous dictator and by shielding Museveni's rebel forces. Papyrus, in its way, helped bring down Amin. If the papyrus swamps had not been there to provide that needed cover, the chilling thought lingers that Idi Amin might still be with us today.

10

Swamps Are the Future

Sustainable development, the process whereby the human race can meet its needs without diminishing the capacity for future generations to meet theirs, is said to be a process whose time has come, and not a moment too soon. The Green Revolution has given way to the revolution of the "Greens." Yet sustainable development must have seemed a normal, natural, everyday condition in the lives of the pre-dynastic Egyptians. After all, they lived within a world whose boundaries were clearly defined—a strip of green that was in stark contrast with the desert, arid hills, and dry mountains on either side. Their Egypt was an isolated land, cut off in the south by cataracts and in the north by a maze of marshlands, tributaries, pools, lagoons, and islands that made up the delta. They were reminded every day of the finite nature of their world. They had no choice but to live within their ecological means.

By all accounts they rose to the challenge. They were a relaxed, tolerant group of people filled with an appetite for life and capable of realizing their good luck, and they treated their natural resources with respect.

Visitors in later years would marvel at the inundation in Egypt. Many of these visitors came from Greece, where the thin, rocky soils meant backbreaking work to till a small field. The layer of silt that the Nile left behind on a wet floodplain must have seemed heaven-sent. Under those conditions the visitors probably thought any fool could reap a bumper crop, that farming in Egypt was labor-free, similar to what one expected in the Golden Age, "where the rich earth, unforced and without stint, bore fruit abundantly." But, as Naphtali Lewis has pointed out, the Egyptian farmer still had his work cut out for him clearing the land, then plowing, hoeing, and cultivating it in order to keep it productive and weed-free. And the work later done on irrigation ditches, sluiceways, and drains would try any man's body and soul.

Prof. Butzer tells us that from 17,000 to 8000 B.C., a wetter climate prevailed. During this period the Nile would swell each summer, becoming a roaring torrent perhaps resembling the Congo in flood. That river comes raging out of the Congo River Valley and into the southern Atlantic with a mighty rush. At any time of the year flying over the mouth of the Congo, you can see the plume of soil and sediment spreading out on the ocean surface before it disappears into the depths of an underwater canyon. Its sediment load is simply carried far out and deposited in an abyssal plain deep inside the ocean. The Congo has no delta because its mouth is so deep—300 feet—like the primeval Nile of six million years ago.

Just as the Congo is a classic example of a river without a delta, the Nile is a classic example of a river *with* a delta. So classic that in fact the term "delta" was coined by Herodotus just for the Nile because the formation so resembled the Greek letter Δ.

Dr. Jean-Daniel Stanley, Senior Scientist Emeritus and Director of the Deltas-Global Change Program at the Smithsonian Institute, has made sediment profiles of the Nile Delta that provide us with a general picture of its evolution. The modern form evolved from around 6500 B.C., when the Nile at the apex of the delta had separated into five branches and, since the sea was still about 30ft lower than the land, the water must have cascaded down the branches onto the delta, which at that time consisted mostly of sand and gravel.

Typically in deltas, the river water cuts its way through previous material and drops heavier sediments, such as gravel and sand, close to shore. The water spilling over the delta also carries silt that spreads out over the alluvial fan, while the fine-particled clay travels in suspension quite far out to sea. There it reacts with salt water and is deposited as alluvial material.

The saying "Nature abhors a vacuum" applies to ecosystems as well as to natural and contrived experiments. At some point, the sand and gravel were replaced by silt and bare mud as the Nile Delta appeared above low water. This new mud was a "vacuum" that would have been quickly colonized by plants and animals. Prior to that time, when only sand and gravel were present, few plants could survive.

The species that first appear on wet mud are appropriately called "pioneers" because their life is a tough one, requiring all sorts of adaptations in order to persist and survive. The largest factor would be the summer flooding since, once rooted, a plant has to just sit and take the deluge. The alternatives are to be ripped out by the roots by the force of the floodwater, or to be left in place to drown. Thus a pioneer plant would have to adapt to extreme water levels and its seeds would have to germinate and grow fast, so that inside of twelve months—by the time the next flood arrived—the plants would be ready to take advantage of their new habitat and take root. They must also be species capable of warding off competition from an increasing array of plants that will attempt to establish a foothold within this newly created ecosystem.

In the earliest days of the delta, when the sediments first appeared above the low-water mark, the water was still fresh—salt water was kept at bay in prehistoric times by shoreline features such as bars and shoals—so the first vascular plants to appear would probably have been riverine grasses and sedges, including papyrus.

Papyrus would have landed there easily enough, as there would have been floating islands of papyrus coming down from the backswamps of the floodplain. Papyrus can also establish itself from windblown seed which germinates and grows quickly on wet mud. In any event, it was a prime candidate for the Nile Delta because it can tolerate flooding, unlike many other plant species. The amazing thing about papyrus is that even though it has stems that grow to 15–20ft tall, they are lightweight. The plant is interlaced with air spaces so that it floats and accommodates itself to the water level. Shortly after papyrus established itself, swamp grasses, reed grasses, and bulrushes followed, species that are common to seasonal swamps. These species can root in mud and wet soil, and grow well in places where the soil occasionally dries out, but they are not as versatile as papyrus.

The first papyrus plants that grew in the delta probably appeared at the very neck of the delta, the place where the Nile first branches out; this is a pattern seen today in the Okavango Swamp in Botswana. The Okavango is an inland delta where the Okavango River empties into a natural inland formation rather than the sea. Papyrus in the Okavango is considered a keystone species in that it grows quickly over any small water body and into flowing water along the edges of the channels, eventually blocking the channels like a dam. It then produces floating islands that break off and travel further downstream, creating havoc as they block more and more channels.[1]

Relief comes in the form of a second keystone species, the hippopotamus, an animal large enough to break through these blockages and release the river water which is otherwise dammed up. If the hippos are hunted down or poached, the blockages get worse, since papyrus is relentless in its advance across perennial shallow water. In the ancient Nile Delta, hippos must have been common enough; in fact, in Merimda, one of the oldest settlement towns close to the apex of the delta, a hippo tibia was found used as a front doorstep.[2] Still, papyrus had its way and was instrumental in slowing the flow of Nile water across the delta and filtering sediment, preventing erosion and the rich delta soil being lost to the sea.

Today one can stand on the banks of the Congo River and see what it must have been like on the early Nile when large and small clumps of vegetation go sailing by on a river unhindered by dams or barrages. Whole trees, logs, detritus, stumps, and weeds wash by on their way to the Congo mouth; and most conspicuous of all are hundreds of islands of papyrus that drift by, with tall stems and feathery plumes acting as sails—yet another clever evolutionary development that allows the plant to find new places to grow and spread its seed.

In the delta, papyrus swamps, grass swamps, and other wetlands would thrive as more silt became available. The ancient delta expanded to become a large formation: 8,500 square miles of freshwater habitats, including ponds, islands, and swamps, that would expand from the apex down to the sea. At the sea edge, salt marshes would soon replace the freshwater wetlands along the coast.

From about 5000 B.C. onwards, the first farming communities were busy in the Nile Valley draining swamps, cutting back thickets, and irrigating the floodplains. Though Butzer placed one center of population growth in the Nile floodplain near the apex or beginning of the delta above Faiyum, he felt that the vast wastes of the delta would remain thinly settled during the Dynastic era until around 2700 B.C., when Egyptians would turn to taming what he calls the "Deltaic Wilds."

In the ancient delta, Prof. Hassan notes, conditions were different from today, since between 10,500 and 2500 B.C. the northern parts of the delta supported far more extensive marshlands and swamps. And so more and more plant and animal species persisted, and a succession proceeded from barren mudflats to a thick growth of riverine vegetation. Thousands of years later, perhaps woodlands or maybe a tropical forest would have appeared, depending on the local weather and the continued accretion of silt and soil. But this normal progression from wetlands to forest didn't happen in the delta. It was stopped and then reversed because of the intervention of man.

Once intensive cultivation began in the delta, more people moved to it; by Roman times, the land cultivated exceeded that of the valley floodplain. Then came canalization of the water supply, clearance and drainage of plots, and finally the complete cessation of flooding and alluvium in 1965 when the Aswan High Dam was closed. The history of the delta from that time is similar to that of Louisiana, where the silt from the Mississippi is held back. Both deltas formerly grew as silt was deposited by either the Nile or the Mississippi, but now they have both stopped growing. They are losing land from erosion, from incursion by the sea, and they are sinking because of extraction of water, oil, and natural gas. This is referred to as "subsidence" or "the destructive phase," since during this phase coastal features such as islands, river banks, and shoals are liable to disappear as the water overtops the land. In Louisiana, this disappearance is often remarked on because it happens within a person's lifetime.

Subsidence in the Nile Delta was best illustrated in the early days by the disappearance of the branches of the Nile. Pliny the Elder identified seven branches. By 700–1000 A.D., the land in the northeastern part of the delta had lowered to such a degree that three of the most eastern branches had disappeared. In addition, large saline ponds, lakes, and lagoons were formed as the sea encroached more and more, turning freshwater regions brackish and then to salt water. The advance of the sea in the eastern side brought about the destruction of Tanis, a major delta town. Hassan tells us that "by the time of the Arab conquest in 635 A.D., Tanis was no more than a ghost town of reed huts."

Before all of that happened, however, as Michael Herb and Philippe Derchain, Egyptologists from the Universities of Cologne and Brussels, tell us in their *Landscapes of Ancient Egypt*, the delta swamps (which were then still freshwater) were intensively used in the Old Kingdom (2600–2180 B.C.) for cattle-keeping, fishing, bird-catching, and plant-collecting. These economic activities were described in pictures and texts from the time of King Sneferu (2614 B.C. and later). They also make a point about the quality of the soil increasing as one goes north along the river, with the best alluvium dropping out as the Nile approaches the maze of canals, natural levees, and blockages in the swamps of the delta.

The first papyrus swamps forming in the delta during that era would become the forerunners of the papyrus swamps that would feed the papyrus paper and rope-making industries in the time of the Ptolemys. Later, during the time of the Romans, the delta marshes and swamps would also provide fuel for the baths in Alexandria, as well as an expanded paper business.

It was almost as if a modern planner had sat down with the delta residents and set out a plan for sustainable development of the region between 3000 and 500 B.C. As agriculture flourished with time, the delta wetlands were used to graze cattle while the perennial swamps, cultivated plots, and farms existed side by side in a balanced cycle, each producing what was needed as civilization began and flourished.

This period is reflected in the sediment cores of Dr. Stanley, who told me that the large (15ft deep) layer of marsh peat laid down in the northwest somewhere around 2000 B.C. was perhaps indicative of the papyrus swamps. Subsequently, this is followed by a layer of lagoon mud and then beach sand from the First Millennium A.D. This perhaps follows the clearance of the papyrus, which marks the end of sustainable development in the delta—but not the end of the plant that made so much of it happen.

〇

How useful was papyrus during these early days in the delta? Could the Egyptian farmer have gotten by without it? As the early observers could see, the famous Nile flood and the deposit of silt were physical processes, events that would go on anyway even in the absence of wetlands or cultivated crops. But the danger of erosion was always present, especially if dry weather followed a flood year. And in ancient Egypt there were some very famous seven-year droughts and famines. During dry conditions, alluvium not covered by crops or swamp vegetation would be subjected to erosion. It doesn't rain that much in Egypt, but when it does it can be heavy. Severe erosion could be caused by the rare rainstorm; but more important, wind erosion was also a serious threat, and still is today. Because of the flat, exposed landscape of the delta, wind sweeps across the terrain unhindered. It has been put to good use in recent years—two large wind farms generating 500 megawatts (MW) have recently been put into operation on the Gulf of Suez.[3] During all those years, the great mass of peat, roots, and rhizomes produced by papyrus stopped a great deal of alluvium from being lost to the sea.

Silt and sediment were also trapped by other wetland species in the delta, and obviously, because of the sheer volume of water that passed through, quite a bit of sediment still ended up in the ocean. But papyrus did a major job of carrying the brunt of filtration, as it does in places like the Okavango, where observers comment on the clarity of flood water after it passes through the papyrus swamps: ". . . the very effective filtration action of the dense reed beds and papyrus groves, results in water of almost startling clarity."[4]

Another action of papyrus swamps and other wetlands is the conservation of water. This is not of much consequence when the whole valley and the delta are inundated, but later, when man developed means of tapping the aquifer by digging wells and boreholes, such water made all the difference in success or failure of a crop during dry years. The role of wetlands became crucial in helping to recharge the fresh water underground, since that same water also slowed or prevented salt water from intruding. Dr. Stanley and his colleague Andrew Warne, from the Waterways Experiment Station in Vicksburg, Mississippi, point out that though papyrus swamps had disappeared, wetlands were still widespread in the northern part of the delta in the 19th century. Their removal and the subsequent construction of levees and drains meant less and less water conservation and recharge. More and more salinization and subsidence went on, and more and more often boreholes brought up unusable water. The result was that farmers walked away from land that had been in production since the time of the pharaohs.

☙

From 10,000 B.C., when papyrus thrived in the delta, until 900 A.D., when the plant disappeared from Egypt, everyone who farmed the delta benefited, everyone who made paper or rope benefited, and the bird hunters and fishermen and craftspeople saw nothing but good from this arrangement. In the early days, the delta was a model of the right sort of development.

When the first Egyptian started clearing papyrus swamps, he had none of the machinery and drainage technology of later years. Large drainage projects would come along late in the Dynastic era, but for many years small areas of swamp were drained and cleared locally. These smaller efforts were perhaps the most efficient way to use swamp resources, since the peat from the swamp, as well as any accrued sediment and silt, could be put to good use as soil amendments. And because the drainage was done on a small scale, enough swamp was left behind to support the established lifestyle of the residents, a lifestyle not seen in other hydraulic cultures of the world. It was a lifestyle that generated export earnings and nourished the local fauna, as well as providing local material for boats, houses, and crafts, with enough left over to provide the dry reeds that were used to fire the baths of Alexandria, an absolute must on the part of Romans who had settled in that city. Without warm baths, life for them would have been intolerable.

What evolved was not simply a riverine ecosystem in the delta, but a whole way of life based on a relationship between a plant and man.

Herodotus tells us that Egypt was a gift of the Nile, but there was as well a second gift—the wetlands of the delta, in which papyrus played a large part.

In the present day, the sacred sedge and many acres of the original wetlands are no longer there to slow the course of the river. Their place has been taken by the modern cultivated and developed landscape. Dams and barrages have canceled the flood regime, captured the alluvium, and now generate hydropower that must be used almost exclusively to manufacture commercial fertilizers needed to replace the natural alluvium. These are the same fertilizers that are poisoning the soil with trace-element buildup.

The final insult comes from the many industrial drains and sewage outfalls that are emptied into the delta lagoons, converting them into sewage ponds. In place of the balanced renewable system of old, we have a system in which delta land is fast subsiding as salt water is intruding and pollution is spreading throughout—and the whole thing exacerbated by the effects of global climate changes. It is also now a system that is not meeting the needs of the people, who are dependent on importing almost half their food, causing prices to rise in a country where political, social, and economic stability has given way to violence and unrest.

∾

With a population of 16.8 million spread over 175 square miles, Greater Cairo is the largest metropolitan area in Africa. As expected, the levels of pollution that result from the "Mother of the World" are gargantuan. Realizing that Cairo takes most of its water from intake points in the middle of the Nile River, how can it be that the quality of tap water in Cairo satisfies most Egyptian and international water-quality standards?

The answer is dilution and diversion.

Prior to the closure of the Aswan High Dam, the dilution factor was huge. The annual flow was then 45 billion gallons per day ($62km^3$ per year in 1964, according to Said & Radwan, 2009). Now the annual flow is reduced to 3 billion gallons per day, but that should still wash out an awful lot of bad stuff in the drinking water.

Diversion also helps, in that the half dozen wastewater-treatment plants serving the Greater Cairo area, as well as the toxic chemical and organic discharge of 329 major factories (which amounts to as much as 660 million gallons per day of untreated effluent), are routed well north of the city by agricultural drains and canals.

This doesn't mean that Egypt gets away scot-free. Cairo's industrial wastewater has made some of the industrial zones inhospitable, and since the wastewater is routed into the Northern Lakes of the delta and the Mediterranean Sea, it has damaged Egypt's shores, coastal fishing, and tourism in this region. Also, the city's water managers must treat drinking water to remove heavy metals such as lead, cadmium, and copper that comes from industrial pollution, a costly process that doesn't get at the root of the problem.

The most worrisome future trouble lies between the Aswan High Dam and Cairo, where 43 towns with populations exceeding 50,000 and approximately 1,500 villages discharge their waste into the Nile.

Programs to reduce Nile pollution are being implemented, but the task is huge and the cost prohibitive. It has not escaped the attention of the planners that filter swamps are a good low- or no-cost solution. There has even been an attempt to use papyrus as one of the component plants in such a scheme. Swamps that are encouraged to grow in polluted water are called filter swamps because they act in just that way. Just like a filter, the water stops moving once it enters a swamp. At that point, sediment and other heavy pollutants settle to the bottom. Swamps are thus ideal for holding back sediment and preventing erosion. Slowing the water also allows papyrus and other plants in a filter swamp to take up and use nutrients. Nutrients and metals can attach to the sediments that settle out of the water. In this case, who knows—the sacred sedge may someday save Egypt from the hand of man.

Meanwhile, there are parts of the delta where pollution seriously affects people's health. In 2005 Dr. Amr Soliman, of the University of Michigan School of Public Health, identified a high incident rate of pancreatic cancer in the northeast Nile Delta region. The culprit was traced to the high levels of cadmium from industrial waste showing up in the local soil, water, and fish. This area has one of the highest levels of pollution in Egypt.

Over time, cadmium accumulates in the body because there are no specific mechanisms for its removal. Its half-life in the body ranges from

10 to 30 years, with an average of 15 years. The serum cadmium levels of residents in the northeast delta region were almost *10 times higher* than those of residents from cadmium-polluted areas in Cairo, and *32 times higher* than reference levels for healthy populations in the United States. This indicates that the water treatment for heavy metals in Egypt is sporadic and that there is an immediate need for cadmium-reduction measures to be put in place. It also calls into question the numbers of people adequately served by treated water. One study, quoted by Susanna Myllylä, a lecturer in Environment at the University of Tampere in Finland, said the official numbers are overestimated and that at least 23% of Cairenes lack access to safe and adequate water supplies.

In the case of water, the alternatives hinted at by Dr. Hassanein were voiced in a report commissioned by the Habi Center for Environmental Rights, which stated that every year some 17,000 children die from gastro-enteritis caused by polluted water.[5] The report also indicated that kidney failure, likely caused by the same polluted drinking water, is four times higher in Egypt than in the rest of the world. Heavy-metal poisoning from polluted water over the long term is already taking its toll in the delta. The danger posed to people eating contaminated fish and drinking contaminated local water was spelled out in 1994 in an assessment carried out by a team from George Washington University and the Smithsonian Institute. They advised that until potentially toxic metals in the drain water and sediments were removed or drastically reduced, fishermen should refrain from raising or catching fish in Lake Manzala, and also advised a prohibition on farming any reclaimed bottomland along the lake edge, both things increasing Egypt's already heavy dependence on imported foodstuffs.

In the future, cadmium and other heavy metals may be on the rise in the Nile due to yet another new pollution threat upstream: oil drilling. Significant discoveries have been made in Sudan amounting to almost 7 billion barrels, in addition to 6 billion in Uganda. Both discoveries could have long-term effects on Nile water since cadmium is one of the heavy metals found in what is called "found water," or "produced formation water," deep groundwater that comes from wells during the process of drilling.

One concern is Block 5A in Sudan, a concession that straddles the swamps of the White Nile. Also worrisome are the Ugandan oil fields that are located in and around Lake Albert, one of the sources of the White Nile.

Although papyrus is absent today from the Egyptian Nile, Egypt is fortunate that millions of acres of papyrus swamp are still acting as one of the largest filter swamps in the world upriver in the Sudd. The wetlands there take up significant amounts of nutrients and act as a buffer to pollution well before the water reaches the main Nile at Malakal. It was therefore a disappointment to hear that, with Egypt's support, plans have been made to dry out these swamps. Egypt wants the water to be diverted directly into the Nile rather than to stay in the wetlands, wetlands that many local people depend on for their living. That way, Egypt increases the water available in the Nile for its use, but at the expense of the people living in and around the swamps—who, by the way, were very upset by the idea. It did not come as any surprise to find out that this wholesale diversion of water was one of the causes of a war in the Sudan, a war in which papyrus once again found itself in the middle.

11

Sarah Starts a War

In Victorian times, the early explorers did not have it easy on their expeditions into Central Africa. Many planned their travel by river, either going east on the Congo or south on the Nile. This allowed them to use their boats as a base of operation, a safer option than camping out among hostile tribes, voracious animals, and disease-infested swamplands.

At that time the one feature most often mentioned in regard to Africa was water, and the fact that once you passed through the northern deserts, the interior seemed to hold immense quantities of it. Given the amount of rain that fell on the center of the continent, travel by boat made sense, and it worked on the Nile, at least until you reached that part of the White Nile (Map 1, p. 17) that spreads out into the Sudd. From there, in order to proceed by boat it was required that a path be cut through papyrus or other swamp vegetation. To cut such a path from the water's edge was, and still is, a formidable task.

Fortunately, explorers like Samuel and Florence Baker could employ legions of Egyptians and local natives. Sam, as he was known to friends, was wealthy and could afford to watch from the safety of the upper deck of his steamer while hired men went into the shallow water, naked but for their loincloths spattered and stained with black mud, to fight their way through the morass. But too often the men needed urging on or had to be protected from wild animals. Otherwise, the boat stuck fast and they had to walk through the swamps on foot, whereupon Sam would find himself wading into papyrus so thick it was the stuff of nightmares. The cutting crew now advanced in front of the steamer, hacking through the dark, pungent rhizomes, while a second crew followed, struggling forward with a heavy grappling hook and thick rope, or hawser. Once hooked onto a mass of plant material, a third crew on deck started a creaking, groaning winch that took up the slack and allowed the vessel to creep forward. Behind them stretched the newly opened channel, in which a flotilla of small craft wallowed, while directly in front of them the water was black with decomposed plant matter dredged from the bottom, and crowded with pieces of rhizomes floating on the surface. The peaceful, fragrant environment of the swamp was shattered as the expedition churned up great bubbles of swamp gas from beneath the swamp which erupted, releasing methane and sulfurous stinks. It was as if they were wading into an enormous pit of sewage.

The Bakers were on their way to discover the source of the White Nile at Lake Albert in Uganda, and on occasion had to abandon their boats and make their way along with the surging mass of humanity that comprised their expedition. At every step they were confronted by vegetation as they plunged forward through rivers or along muddy swamp bottoms or flooded lowlands; and their baggage didn't help matters. They had brought with them tons of provisions, rifles, ammunition, spare clothing, 21 donkeys, 4 camels, 4 horses, and 80 bushels of grain as a food supply for the 90-man army and boat crew. They were also saddled with crates and barrels of trading goods to barter their way through the kingdoms of the unknown. And they expected at any moment to meet tribes of savage people as they made their way east toward Uganda, looking for the lake said to exist somewhere in the western Rift Valley.

Always on the move, their passage through valley swamps made my forays into Nakivubu swamp look like a picnic.

My wife had never stirred since she fell by the coup de soleil, and merely respired about five times in a minute. It was impossible to remain; the people would have starved. She was laid gently upon her litter, and we started forward on our funeral course. I was ill and broken-hearted, and I followed by her side through the long day's march over wild parklands and streams, with thick forest and deep marshy bottoms; over undulating hills, and through valleys of tall papyrus rushes, which, as we brushed through them on our melancholy way, waved over the litter like the black plumes of a hearse. (Sir Samuel W. Baker, The Albert N'yanza, Great Basin of the Nile, 1866)

They both survived the ordeal, as did their observations on the swamp plants of the Sudd, where they measured the heights of selected papyrus plants at 18ft and also found that the average umbel was 4ft one inch in diameter. They were made even more aware of the umbels because they provided a modicum of shade. If they were hacked down or pushed aside, a gap opened through which the sun blazed directly. The heat, and many days of trudging through endless papyrus swamps, must have been a living hell for them, but they survived and in the end it made them famous.

❧

I've often wondered what would happen if the Bakers were to make the same trip today. In some ways it would be an entirely different experience, but in other ways things wouldn't have changed much. On their 1862 expedition, setting out from Khartoum they met armed resistance in many places in the south from Arab slavers; then deep into the region they found themselves embroiled in tribal wars, which were a serious problem and a daily threat to their lives. Once they crossed the border into Uganda they fell into the clutches of Kamrasi, an early murderous king of what was then called Unyoro.

Today, the same region of Sudan is fraught with danger as armed aggression persists between North and South. And once you reach Uganda's northwest border, Joseph Kony and his Lord's Resistance Army still roam at will. The easiest and safest way to traverse the region is to fly over it. I can picture Sam and Flooey (his pet name for Florence) as they take off and fly to the shores of Lake Albert (named by Baker and dedicated to the Prince Consort). Their light chartered plane would land at Pakuba airstrip in Uganda's Murchison Falls National Park (named by Baker after the president of the Royal Geographical Society). In organizing their flight, it would be best to fly out of Malakal in the Sudan, since that would take them right over the Sudd. We know Sam would be able to afford this because in Khartoum, in addition to his small private army, he bought a paddle steamer, tons of provisions, and two sailing barges to carry his expedition south—an expensive operation even by the standards of those days.

One hitch in his travel plans today might be the fact that charter flights could be difficult. There are exceptions, such as Air Cess, a small airline operated for years in Sudan by the recently jailed Viktor Bout, the arms dealer nicknamed "the Merchant of Death." It happens that he was not the first to bear that title. Alfred Nobel, the inventor of dynamite, was called that in a premature obituary and was so upset by the moniker that he was inspired to create the Nobel Prizes.

On their hypothetical flight, I'm certain Sam would relax over a cold beer as he watched the papyrus swamps sweep by down below. He loved beer. On the eve of his departure from Africa in 1865, he marked the end of his four-year near-death cycle of wild adventure by staying at an English hotel in Egypt where the hotelkeeper had "Allsopp's Pale Ale on draught."

Their only contact with the Sudd on their modern air trip would be the photos they would take from the plane's windows, or the view that the modern traveler has flying over such an exotic tropical region. And they would have had the pleasure of seeing papyrus from a distance.

There is something about flying over papyrus that excites the imagination in a pleasant way, versus how the imagination runs wild with darker thoughts when trying to move through it, whether it's over the Sudd, or the swamps along the shores of Lake Victoria, or the inland valley swamps of Uganda, or the wide green bands of papyrus that nestle along the banks of the Victoria Nile. Those light feathery umbels from the air look like soft green fluff down below, an impression that is heightened by the thought that this is a rare sight. Like virgin rain forest, tropical savanna, tundra, or the spruce forests in North America, you are looking at a vegetation type that has not changed in hundreds of years; and if it does change, chances are it will never look the same again. In 2009 the British movie and TV star Joanna Lumley flew over the Sudd on a trip from Khartoum to Juba and photographed what the Bakers would have seen on a similar trip.[1]

⟋

In the 21st century, European birds on their way south to Africa are mightily in need of food and a quiet, safe place to sleep after passing through the deadly air of southern Europe. Fumes pumped out of refineries into the sunny Mediterranean atmosphere turn into a toxic haze that affects any bird that lingers in the region. The Eurasian cranes that make it through have been on the road for 2–3 months, passing through Germany, Hungary, Bulgaria, and Turkey, riding thermals and flying with slow, powerful strokes, traveling at 45mph as they search out a safe route through the Levant.

White storks follow the same route but have a much longer way to go; their migration to South Africa will take them on a journey of 6,200 miles. Both cranes and storks follow thermal air currents that are not found over the oceans, so they must find one of the flyways on land that will carry them through the Middle East and down into the Jordan Valley. The cranes travel in pairs; a crane couple may flank their young on either side during migration flights, whereas storks, though monogamously attached for life, do not migrate or overwinter together. As they land in the swamps in the Jordan Valley, the crane couple and their young will probably find much company, because 25,000 other Eurasian cranes overwinter in a place there called the Huleh Valley. Many roost in the shallow water of close-by Lake Agmon, shaded in the evening and early morning by papyrus, which is now encouraged to grow there. The cranes have become such a valued tourist attraction that they are fed by the Reserve staff; this serves also to keep them away from neighboring fields and from damaging local crops.

The white storks will probably not hang out more than a day or two at the Huleh Swamp "bird motel." After resting for about 12 hours they will push off, perhaps stopping along the way in one of the brackish, highly polluted marshes of the Nile Delta, such as Lake Manzala. Shortly thereafter they will make their way south along the Nile to the great papyrus swamp of the Sudd. This is where millions of other birds overwinter or pass through on their way south. The Sudd is the least polluted of any stop so far on its route, and right now it's probably a very quiet place.

It was anything but quiet on the 10th of January in 1983 when "Sarah" was very much alive. But who (or what) is "Sarah?" Sarah is—or rather was—one of the largest freestanding machines ever built. In 1983 Sarah appeared in an article in *Time* magazine, and the world then learned how she had been brought to the Sudan to cut an open canal 220 miles long in a province called Jonglei. The canal would be 15ft deep by 170ft wide, the longest open, continuous ditch in the world, a ditch whose express purpose was to divert water from the Sudd.

The concept of a Jonglei Canal has been floated since colonial times, the idea being that a canal bypassing the Sudd would result in a great saving of water in the main river, since 60% of the water of the White Nile is lost here through seepage and evaporation. Bypassing the swamp would increase the water in the main channel of the Nile by at least a trillion gallons per year. Northern Sudan and Egypt would benefit from this; indeed, they had already begun including this gain in their onward planning in anticipation of the completion of the Canal, and hundreds of thousands of acres of land to be irrigated were set aside within their parched landscape just for this.

Egypt especially was in need of water, as it doesn't rain there. The only water Egypt receives is from the Nile, so Egypt is constantly looking for new ways to increase the flow of the river. The population growth in Egypt has long outstripped production of food and, as mentioned previously, this population growth, combined with neglect of the water supply, land, and industrial pollution, has left Egypt as one of the world's largest food importers. They buy about 6.5 million tons of wheat a year. They also lose a great deal of their own water due to pollution, so they are in constant need.

The contract to dig was awarded to French construction and investment companies, and by 1980 Sarah had been assembled and was hard at work. She was named after the daughter of a Sudanese official, and had originally been built for use in Pakistan to dig a large open canal between the Indus and Jhelum rivers. The "roue-pelle," or "bucketwheel," had several large self-propelled sections joined to each other with girder-like connectors. The working head was a 40ft-high wheel with 12 buckets that plunged down into the soil, lifting 3 tons with every scoop. The scoops were emptied onto a conveyor belt and the soil carried to the embankment, where it was dumped.

In the course of a single day, 25 operators were required to work three eight-hour shifts, and it used 10,500 gallons of gas every 24 hours. Eight stories high and weighing over two thousand tons, it required a million spare parts, and must have been a joy to the owners when a buyer was found.

The local tribal people would stand and watch it in wonder. To top it off, oil had been discovered not far from the region and Chevron had been given the go-ahead to start pumping crude into a pipeline that would take it to Port Sudan for export. All boded well, though in the process the Northern Sudanese government had consulted only Egypt and the World Bank, a necessary step as financing was needed for the canal. Egypt ultimately invested $100 million, and presumably international donors provided the rest of the $260 million required to start it up. By January 1983, when the *Time* magazine story was published, the canal was already visible as a straight line on satellite images. Sarah could be detected as a dot on the end of a very, very long exclamation point.

The only thing lacking in all this was any response from the Southern Sudan, other than some grumbling. Perhaps it was assumed that, since the oil and water were to be extracted from the South, the South would profit from spin-offs of one sort or another, and thus be placated. Exactly how this would happen was not spelled out to the public by Northern Sudan or the Egyptians, whose business interests in their race to reel in the extra water and profits therefrom left them with little interest in the discontent of others.

Toward the end of 1983 the South finally let everyone know their feelings, and they were not good.

The first sign of trouble was a kidnapping that took place in November 1983. Following that, the canal workers were apprehensive, and rightly so, as the following year eight workers were kidnapped by the Sudan People's Liberation Army (SPLA) and the machine was attacked. It stands today, bullet-pocked and rusting on the spot where it came to a halt. The SPLA also attacked the oil-drilling installation in February 1984, kidnapping and later killing three of Chevron's employees. In 1985 Chevron closed down its Sudan operation, by which time the Second Sudan Civil War was in progress. It lasted 22 years, during which time 1.9 million people were killed and 4 million had been displaced. But what exactly had driven the South Sudanese to such initial acts of violence? And how did it escalate so quickly?

It all comes back to water and what makes a "water war." The North Sudanese and the Egyptians did not realize (or care), but the South was very much aware that drying out the swamps would open up the entire Sudd area for irrigated mechanized farming. The mechanized farming schemes, mostly managed and owned by Northern Sudan businessmen, would lead to a land takeover and a disruption of traditional life. In addition, many felt that draining the swamps would allow Northern government troops to move military equipment and troops more quickly into the South, where tensions had already been brewing. At least 1.7 million Dinka, Shilluk, Nuer, Murle, Bari, and Anuak live in the region and would be directly or indirectly affected.

According to Dr. Mohamed Suliman, Director of the Institute for African Alternatives (IFAA), if the South lost the water, they would lose the war. He felt that the ecological degradation that had gone on unabated in the North would happen in the South as well if the swamps were drained. Water for irrigation was one of the most important factors in the war. Oil was also important, but not as important as water, and he felt it was significant that the first attacks by the SPLA were directed against the Jonglei Canal, not the oil exploration companies.

Today, Sarah sits beside the unfinished canal, like the statue of a widow grieving the aftermath of a war in which her whole family was lost. Events have passed her by. The Southern Sudanese held elections, elected a president, and also passed a referendum that made them independent. Discussions continue on the fate of the Jonglei Canal and the permanent and seasonal swamps of the Sudd. Although ethnicity, cultural identity, and religion were major elements among the causes of the war, so was a "justifiable mistrust of the project from Southerners who saw the North and Egypt benefiting while their own lives were irreversibly changed" by the draining of the Sudd.

One large concern on the part of environmentalists throughout the world is the prediction that if the canal were to be dug, the swamps are bound to suffer. If the seasonal swamps of the Sudd were allowed to dry out, what would be the fate of the 450,000 Dinka, Shilluk, and Nuer who use the seasonal swamps as dry-season forage?[2] Many thousands of them gave up their lives in defense of the swamps.

And what about the migratory birds and other wild animals who feed in the seasonal swamps and take refuge in the permanent swamps? The canal planners had commissioned studies that predicted that the canal would have a larger effect on permanent swamps than on the seasonal swamps. Papyrus dominates the permanent swamps and therefore would be the most affected. Was it a good or bad option that the wild animals associated with papyrus would suffer more than the humans? It seemed like a choice made by the Devil.

The original plan for operating the canal held out the promise of a compromise, which some people viewed with suspicion. It called for managed flooding of critical areas. Managed flooding meant that floodplain areas could be watered where cattle would drink and forage grasses would grow. On the other hand, it encouraged farming of some swamp areas that would definitely be allowed to dry out.

Despite the project planners' careful calculations based on prior wet and dry cycles, the real results seemed impossible to predict. In the conclusions of the extensive impact assessment of the canal made in the '70s and '80s, it was stated that "A simple hydrological model of the kind described is certainly *not the perfect and ultimate way of predicting the effects of varying the throughput*. But the implications are extremely significant and *suggest the need for imaginative operating regulations* if the economic interests of the people of the Jonglei area are to be taken into proper account. There are guidelines here for any future canal authority; *those who control the sluice gates . . . will, to a large degree, control the environmental conditions of the Sudd region* [emphasis mine]."[3]

Considering also, as stated in the impact assessment, that there were "weaknesses in the powers and structure" of the managing authority, and relations that were "far from harmonious" between the governing bodies, there is a danger that without a rigorous management scheme, a reliable (and costly) computer model, and a staff trained to carry it out, managed flooding by the canal operators could be a very dicey proposition.

In the impact assessment, little attention was given to the question of what would happen to papyrus in the Sudd if the swamps were allowed to dry out and die. Presumably these swamps have been in place since before 12,000 B.C., and we know that papyrus is a great producer of peat. In Uganda and Rwanda, the depth of organic peat material laid down by the plant can be extraordinary. In the Egyptian delta, the peat that was left behind by the ancient swamps still survives in a layer of up to 10ft, covered over with a layer of soil 16–43ft deep.[4] In the Sudd, the peat is close to the surface and there is little information about how much is there. One survey, done by a team from the US Dept. of Interior in 1983 in search of energy sources, mentioned a report of "peat-like soil" in the region to depths in excess of 3–4ft.

It could be that there is a massive deposit of peat under the Sudd swamp, which in turn would mean a great potential for a peat fire that would end all peat fires. Leaving so many factors to the unknown does not inspire confidence in the canal project, especially when combined with the inevitability of a drought. When dealing with a legacy of peat, a lengthy period of drought can be dangerous when there is no papyrus swamp to keep it fairly moist throughout the drought season. In Indonesia in 1997, an extended drought was responsible for speeding up the drying of peat in a 2.5 million acre project designed to clear swamp forest and plant rice. The result was an ecological nightmare.

In Indonesia, burning is used as an easy way of getting rid of tree stumps in swamp forests, but once the dry peat caught fire, a plume of smoke (white in the spectrometric scan carried out by NASA) rose over the land and remained stagnant over Southeast Asia from 1997 to 1998. Another product of burning dry peat is smog, tropospheric low-level ozone (green, yellow, and red in the same scan) that spread rapidly across the Indian Ocean toward India. The color scan done by NASA that detected the extent of the Indonesian disaster looked like a color photo of an atomic explosion!

In 1997, due to the smog at the height of the peat burn, a Garuda Airways Airbus crashed, killing all 234 people onboard. Low visibility prevented the pilot from seeing a mountainside. Thirteen airports in the area were closed for two months, people were advised not to go outdoors without protective masks, and ships collided on two occasions in the Strait of Malacca; one collision left 29 crewmen missing, presumed drowned.

The burning peat also had an unseen effect on global climate. It is estimated that the peat and forest fires in Indonesia in that year (1997) released between 0.81 and 2.57 billion tons of carbon, equivalent to 13–40% of the amount released by *global* fossil-fuel burning, and greater than the entire carbon uptake of the world's biosphere.

The managers of the Huleh Valley swamp drainage project in Israel in the '70s found to their chagrin that clearing a papyrus swamp of only 15,500 acres could lead to dust-choking chaos. What would happen if *two million* acres of swamp in the Sudd were to go in the same direction? If a worst-case peat-fire scenario were to play out in the Sudan, it would be catastrophic not just for Sudan, but for the world.

If another African drought set in, such as happened in 2008 and 2009 when the level of Lake Victoria dropped to historic lows, and if the Jonglei Canal were completed as planned, a die-off of permanent swamp in the Sudd could occur. This translates to a die-off and drying out of approximately two million acres of swamp, almost exactly the size of the Indonesian rice scheme that so badly affected the world in 1997. Agreed, the peat layers in Indonesia are extremely deep and papyrus peat layers in the Sudd are still unknown, but who knows, papyrus might rise to the occasion to avenge its destruction. The fires would rage for years.

Peat fires would be only part of the problem in the Sudd. As in the Huleh Valley (to be discussed below), the birds would go elsewhere, the wild animals that take refuge in the Sudd, especially the elephant herds, would move on, while hundreds of thousands of tribesmen and their cattle would lose a hefty portion of the flooded grassland that they depend on for dry-season pasture.

Bad news heaped upon bad news, and still more bad news. The recent oil discovery in Uganda of six billion barrels under and around Lake Albert signifies a major pollution problem in the immediate offing. Lake Albert is one of the sources of the Nile, as Sam and Flooey discovered more than a century ago. After leaving the lake, the beginning Nile River flows on to the Sudd. If the Sudd were bypassed by a canal, any pollutants that found their way into the river would flow directly into the main Nile, and from there the toxic load would be carried downstream to Lake Nasser-Nubia. Within 40 days it would arrive at Cairo, the largest metropolitan area in Africa, which as we know takes its drinking water directly from the Nile.

Often, wetlands go unnoticed because their important filtering capabilities go on without any fanfare; it all happens as the runoff water passes through. In the process the wetlands also act to slow down the release of surface water, a braking action that lowers flood heights and reduces erosion. The bottomland hardwood-riparian wetlands along the Mississippi River once stored at least 60 days of floodwater. Now they store only 12 days because most have been filled in or drained.[5]

Without the papyrus swamps to filter the water upstream, Egyptians will become as dependent as Louisianans are today on the good faith of transnational petroleum companies.

The Sudd to this day is one of the largest filter swamps in the world in which papyrus is a star performer. But this only happens if it is left undisturbed to work its environmental magic.

12

The Revenge of the Sacred Sedge

To a hungry migrating bird making its way south to its winter quarters, a swamp must appear like McDonald's golden arches rising on the dusty horizon after a full day's journey on a barren highway. There was such a swamp "rest stop" just 50 years ago, located in the middle of the Huleh Valley (see Map 4, p. 126), a productive region that straddles the upper Jordan River and sits just below the Golan Heights, north of the Sea of Galilee. That swamp, the largest and most diverse freshwater wetland in the Middle East, was described in 1865 by the Rev. Henry Baker Tristram, English clergyman, Biblical scholar, traveler, and ornithologist, as teeming with bird life. He was there between November and March when migrating birds from tropical and temperate regions made that swamp their winter home. He said it was the most vast and impenetrable swamp he had ever visited, comprising 15,500 acres that included a papyrus swamp, a small lake, and some neighboring wetlands. In the Bible it was known as the "Waters of Merom," famous as the place where Joshua defeated the Canaanites.

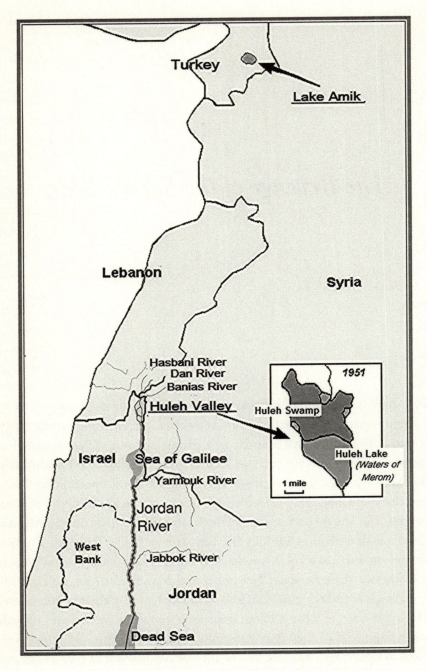

MAP 4: *The Jordan River, Huleh Valley, Huleh Swamp, and Lake Amik.*

The Waters of Merom were left in peace until 1954 when the Huleh Swamp and Huleh Lake were drained, leaving behind only a token papyrus swamp of 865 acres. More bad news followed in 1966 when Lake Amik—the only other freshwater habitat in Turkey—was completely drained to provide farmland and, later, an airport. The birds were forced to stop elsewhere on their migratory routes; the few that hung on in the valley were not welcomed by the new developers, and they were probably witness to two calamities that might have proved fatal if they were caught up in either.

The first was the 1967 Arab-Israeli War, a war that opened on the Syrian Front with a massive shelling of Israeli towns and farms in the Huleh Valley. A search-and-destroy mission was then successfully mounted by Israeli forces across the Golan Heights. By the war's end over 22,000 had been killed, and Israel was about to settle down to enjoy the waters of the Jordan River when the second calamity came to pass, the disaster of the Huleh Swamp.

By draining almost the whole of the papyrus swamp in the Huleh Valley, Israel had set off a chain of environmental events that turned a large part of the region into a dead zone. This came as an unpleasant surprise for the developers, who had until then boasted in press releases and media coverage about the fact that they had wiped out a weed, a miscreant that was now nothing but a bad memory.

The only problem is that papyrus leaves behind more than a memory. It leaves a legacy of peat.

According to Tamar Zohary, coordinator of the research program that followed the events in the Huleh Valley, and her colleague, David Hambright of the Zoology Department, University of Oklahoma, swamps have existed in the valley for about 34,000 years. Though papyrus has been present only for the last 5,000 years, there was still ample time for it to accumulate the deep layer of peat that would later cause innumerable problems.

The Huleh Valley has had a long history of human settlement, and the few travel journals that mentioned it in the 1870s were lavish in their comparison of the valley to the most productive spots on earth. It was on land so holy that the Talmud said that merely walking in it can gain you a place in the "World to Come." Within the basin, the Huleh Lake and

Swamp were seen as nothing more than bottlenecks along the road to development of the valley itself. Not that the original inhabitants would think of it as heaven. In the 1830s, long before it became a region of focus, the population of the Huleh Valley consisted largely of Bedouins, Mesopotamians, former Egyptian soldiers, and runaway slaves. The Bedouin residents were described by Victorian travelers as "stunted and dwarfed, though industrious," with fever-stricken children.

They subsisted principally by dairy farming and making mats from local papyrus stems. Malaria must have been endemic in the region, and the swamp could hardly have been thought of as anything but an evil place. Many lived in reed huts that resembled those built today by the Marsh Arabs in southern Iraq and perhaps those built in pre-dynastic Egypt.

Bedouin women carrying papyrus stems and weaving papyrus mats in the Huleh Valley, 1900s (Lib. Congress).

With the arrival of Jewish immigrants from war-torn Europe in the 1950s, action was called for; it was time to get rid of the bottleneck. Glenna Anton, a doctoral student in geography at the University of California at Berkeley, said the drainage project that resulted was heralded as a chief wonder of the Zionist effort. Once the drainage was complete, people were elated. Within a few years they had made a significant savings in water

(7.4 billion gallons per year), eradicated many acres of anopheles mosquito habitat, and reclaimed appreciable land for farming.

Through the years, farmers on the slopes of the Huleh Valley have valued their deep, rich alluvial soils that are brown or gray in color. As you get closer to the bottomlands, they became more productive and darker, almost black. From films made in the '50s during this drainage operation, it was obvious that great things were expected once the papyrus had been cleared and the swamp bottom exposed. The dark, glistening layer of organic matter they found looked like it would grow anything and everything. They thought they had struck gold. And who could blame them? Aren't we told in gardening manuals that dark, rich organic soil is the ideal? Amateur and professional gardeners alike are encouraged to aim in that direction. But whether anyone could farm this newly exposed swamp bottom was another matter. The dark material turned out to be a deep layer of fine organic matter similar to the peat found in bogs throughout the Northern Hemisphere, most of which are sphagnum bogs, created by the aquatic moss that can hold from 16 to 26 times as much water as its dry weight. The peat they uncovered in the Huleh Valley was composed of the organic matter that had been deposited by papyrus plants over thousands of years.

Perhaps this was the point at which the developers realized they had a problem on their hands, because peat, though excellent as a soil additive, is not a soil in itself. It doesn't have the substance or structure. For papyrus this is no problem because the plant is able to grow *on top* of the peat. It does this by sending out rhizomes, strong horizontal stems that spread out in a plexus or matrix that provides support to a mass of vertical green shoots. But any of the horticultural crops that people intended to plant on this newly exposed peat would have trouble because the peat would never be able to support the roots of these plants on its own; it would have to be mixed with soil.

What they now had was 15,500 acres of peat. Deep peat. Flammable peat. Measured in cubic yards, it would amount to trillions. It was like a nightmare where you win a prize on a TV show that allows you to have as much peat as you could fit into a dump truck, only to remember while driving home that you live in a small second-floor apartment.

One solution put forward by the developers was to dig the peat out, dry it, bag it, and sell it as a soil amendment. At least that would allow them to get down to the clay soil, which generally lies deep underneath papyrus swamps. This scheme never got off the ground, though there may have been a good market for peat at that time. It is ironic that since then, Israel has developed an active greenhouse industry that uses tons of peat, all imported from Ireland.

In the '50s, with so many problems in Israel demanding solutions, the obvious course was to put aside the peat problem—and perhaps that was the worst thing they could have done, because with time the peat began to dry, after which the problems began in earnest. Instead of pumping water out of the swamp, they should have left enough water to keep it wet until they had time to dig out the peat, or not bother. Perhaps conservation of the land might prove the most efficient use, rather than agriculture. Over the next few years it became clear that the project was headed in the direction of a massive ecological meltdown. The first indication of trouble appeared in the middle and southern parts of the basin, where severe problems began to develop because of the peat.

Peat, when found fresh in nature, is an extraordinary substance. It could almost be considered a living organism because of the way it functions. Composed of bits and pieces of the bog or swamp plants that grow in it, it pulls in everything. Like Audrey II, the voracious plant in *Little Shop of Horrors*, if peat could speak, its first words would be "Feed me!" As the plants and animals of a swamp die and fall into the peat, be it papyrus or sphagnum moss, the dead bits turn dark brown, and the fragile and more fleshy parts disintegrate and then decompose, feeding the organisms that live in the substrate. "Living" peat teems with life, small animals that live out their whole lives there as do worms in garden soil—and, like garden soil, peat is always "working," or "being worked."

Oxygen is depleted within peat, sometimes within inches of the surface. As the oxygen disappears, so do the organisms. As you go even deeper, chemical reactions take over so that in some bogs the ultimate product, way down deep, is coal.

Everything that enters the peat stays there, similar to quicksand or tar pits; nothing leaves except as a gas or by being washed out. And because oxygen is lacking and tannins are present, anything falling into the peat—especially in cold bogs—will sink down and be preserved. Bodies recovered thousands of years later are preserved fully clothed and intact, such as the 4,000-year-old man preserved in an Irish peat bog, the oldest European body ever found with skin still intact.[1] Or the Tollund Man, a naturally mummified corpse of the Pre-Roman Iron Age found in a peat bog in Denmark, which was so well-preserved that he was mistaken at the time for a recent murder victim![2] Peat also holds on to inorganic nutrients, binding them to molecular surfaces or locking them into organic material, so that, as long as it stays wet, peat serves as a marvelous and efficient storehouse, which is why it is such a great soil additive, if not a soil replacement. But let it dry and it changes. You see this when you use dry peat in a garden or try to mix it with soil to fill flower pots. It stays fluffy and light and takes forever to wet. Once wet, it becomes useful as a soil additive. If it dries out, it dies and then fragments into fine particles and dust that are easily picked up by the wind. The Huleh Valley disaster was directly related to the drying of peat, and it was almost as if papyrus had planned its revenge.

As the groundwater level fell in the drained swamp, air penetrated this layer of peat, drying it and setting off microbial decomposition of the organic matter in a big way. Zohary and Hambright told me that, essentially, microorganisms were "eating" into the peat. As the mass of material diminished, the ground literally collapsed, dropping by up to 9ft in some regions. At the same time, the high rate of decomposition, like an infection, caused the temperature to rise to a fever pitch. The peat became hot enough to cause spontaneous combustion and uncontrollable underground fires that consumed surrounding material and created dangerous smoking caverns. Anyone walking on the peat at that point was in danger of falling in, and the deep, glowing pockets offered no hope of escape. After the fires, the weathered peat generated black dust that swept through the newly cleared valley in dust storms severe enough to damage crops. Other bad effects recorded by Zohary and Hambright were the disappearance of millions of migratory birds and many freshwater plants, and the loss of 119 animal species, of which 37 disappeared from Israel entirely.

An indirect problem that came from the drying was the proliferation of field mice; they burrowed into the warm, dry peat, multiplied in an uncontrolled fashion, and wreaked havoc in the valley by stripping seed crops in the fields and contaminating stored grain. Over time, farmers abandoned more and more of the drained swamp area because cultivation was no longer profitable, thereby further enhancing the rate at which these soils deteriorated.

☙

In 1978 I was invited to tour the Israeli National Water Carrier that had been completed in June 1964, and I was impressed. This is a system designed to channel about 125 billion gallons per annum of water from various sources into the Sea of Galilee, which acts as a reservoir for the nation. In the '70s, this water would be used for irrigation and production of electricity; only a small portion would be used for drinking. The Carrier was a massive undertaking and showed how serious the people in Israel were about efficient water use and living within their means.

Much of the water to be tapped came from the Jordan River, which draws its source from three rivers in the north (Map 4, p. 126): the Dan, Banias, and Hasbani near snow-capped Mount Hermon. The Jordan River contributes 225 billion gallons per annum to the water needs of the nation—a significant input. It was therefore a matter of concern when the water planners found out that the decomposing peat in the drained swamp could no longer hold on to inorganic nutrients, such as nitrates, phosphates, and sulfates. All of these nutrients were being washed out of the peat with the winter rains and had nowhere to go but downstream. In essence, the papyrus peat was now polluting the Sea of Galilee. Not only had papyrus taken its revenge with the initial clearing of the swamp for agriculture, which the dried peat sabotaged, but it was still at it nearly twenty years later.

Lakes and ponds in remote regions of the northern USA and Canada often remain crystal clear because of the absence of nutrients and the cold temperatures that prevail. In such water, the growth of algae is suppressed and the lakes are often described as "pristine." Once nutrients are introduced in quantity into water, especially water that is warmed up, a rapid buildup of blue-green algae occurs in a process known as "eutrophication." This is not a welcome sign in water; these algae are referred to as "coarse algae" for a reason. Single-celled and bacteria-like, they form filaments and slimy clusters that clog filters and require the water engineer to add more and more disinfectant. Some of the blue-green algae are toxic to fish and humans, and, as often happens, even when they are not at harmful levels they give the water a bad, musty taste.

The first signs of eutrophication are "blooms" of algae that soon die back, leaving dead cells and encouraging bacterial growth. This consumes oxygen and turns the water cloudy; light no longer penetrates the water, and as a result the normal aquatic fauna and flora, microscopic animals and plants, die off or are replaced with "coarse" species. The overall effect is to turn the water into a turbid green soup with high bacterial load and increased dissolved and suspended organic matter. This makes for poor drinking water, and it is a disaster for recreational purposes (which is often the base of tourism, itself a powerful foreign exchange earner), as well as choking out any native flora and fauna.

The Israeli Foreign Ministry tells us that water is considered a resource of utmost importance in a nation where they have suffered from a chronic water shortage for years. In recent years the situation has developed into a crisis so severe that it is feared that quite soon it may be difficult to adequately supply municipal and household water requirements. The current cumulative deficit in Israel's renewable water resources amounts approximately to 2 billion cubic meters, an amount almost equal to the annual consumption of the country. In Israel in the earlier days when the water was used primarily for agriculture, eutrophication in the Sea of Galilee might have had little impact; but now with the large increase in today's demand for potable water, that kind of pollution can no longer be allowed. Yet the swamps that had once filtered the water—as well as stabilized the region and provided a natural balance in the Huleh Valley—were gone; papyrus had all but vanished. To reverse the effects, essentially to reestablish wetland plants like papyrus and allow them to do what they have been doing for thousands of years, would be an expensive operation, but it would still be cheaper than the construction of additional conventional (i.e., chemical) sewage-treatment facilities.

The future was clear: the plant that started it all would have to be brought back, and apologies would have to be made. It is now clear that reversing the damage was a positive step for everyone, a win-win situation. The first thing was to create a new reserve area in which papyrus was left to grow and reproduce. That resulted in a new atmosphere where local farming, tourism, and nature protection authorities began working cooperatively. Another factor was that there was a diversion of peat water and local sewage into treatment plants and subsequent use for irrigation, all of which will reduce the flow of nitrates into the Sea of Galilee.

The new Reserve also provides a rationale for expanding commercial tourist resources within the region. This translates into a movement to provide even more habitat for seasonal birds and ensures that the Huleh Valley will be one of the most bird-rich places in the Middle East.

Luckily, the Huleh Swamp disaster was reversible. Other such papyrus-clearance schemes are often not so fortunate. The foremost example of papyrus clearance that caused permanent damage is the delta region in Egypt. Papyrus, the plant once adored and revered by ancient Egyptians, was cleared from the delta over a thousand years ago and replaced in part by other wetlands that have since also been decimated. In the modern era, the delta has been systematically degraded so that the northern and eastern areas are on their way to becoming a no-man's-land, a place where fishermen are afraid to eat their catch and farmers are unable to use the local land or drink the water.

Egypt can't afford this. The Nile Delta represents about 60% of the nation's total arable land and is home to about 30 million people. Engineered wetlands designed to filter pollution are now being built in the delta on 245 acres of land set aside for that purpose. The idea is to help stop and reverse the march of land loss and salinization. Papyrus has been brought back to Egypt, where it might once again be used and cultivated in protected plots in order to help reverse the ravages of man. This battle for survival has just started as the country braces itself to reclaim much-needed agricultural land from an encroaching desert, feed its growing millions, save water that is being wasted in enormous quantities, and fight back the sea that is swallowing the delta—a battle that will worsen as global climate change takes hold.

In this struggle where every resource must be mobilized, papyrus may yet have a role to play in helping Egypt survive the 21st century. Today, papyrus is part of the world community of wetlands that works within the biosphere to help complete the global cycle of elements in nature. Wetlands are said to be the tough guys of the plant world because all along the world's coastlines, they have to bear the brunt of hurricanes and oil spills. Inland wetlands that line rivers and lakes have to act as the front line in filtering pollution and moderating flood events. Their impenetrable green wall shelters birds, fish, and endangered mammals, and acts as nurseries for commercial species like shrimp and crabs. But wetlands only show up on the front pages when the heat is on.

They were in the news during the BP Deepwater Horizon platform accident, the worst environmental disaster the US has ever faced. Today, years after 5 million barrels of crude oil were spewed into the sea, the Gulf ecosystems are miraculously recovering. How did that happen? The story now emerges that bacteria in the open water, microbes that cluster at the bases of the wetland plants and those that inhabit the mud of the swamps and marshes, are doing their job. The wetlands that harbor these microbial wonders metabolize enormous quantities of oil even as they continue to provide nursery grounds for economically important coastal fish and shellfish and a fall and winter habitat for over 13 million birds. And they do all this without fanfare and after many pictures of the brown pelican of Louisiana had captured the Gulf oil spill headlines.

There is no component of the biosphere that works harder than wetlands to restore order and maintain equilibrium in the natural world, yet they are losing ground every minute of the day. In Louisiana it is obvious that the levees are holding back the silt that used to flow out over the wetlands, while at the same time oil extraction from the deep regions causes the land to sink. Both processes are causing the rooted wetlands to disappear under the water. This loss of Louisiana wetlands to what is called "subsidence" is no idle threat; 40% of the wetlands in the US occur there, and these are now lost at the rate of 35 square miles or more each year. This translates to over an acre an hour for the last half-century or more.

If wetlands are lost at such rates in the First World, what chance do they have elsewhere? Papyrus still grows in Africa in swamps up and down the Rift Valley, in war-torn Southern Sudan, across the African Great Lakes region, down into the Copperbelt of southern Africa, throughout the Congo Basin, and in the southernmost reaches of the Okavango River in Botswana. Since its natural habitat is the rivers and swamps that often form the boundaries between countries, papyrus is found in some of the most politically and economically unstable places in the African world. This makes it even more difficult to conserve. When bullets and artillery shells are whizzing overhead, preservationists and planners are not likely to pay attention to the message that papyrus, the plant that was used in ancient Egypt to make paper, is still a priceless and unique ecosystem.

Thus far, papyrus has been our constant companion in a historical narrative, and until now we have treated it as a curious relic of our ancient past, from the Egyptian marsh men and scribes, to military and civil war hideaways, as water saviors, and finally as vengeful, peaty wraiths. In the next section we will see it in a new light: as a rescuing force in the modern age where pollution and degradation of nature have become the new scourges of mankind.

Part III

Papyrus Swamps, the Last Frontier

13

The Congo, Economic Miracle or Pit of Despair

The migration of millions of birds in the winter was one of the most well-kept secrets of nature until the 20th century. Prior to that, according to Frederick Lincoln, the pioneer bird bander who spent 26 years banding birds with the Department of the Interior, people thought birds simply went into a torpid state and hid in hollow trees or burrowed into marsh mud for half of the year. This despite the clue offered by the Bible in the Book of Job (39:26), where we find a leading question that gives it all away: "Doth the hawk fly by Thy wisdom and stretch her wings toward the south?"

Still, the answer to the puzzle had to wait until another, more vivid clue was dropped, one worthy of Agatha Christie—the appearance of several storks in Germany with African arrows embedded in them. The oldest of these *Pfeilstorche* (German for "arrow stork") was a white stork shot on an estate near Mecklenburg in 1822 that had its neck pierced with a 32-inch African arrow. More were to follow. To date, around 25 have been documented.

African arrows are distinctive. I have one that I bought off a tribesman in Botswana. I was tempted to bargain for it until he told me that it still had dried poison on it. At that point I knew I had to have it at all costs. It is made from a dark, tough, springy wood carved and polished and fitted with a razor-sharp metal point. It has a cluster of five feather fletches on the notched end and looks positively deadly.

How a bird pierced with such a thing would have survived is a wonder, especially one that had to fly thousands of miles back to Europe with it hanging from its neck, but the plight of the *Pfeilstorche* was not in vain. By 1900, migratory patterns had been worked out showing that some birds, like the Eurasian crane, and the white stork that we followed earlier, come to Africa along the eastern flyway, which takes them to the Jordan Valley, then south toward Lake Victoria. Other birds, like the great white pelican (*Pelecanus onocrotalus*), head southwest coming from Europe and fly on a direct line overland to the Congo region, where they join a large resident population that lives in the wetlands there.

Flying as they do on thermals at great altitudes (9–12,000ft), their view of the Congo River would be much like that of most people who see the river on a map for the first time (Map 5, p. 141). That long, lazy loop, the classic "bend in the river," jumps out at you as it cuts right across the middle of the continent and passes through the heart of the land mass.

"An immense snake uncoiled," thought Conrad's narrator, Marlow, looking at a map of it in the window of a bookshop, "its head in the sea . . . and its tail lost in the depths of the land. . . ." He went along Fleet Street but could not shake off the idea; "the snake had charmed him."[1]

A closer look at the same river on a detailed topographic map reveals myriad tributaries, thousands of them bending toward the main stream. As impressive as maps are, the enormity of the Congo River doesn't come home until you fly over it in a light plane. From the same height as our great white pelican you will see one of the last untamed rivers, with a torrent of water in its lower section that widens into a broad moving sheet ranging in width from 0.5 to 10 miles.

TOP LEFT: Hapi from the South and North with lotus and papyrus crowns, a common temple relief. Tying both plants together—joining Upper and Lower Egypt. MIDDLE LEFT: Birdlife at the edge of a papyrus swamp. BOTTOM LEFT: Papyrus canoe on Lake Tana built using an ancient design. RIGHT: Papyrus stems and rhizome from an African swamp.

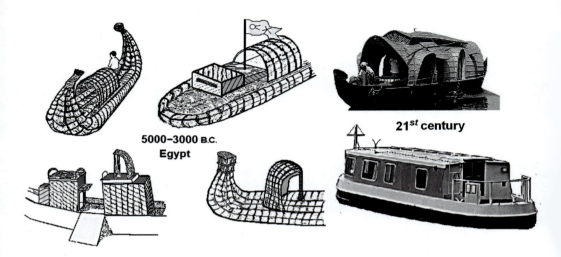

Shed, vaulted, and cupola-roofed cabins on papyrus boats that served as housing for some Egyptians in pre-dynastic times (after Badawy) compared to a modern thatched tour boat in Kerala and a modern European houseboat.

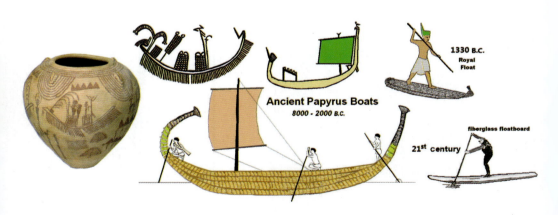

The first sail boat, an ancient papyrus vessel with papyrus sail, after vase paintings (3500 B.C.), a papyrus float of King Tutankhamun's time (1330 B.C.), and a modern fiberglass floatboard.

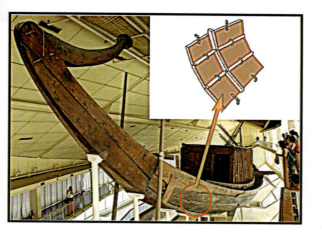

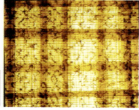

TOP LEFT: Cheops's famous solar boat reassembled with stitched planks (after Alex Lbh). MIDDLE LEFT: A piece of papyrus paper and looking at it against the light. RIGHT: Stems of papyrus in Uganda to be used by matmakers (Denny, 1987). BOTTOM: Ropemakers in a workshop near a papyrus swamp. On the workshop wall are coils of rope, tools, and supplies. The stones hanging on the ropes were used to gauge tensile stress (adapted from a drawing in Khaemwaset's Tomb, Saqqara).

The great colonnade at Luxor, looking through to the hypostyle hall in the near distance.

Lake Chad
21st century

Nile Valley
3000 B.C.

Twentieth century Yedina in papyrus skiffs on Lake Chad swimming cattle, much like Egyptian cowboys of 5,000 years ago (based on Macleod and Erman).

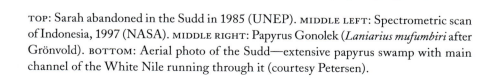

TOP: Sarah abandoned in the Sudd in 1985 (UNEP). MIDDLE LEFT: Spectrometric scan of Indonesia, 1997 (NASA). MIDDLE RIGHT: Papyrus Gonolek (*Laniarius mufumbiri* after Grönvold). BOTTOM: Aerial photo of the Sudd—extensive papyrus swamp with main channel of the White Nile running through it (courtesy Petersen).

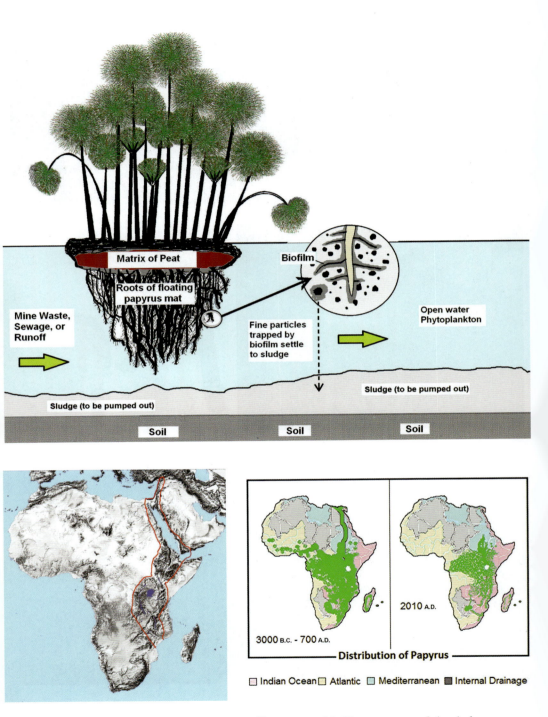

Labels within the figure:

Matrix of Peat

Biofilm

Roots of floating papyrus mat

Mine Waste, Sewage, or Runoff

Open water Phytoplankton

Fine particles trapped by biofilm settle to sludge

Sludge (to be pumped out)

Sludge (to be pumped out)

Soil   **Soil**   **Soil**

3000 B.C. - 700 A.D.

2010 A.D.

Distribution of Papyrus

☐ Indian Ocean ☐ Atlantic ☐ Mediterranean ◼ Internal Drainage

TOP: Floating mat of papyrus serving as a filter swamp, biofilm on roots and the sludge settling process. BOTTOM LEFT: The Great Rift Valley from Turkey to Mozambique. BOTTOM RIGHT: Distribution of papyrus years ago and today.

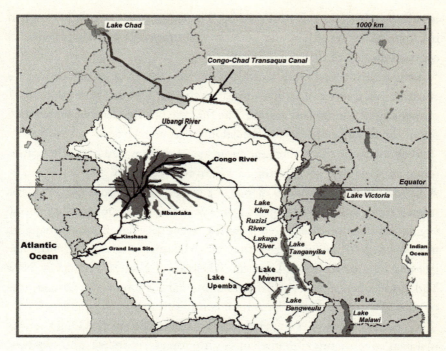

MAP 5: *The Congo River catchment, central wetlands, and sites of the Grand Inga Dam and Transaqua Canal.*

The Congo has recently been found to be the deepest river in the world—750ft in some places. The Mississippi is 200ft deep at its deepest point, while the Nile averages only 33ft. Constantly moving, the Congo swells in May and December, but still flows during all seasons because the basin is so large that there is rain falling someplace within the system every day of the year. An annual rainfall of 6–8ft in the basin results in over one million cubic feet of water that flows into the South Atlantic every second.

Another unusual feature of the river is the constant parade of plant material that travels downstream. Whole trees, logs, huge rafts of floating aquatic weeds, water hyacinth (*Eichhornia crassipes*), and water lettuce (*Pistia stratiotes*) and other plant matter goes drifting by unhindered. On the lower Nile, or on the Zambezi, there is no similar parade because both are well dammed. Watching from the banks of the Congo, the most conspicuous plant in the flotsam is papyrus. Small clumps as well as immense islands weighing several tons pass by. The stems in every case are topped by umbels that stand out and identify this unique plant that generates a constant stream of floating biomass.

Below Kinshasa, before it reaches the sea the river passes through a constriction, a series of rapids and cataracts that will tear apart and break up any large mass of plant matter. The floating bits that survive are washed out of the mouth onto the beaches along the north coast.

Walking along that strand one sunny day, I was amazed to see thousands of old papyrus rhizomes drying in windrows in the sun.

Offshore I could see a few islands of papyrus floating out to sea. Papyrus is sensitive to salinity and wouldn't survive in the ocean, but tons of riverine vegetation must be discharged from the river every day. So much papyrus passes down the main stream that Dr. Melanie Stiassny, an ichthyologist and curator with the American Museum of Natural History in New York and leader of a recent fish-collecting expedition on the Congo, was prompted to ask me, "Where is it all coming from?"

The answer is easy if you fly upstream along the river. Along the way you pass over an amazing vista of swamp forests, marshes, and swamps, among which papyrus is easily distinguished. It grows along the edges of bays or places in the floodplain wherever water is slow-moving. From the air the form of the plant makes an impression, as it appears to be an even carpet of light green that covers the valleys and smaller bodies of standing water.

As you go further south, deeper into the basin, along the shores of Lakes Upemba and Bangweulu you come to the source of the Congo, where papyrus grows unhindered among the lakes, ponds, and riverbanks, and in the valleys of the tributaries. It is here that the headwaters of the Nile, Congo, and Zambezi come close to meeting. This watery region constitutes only a small part of the 1.4 million square mile catchment of the river, but within the Congo Basin, during times of drought, it is vital. Papyrus swamps are so plentiful in this region that it is hard to escape the conclusion that the swamps are the long-sought Holy Grail of the Victorian explorers: the cradle of African waters.

In the 1960s, during the early days of African independence, the key word in swamp preservation was "isolation." The low density of people in the Central Congo Basin, and the large expanses of flooded terrain, meant that there would be few people to even begin clearing these areas; and if they did begin clearing, the effects would be insignificant.

Things change. Civil disturbance in Africa drives local people into desperate circumstances, forcing them to become refugees. Rebel troops, the *mai-mai*, roaming the borders of the Congo rape, kill, and plunder. In an effort to escape, the refugees seek out national parks where game is available for food. Beyond the havoc caused among humans, rebels equipped with automatic weapons also slaughter game to feed their troops or else sell the carcasses on the black market, and in doing so further disrupt any effort at conservation.

To the east of the Congo, in Rwanda, on the Kagera River and in the Akagera National Park, land was taken over by refugees who had been driven out of Tanzania. They flocked there because the land was unoccupied, they were hungry, and they needed soil to raise crops to survive. This park contained some of the few untouched papyrus swamps left in Rwanda, preserved until then by isolation and park supervision. Today, much of the savanna region within the park is settled by the refugees, and at a national level the government has begun the process of repairing damage done by civil disturbance. The papyrus swamps survived; though the armed struggle is not over, the *mai-mai* have shifted operations to the eastern Congo region where they are still operating to this day.

It comes as a grim surprise to hear that in order to get away from the *mai-mai*, 8,000 refugees—mostly young people—voluntarily moved onto papyrus islands in Lake Upemba in the upper reaches of the river (Map 5, p. 141). According to a report by NPR journalist Jason Beaubien on *All Things Considered* (Feb. 2006), they felt safer on the islands despite the difficult conditions there. "The islands are almost like swamps," Beaubien said, "the ground sinks under your feet." This is similar to the papyrus swamp hiding places seen by Dr. Livingstone on the Shiré River and is physically not far from the Lake Bangweulu swamps of the Batwa who were visited by Count von Rosen.

On Lake Upemba, the largest concern of the relief agency Doctors Without Borders (*Médecins sans Frontières*) is that the swampy conditions are ideal for water-borne diseases. Outbreaks of cholera and malaria are rampant and made worse by the rains, which fall from October through May.

The only good news is that small gardens can be fashioned on the islands by importing soil and heaping it into mounds to grow onions, tomatoes, and squash. But manioc, their staple food, cannot be grown here; instead, they have fish, which are plentiful, and they have papyrus, *ndago mwitu*, the "people's sedge," which is one of the dominant plants in the Upemba wetlands. And the people who live there know that in an emergency the base of the green stems can be chewed like sugarcane and the rhizomes can be baked. Also it is useful to know, as did the ancient Egyptians, that the stems of papyrus can be used for thatching and weaving mats, baskets, and other household products. And the dry stems, once spread out, act as a substrate to walk on as well as providing floors inside papyrus huts. Dry stems also provide kindling to ignite dry rhizomes, which can be used as a wood-like fuel.

Many of the refugees will presumably move back to their villages if peaceful conditions ever come about, but that may not be for some time. In an interview with Beaubien, I was told that during the past ten years more people have lost their lives in this region than in all of World War II. Over four million have died so far, and a quick end to hostilities is not in sight. The swamps turn out to be useful in emergencies, but it's best to look elsewhere for a place to live—unless one is of a rare breed like Mr. Onyango on Lake Kyoga and makes the floating papyrus swamp his permanent home.

❧

Regardless of what one's Cajun friends may say about living in a swamp, it is not something that people should undertake lightly. The largest problem is the mosquito. Though not common deep inside natural papyrus swamps, where abundant wildlife prevents eggs from ever hatching in the swamp waters, mosquitoes are devastating along the edges of papyrus swamps. The early inhabitants of the swamps in Egypt used oil from castor beans (*Ricinus communis* L, called *kiki*, according to Herodotus) to ward off the abundant flies and mosquitoes. "They sow this plant . . . on the banks of the rivers and lakes . . . it produces abundant fruit, though malodorous; when they gather this, some bruise and press it, others boil after roasting it, and collect the liquid that comes from it. This is thick and useful as oil for lamps, and gives off a strong smell." In India years ago, castor oil was said to be among the best of the lamp oils, giving a white light far superior to most others. It is used in modern herbal insect repellents, such as that produced by Burt's Bees, which also contains just about every essential oil known to man. Caution must be exerted, especially around food, since some people are very allergic to the castor plant and its products.

It happens, then, that in refugee camps or huts on the edges of papyrus swamps malaria is the number one cause of death. And it is a secret killer, because although adults suffer from infection, the population at first seems hardly affected, since infants and young children are the first to succumb and so the toll is not easily seen. In her book *Lake Chad*, Sylvia Sikes tells us that many of the Yedina who used to live in the papyrus swamps on Lake Chad used bed nets, but still infant mortality was high, so high that an infant was not named, nor its sex disclosed, for several days—a custom that insulated the mother from repeated disappointment and disgrace.

In Africa, the largest danger to marsh and swamp dwellers is the anopheles mosquito, *Anopheles gambiae*, one of the most common transmitters of the dangerous form of malaria, *Plasmodium falciparum*. Fortunately, many cures and preventatives exist today so that one need not die of malaria. The only problem is one of cost.

Fiammetta Rocco's fascinating book *Quinine* tells the story of the natural drug that was first used to treat and prevent malaria and how it was obtained from the bark of cinchona, the "fever tree" found in the jungles of Peru: "The tree that was as crucial to the art of medicine as gunpowder had been to the art of war."

She also makes the point that, after many years of development of synthetic alternatives, there is still a great need for quinine in Africa, since new formulations, though cheap in local drugstores in the West, are priced out of the reach of rural Africans. This leaves quinine, because it can be manufactured and distributed locally, as the most cost-effective treatment.

Cinchona ledgeriana, from which it is produced, is grown in Africa in the eastern Congo, and the bark is processed in the town of Bukavu by the company Pharmakina. Pharmakina persisted in growing and producing quinine in the face of the Rwanda-Congo war, which was in itself something of a miracle. How the company survived is a story told by Rocco that reads like a scene out of the movie *Hotel Rwanda*. Whereas thousands were affected by the intercession of Paul Rusesabagina in his well-known hotel in Kigali, Pharmakina saved the lives of millions. This is because so many in Africa are dependent on the production of the company, which is still very much in business and active in the development of the region.

Quinine interferes with the parasite's ability to break down and digest hemoglobin. It literally starves the parasite. Of interest are the discoveries of several other natural compounds, including Artemisinin, which is extracted from a common weed, wormwood, *Artemisia annua*. Native to temperate Asia and naturalized throughout the world, it has been known for 2,000 years for its curative effects on fever, hemorrhoids, and skin diseases. The latest research has shown that it also has strong effects on malaria. The active ingredient Artemisinin effectively treats malaria in human subjects with no apparent adverse reactions or side effects.

Another natural drug, Tazopsine, comes from a tropical forest tree that grows in Madagascar. Unlike quinine, which acts at the level of the blood, Tazopsine is active at the early stage of infection in the liver, and therefore may lead to a cheap effective malaria prophylactic—a godsend to those at risk.

In places where malaria is prevalent, it is possible to develop a limited immunity to the disease. This does not prevent one from developing malaria again, but does protect against the most serious effects. One could develop a mild form of the disease that does not last very long and is unlikely to be fatal. Early in my career in Africa, I came down with a mild dose that persuaded me to take chloroquine on a regular basis, as I would be spending so much of my time in the swamps. After a while I came to realize that I was, paradoxically, in more danger *outside the swamp* than inside, where there were few mosquitoes. The malarial carrier *Anopheles gambiae* doesn't breed in the interior of papyrus swamps because the mosquito larvae are preyed on by dragonfly larvae and predacious water beetles (*Dytiscidae*).[2]

Mostly the larvae breed on the periphery, in hoofprints at cattle drinking places and other disturbed areas or in open natural pools. Rocco's book describes her family's battle with the disease during the years when she was growing up on the shores of Lake Naivasha, along the edges of papyrus swamps where the most dangerous places are.

Anti-malarial programs during the years just after World War II included aerial spraying of papyrus swamps as a precaution against the disease. Now the experts say that the spraying of the swamps was a waste of time and money, and may even have made it worse because the chemicals that kill the mosquito larvae are the same that kill off the natural predators of the mosquito, such as beetle and dragonfly larvae. It is best then to limit the spraying to the swamp margins, where the incidence is highest. Humans who move into the edges of papyrus swamps do so because they are attracted by the safety that the swamps provide, but within a short period of time they realize that in many ways, it is its own sort of death trap.

14

A Tragic Irony

It is a tragic irony, that the Great Lakes region of Africa, which has been the theater of the most brutal genocide in modern history, could be the center of the greatest economic prosperity on the continent. A magnificent proposal exists, which could provide the basic energy and transportation infrastructure to transform one-fourth of the continent, into a flourishing economy, and lay the basis for integrating the entire continental economy for the first time in history.
—Muriel Mirak-Weissbach, 1997.
Transaqua: An Idea for the Sahel.
Exec. Intelligence Rev.

The Congo River has fascinated developers for years. Stanley saw it as the way into Africa: "This river is and will be the grand highway of commerce to Central Africa." Other early travelers concurred, including one with an unusual name for someone venturing into unknown territory—Lt. Emory

Taunt of the US Navy. Lt. Taunt landed at the mouth of the Congo River in 1885 and explored the region while his ship toured the coast. He spent an exciting six months fighting off hostile natives, cannibals, and debilitating fevers, and was able to get back to his boat and later report to the Secretary of the Navy that ". . . when in camp, the American ensign was hoisted over my tent, and while on the Upper Congo my flag was always, from sunrise to sunset, hoisted at the bow of the launch."

Taunt returned to the Congo in 1888 as the official US Agent and died there three years later. He concluded that although the Congo Valley was rich in natural products, and was as yet totally undeveloped, a demand existed for American cotton products, canned goods, and lumber, and it was a demand that increased every day.

In later years, while diamonds, gold, oil, and other precious natural resources from this region held the attention of the world, dry African countries to the north were intrigued by the one natural resource that has since become even more precious to them than all others: water.

What bothered them was the great quantity of water debouching from the river into the South Atlantic, like blood hemorrhaging from an open wound. Ideas soon surfaced on how Congo water could be put to better use. In the late 1980s, the most interesting concepts came from Italy, where the Società Bonifica had been tasked by its host agency, the Italian Institute for Reconstruction, to promote a series of initiatives for African development. From such beginnings evolved the Transaqua Project.

Like some exotic tropical plant, it blossomed and grew and thereafter developed into the scheme that Muriel Mirak-Weissbach, an international activist and writer on global affairs from Winchester, Massachusetts, described as ". . . unlike any commercial proposal made for infrastructure development of any part of Africa, for the simple reason that the motivation behind the project is not monetary profit, but actual development."

Her reasoning is based on the fact that the Transaqua investment costs are not only millions of dollars in foreign investment, but the absence of wars, the millions of human lives saved from starvation, and the social peace and international conscience that will come when it is up and running.

The original project design in 1988 was based on the idea that the northernmost reaches of the Congo Basin overlap with the southernmost part of the Lake Chad Basin and the headwaters of the Chari River that feeds Lake Chad.

By 1997 the concept of a "riverway" had evolved, a broad 1,500-mile navigable canal that would wind along the northern crest of the Congo Basin. It would intercept the drainage of the Congo in the region of the Ubangi River and connect it to 800 miles of existing river channel that would take it to Lake Chad (Map 5, p. 141). In recent years, the Lake Chad Basin Commission has presented a more reduced scheme that would link the water transfer to the proposed Palambo Dam, a hydropower dam to be built on the Ubangi River near Bangui, one of the major tributaries of the Congo River. The dam is a structure proposed by the Central African Republic in coordination with the Democratic Republic of the Congo. The connection between the dam and the Chari would be made via a 114-mile tunnel that would draw water from the dam impoundment. As a result, the Congo would lose 5% of its flow, but once it reached Chad, Lake Chad would act as a reservoir for development.

Since they share Lake Chad and some of the rivers leading in and out of it, in one stroke irrigation schemes in Niger, Nigeria, Chad, and Cameroon would gain a perennial source of water; the fisheries on Lake Chad would be revived, allowing the people to again take up their lives in and around the Lake; and, last but not least, the papyrus swamps would be saved, on which many of the Yedina people are so dependent.

Heads of state of the Lake Chad Basin Commission committed themselves to the project and commissioned a feasibility study in 2009. The project became even more attractive on paper by incorporating all sorts of multiplier effects. Planners in the early stages saw the potential for linking it to other major schemes, including a "hub" that would be created where the canal connected to existing rivers. The hub would be a river port served by the Trans-Africa Highway, a road planned to cross Africa from Mombasa to Lagos, and tied to international rail lines that are projected to serve the region. A free-trade-zone industrial park featuring agricultural, food, and woodworking plants, textile mills, and marketing facilities would be the centerpiece of the hub. The Lake Chad Basin would also gain 12–17 million acres of semi-intensive irrigated land, and the riverway and a road connection would allow for transit to the Atlantic (Lagos), Pacific (Mombasa), and

Mediterranean (through Tripoli) ports. All of which would make Central Africa a world center for hope and development.

Would it work?

On paper, yes; in practice, however, it would require a major push on the part of Africa and the international community to get it started. But it has two things going for it: the water is there in profusion, and the gradient is downhill from source to sink.

Economically it promises everything; technologically it is innovative and timely; but environmentally there would be a great many problems. The prospect of digging a 114-mile tunnel is daunting in itself, but the second phase would require the widening and strengthening of 700 miles of existing riverbeds, following which would be the construction of canals and control structures in order to implement 12–17 million acres of irrigation projects. But with so much at stake in the Sahel, and with Lake Chad in an advanced state of environmental decline, the project right now seems to be the only solution.

In many ways it reminded me of the Tennessee Valley Authority (TVA) program in the United States. A federally owned corporation created by congressional charter in May 1933, the TVA's service area covers a diverse region including ten states in the US, and a TVA international program extends the concept of integrated river basin development throughout the world. In the '70s and '80s, the international program suffered a number of failures that were ultimately corrected. It now has succeeded far beyond the expectations of most of its supporters, among whom are counted many conservatives and liberals in a refreshing case of bipartisanality. Today the TVA brings nations and international developers together with the goal of modernizing Third World agrarian societies using the TVA scheme as a model.

The Transaqua project is an excellent example of what was discussed by Dr. Marcel Kitissou, historian and political scientist at George Mason University in Virginia. He noted that the rise or decline of nations goes hand in hand with their ability to master water. In the time of the pharaohs, this meant digging canals using local labor, the cost of which was reckoned cheap though thousands died in the process. As an example, the Transaqua project planners cite a Russian proposal to change the flow of rivers that now empty into the Arctic. The water instead would be diverted to the dry regions of Kazakhstan and of Uzbekistan by means of a 1,400-mile navigable canal, at a cost of about $18 billion. But the environmental cost of such canals might far outweigh the construction cost. Consider, for example, the Qaraqum Canal, an 854-mile-long legacy of the Soviet Union that is the longest canal in Central Asia and one of the major causes of the Aral Sea disaster. This canal was never lined; as a result it loses water at a rate of 30–70%—a horrendous loss further exacerbated by the water that seeps out and then evaporates, causing widespread salinity in local soils.

Diverting the Congo to save Lake Chad is attractive only if the environmental impacts can be surmounted. There is also one large drawback which has be addressed and lies at the root cause of the Lake Chad disaster itself: the fact that the disappearance of the lake was caused not only by the extraction of water from the river but also by the general drying of the region due to weather and man's activities, especially the extensive cutting and clearing of vegetation in the basin.

That all has to be brought under control, if only to demonstrate to potential donors that lessons have been learned from past mistakes. This means that the Transaqua Project must be preceded by a major conservation effort. A "business as usual" approach will no longer work in the Sahel with global climate change staring everyone in the face.

The place to begin this effort is not in the riverbeds but on the land, where overgrazed, treeless dry depressions must be reclaimed. The terrain in the Sahel is often so arid-looking that people forget that water does exist underground; it comes from the runoff created by rainstorms or flash floods. In areas that are reforested, the aquifers are recharged more easily. If water is brought back to the region, these shallow aquifers can be supplemented by water seeping into them from the Chari River, Lake Chad, and the surrounding wetlands.

Why is this groundwater so important? Because it will supplement the water flowing from the Congo during good times, and will be the lifesaver in the event that the river ever runs low or dries up during droughts that are sure to happen with greater frequency in the future. To ensure that the groundwater will recharge, it is especially important to have a working program that manages the trees, shrubs, grass, and wetlands of the region in a responsible way.

Groundwater resources are used daily in many parts of the Lake Chad Basin, even now after the lake has dried up. And it's old news that groundwater buffers the effects of dry seasons and droughts, but in an arid region this cannot be overstated.

> The ability to exploit groundwater in arid regions can determine the livelihood of communities, whether they are small rural or larger communities that practice modern intensive agriculture or industry . . . the processes governing flood water infiltration is the key for sustainable water management in arid environments. (From: Groundwater Recharge in Ephemeral Rivers of Southern Africa International Workshop, Cape Town, South Africa, 2007.)

Technologies are already in place in the Chad Basin that are going forward: rain harvesting, sand dune stabilization, windbreaks, agroforestry using native trees, green belts, and protection of the fauna and flora of national parks are all in place. But they must be intensified in order for the development objectives of projects like Transaqua to work.

The largest user of water in the region, the irrigated farming sector, must also demonstrate that it can change from wasteful water practices now in use, such as overhead sprinkler irrigation, to drip irrigation, a cheap, easy way to cut water use by 25–50%. Drip or trickle irrigation does away with sprinkler pumps and costly piping. In addition to saving water and power, it improves yield and the quality of produce. Equally important will be an ongoing effort to drain fields using perforated, corrugated plastic tubing to prevent salinity, and larger drains to channel end-user runoff water into fish farms, and above all the use of filter marshes—places where the newly acquired Congo water can be refreshed.

❧

Where is the place for papyrus in all of this? A recovery of Lake Chad would give life back to the lake-edge swamps and a return of the lifestyle of the Yedina; but more important, it would provide an opportunity to use papyrus in even more contemporarily relevant and productive ways. Presumably the Transaqua Riverway, with its canals, newly opened irrigation schemes, and transit corridors, will bring about major changes in water quality and a steep rise in pollution. There will be a need to keep pollution in check and to refresh water that is gained at such great cost. This means water treatment will have to be in place, for which more and more engineers are recommending the use of managed wetlands or filter swamps.

The American Society of Mechanical Engineering's online magazine reported recently that construction and operation of such wetlands typically comes to one-fourth or less the cost of conventional waste treatment systems. Also, the wetlands are said to be completely free of objectionable odors, because the sludge is kept aerated. They cite one example of a reed bed constructed at a cost of $45,000 that performs so well, it eliminates the need for a conventional installation with an estimated cost of $200,000 to $500,000.

During the design and implementation of the Transaqua Project, papyrus filter swamps could make an important difference, mitigating many of the impacts, conserving precious water, and providing more habitat for nature tourism, an area of development that will surely follow as Central Africa is opened up to the world at large.

❧

On a field trip into the Congo Basin years ago, flying west from Kinshasa the plane dipped low and the pilot said to me, "Inga," pointing to the Congo River and a barrage across a side branch of the main stream. I was properly impressed. Inga is the name of the town where a barrage called Inga-1 was built in the early '70s. Later, Inga-2 came along. Both taken together affect only a small portion of the river at the place where they were installed. Designed to generate 1,775 MW of electricity, they have had little effect on the papyrus swamps or other wetlands up- or downstream. Then came news of a dam called "Grand Inga," to be preceded by a smaller project, "Inga-3." Together, they are designed to span the entire river and divert the flow into a neighboring dry valley. When the two are completed, 52 turbines would generate up to 40,000 MW, more than twice the production of China's controversial Three Gorges Dam.

Grand Inga would not only affect all of Africa but would play a role in the future of southern Europe as well. The amazing thing is that this project follows on the heels of Transaqua, a project that itself has the potential to affect over one-quarter of the continent.

My initial reaction on hearing this was: "Here would be a problem if there ever was one." For the first time, the mighty Congo River would be brought to heel. What would happen when such a large body of water was slowed in its course to the sea? The amount of water involved is so large that local or even global water cycles would be altered. A case in point is the building of the Aswan High Dam, which had adverse effects on Egypt and the downstream Nile, where it caused increased rates of erosion, salinity, and the spread of disease. Its effects were compounded by a negative impact on the Mediterranean. The Aswan High Dam so diminished the annual flood of water and silt into that sea that it markedly depressed the marine fisheries, an effect that continues to this day.

How would papyrus swamps on the Congo be affected if the river backed up into the interior part of the basin, the region that now contains the existing wetlands (Map 5, p. 141)? What would happen? My guess was that papyrus would initially adjust: the swamps would float or grow up to the new water level. But if flooding continued and a lake were formed, the new growth exposed to open water would be battered by wave action and much of it would break apart and float downriver, causing problems there. All thoughts about the region being so remote that things would remain unchanged vanished. Nowadays, no place is safe.

Then came the good news. It seems that because the flow of the Congo River does not show the seasonal variation so obvious in other rivers, it is possible to build Inga-3 and Grand Inga as "run-of-river" systems in which sizable impoundments would not be required. Run-of-river systems, instead of holding back water, simply divert the water into large pipes or tunnels called penstocks. The penstocks then feed water to power station turbines that in turn generate electricity. The water leaves the station and is returned to the river without altering existing flow. This eliminates the need for costly storage dams and the need to flood large areas. In turn, this means there would be no change in the flood regime and few, if any, upriver effects.

Better yet is the prediction of the developers that the energy derived from a run-of-river project would qualify as "green" energy in terms of the Kyoto Protocol on Global Warming. Thus, carbon credits sold to developed countries would become an additional source of revenue for the Democratic Republic of the Congo (DRC).

So, the news was better than expected. But not long after initiation, plans for Inga-3 and Grand Inga became muddled, as the DRC promised a large share of the newly planned electric output to an Australian company, BHP Billiton, in order to power a very large aluminum smelter. Hardly a sustainable use of new "green" power, especially as the process of aluminum smelting is a notorious polluter of air, water, and soil. Recently that deal has also fallen through, leaving the project hanging.[1]

Another idea floated was to build a 3,700-mile transmission line through tropical rainforest, across the Sahara and Darfur, through Egypt and across the Mediterranean to bring electricity to . . . not poor Africans, but wealthy European consumers!

Although the Inga project in the long run will conserve papyrus and wetlands, it does no good if the wetlands are not incorporated into part of a national sustainable development effort in which everyone is involved. Another large drawback of the project, as it is presently designed, would be the overall effect on the country's economy, and the perennial problem of where the money would wind up. That seems to be the question on everyone's mind. Unless the government and the economy are in sync with the needs of the people, no new era of change or lasting development will happen.

15

The Battle for Lake Victoria

*The Papyrus Yellow Warbler (*Chloropeta gracilirostris*), White-winged Warbler (*Bradypterus carpalis*), Carruthers's Cisticola (*Cisticola carruthersi*), Papyrus Gonolek (*Laniarius mufumbiri*) and Papyrus Canary (*Serinus koliensis*) are all five confined to swamps in the western arm of the Rift Valley and around Lake Victoria, spending most, if not all of their time in papyrus swamps.*
—A. Owino and P. Ryan, 2006,
African Jour. of Ecology

One day while waiting at JFK airport in New York for an onward connection, I turned to the best seller *Passages*, by Gail Sheehy, to while away a few hours. This was the original narrative about predictable crises in life. Not usually my kind of book, but I was at a stage where I had to make decisions about my career, and someone had told me to read Sheehy's book: "It might help."

In a way, it did, as it reminded me of how many phenomena in nature are geared to cycles. Even the "seven-year itch" in marriages could be due to external forces, much like the effect that sunspots have on the weather. This was an idea that definitely rang a bell. I'd always been curious about the extremes that are so obvious in Africa, where once a drought sets in it lasts for about five or more years; then comes rain unlike anything you can imagine, causing floods that set everything awash for another half dozen years. It's truly feast or famine, and it takes about eleven years for these cycles to complete themselves.

This is the basis for the theory that the weather in Africa and elsewhere is correlated with sunspot eruptions, which happen about every eleven years. The first indication is an increase in magnetic activity in the atmosphere, followed by rain, then a rise in lake levels. The theory has still to be proved, and any mechanism behind it, if it does exist, is still uncertain,[1] but recent research found that all nine of the past century's sunspot maxima coincided with maximum water levels in Lake Victoria.[2] When I began writing this book, the next peak in the sunspot cycle was predicted for 2011, when heavy rains were expected to pummel East Africa—which they did. Prior to that time, drought had set in and lakes had been drying up. Lake Chad, the papyrus-fringed lake in the arid zone of North Africa, had shrunken until it was only a shadow of its former self. The Kenyan lake, Lake Naivasha, followed suit. Also of note was the decrease in Lake Victoria. At 26,563 square miles, it is the largest freshwater lake in Africa. In 2006 it dropped by *over seven feet*, reaching its lowest level in eighty years!

Where was the water going? The only way in which such an enormous drop in level could happen would be if water were lost through the Victoria Nile at Jinja, which is the only exit for the lake. But when asked about such things, the authorities in Uganda who control the flow through the dam at Jinja turned a deaf ear. Even as the Ugandan weekly, *Sunday Vision*, reported that the water level at Entebbe had dropped by over 3ft and the shoreline had retreated by more than 120ft, the Uganda Electricity Board in 2006 continued to blame the loss on drought, global warming, and excessive evaporation from the lake itself.

"Until it stops I don't know how we could stop the water levels from falling," said Dr. Frank Sebbowa of the Uganda Electricity Regulation Authority.

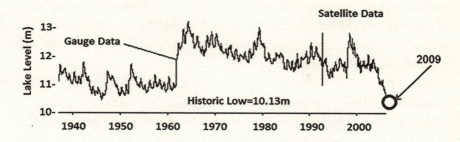

Water levels in Lake Victoria were unusually high from the mid-1960s until December 2005. Since then, water levels have dropped significantly (Simmon and USDA).

The *East Africa Business Week* (January 2006) disagreed. They accused the water authority board in Uganda of simply disregarding the rules and spilling water through the Nalubaale Dam, the only exit from the lake. This is a hydroelectric facility located at a place formerly called Owens Falls. Nalubaale, together with the smaller Kiira station downstream, is operated by a private firm that is supposed to release water in accordance with what is known as the "Agreed Curve." The Agreed Curve is the adopted policy ensuring that the water released through the dam corresponds to the natural flow of the Nile River. It was adopted by the British and Egyptian governments to ensure that the water released from Lake Victoria for downstream users is released at a rate based on the flow before the dam was constructed in 1954. In this way, Egypt would be guaranteed a water supply while the lake level would be maintained at some reasonable level.

In June 2006 Daniel Kull, a hydrologist with the UN's International Strategy for Disaster Reduction in Nairobi, in an online newsletter dealing with current water issues, reported that it was clear that "The Agreed Curve is no longer being adhered to, and the resultant over-release of water from Nalubaale and Kiira is contributing to the severe drop in water level in Lake Victoria."

By now, papyrus swamps on the edge of the lake had begun to dry out. Since 30 million people, one way or another, depend on the lake for water, concern was soon voiced and photos appeared in the local press showing lakeside villages high and dry and fishermen with boats abandoned in the middle of mud flats far from the water's edge. It was clear that the reason the lake was drying was the fact that Uganda was ignoring its responsibility of maintaining the natural lake balance. The result was a great deal of ill feeling in a country with years of hostility from Amin's reign of terror still bubbling beneath the surface.

Since the lake is a shared resource, and Kenya and Tanzania intend to use the waters for their own development projects, it came as a shock to discover that from now on the level would simply go down, inexorably dropping every year. While resource managers in Tanzania and Kenya were being bombarded by questions from fishermen and tour companies, the media were firing off a continuous round of crisis messages about the death of the lake along with headlines blasting Uganda for stealing the livelihoods of thousands. Worse, politicians in Tanzania and Kenya found there was nothing they could do about it. As lakeside residents in all three countries stood by and watched the level drop, no explanations, no excuses were forthcoming, though activists even in Uganda were not slow in pointing the finger. "This dam complex is pulling the plug on Lake Victoria," said Frank Muramuzi of Uganda's National Association of Professional Environmentalists.

As the crisis deepened, the message came home to the world that papyrus swamps made up an important part of the wetlands that surround the lake. An estimated 2,300 square miles (1.5 million acres) of papyrus swamps (about half the total of 4,000 square miles of wetlands in the basin[3]) extend along the lake shore and up local rivers into nearby valleys. Because environmental education is now well established in East African schools, and the general public is nature-conscious, there was never any argument locally about the value of swamps to conservation. On the Ugandan side, two papyrus swamps have even been designated Ramsar sites. Ramsar sites (named after the Ramsar Convention, an international treaty) are internationally recognized wetlands. One site, the Mabamba Bay Wetland System, is located along the lake shore west of Entebbe International Airport (5,990 acres) and the other, the Lutembe Bay Wetland System, a shallow swamp area (242 acres), is at the mouth of Lake Victoria's Murchison Bay.

Conservation of these swamps has become critical because of new evidence regarding the ability of papyrus to act as a nutrient "sieve" and a physical barrier to sediment. The concept is based on the use of vegetation to filter effluents as a step in naturally purifying outflows from sewage plants. Known as water "polishing" by water engineers, it is a widely accepted technique, similar to the concept of filter marshes used in the Everglades.

In the Lake Victoria region, urbanization is going forward in a big way and towns along the shore have experienced significant growth in urban population. It is predicted that the growth rate around the lake will not let up, which means that more and more people in the future will depend on the lake's water level being held close to normal.

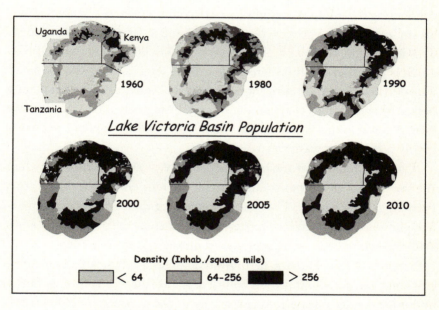

Population density in the lake region (UNEP/GRID).

Not only is this necessary in order to provide access to fisheries and tourism, but there is a need to provide dilution of the many forms of pollution from runoff and urban sewage that go directly into the lake. Even in urban centers such as Entebbe, Kampala, Mwanza, and Kisumu, the swamps are the only backup when municipal sewage systems cease working because of power outages, flooding, or overloading, which happen frequently.

Under such conditions, the benefits from the filtration by papyrus swamps—and their protection from drying out due to dropping water levels—could be the most significant thing happening to the lake over the next decade.

Filter Swamps—Harvesting and Management

The role of papyrus in filtering sewage is illustrated by the work of several teams studying the effect of wastewater discharge on local flora. Papyrus was selected as one of several plants studied because it is considered to form one of the most productive plant communities on earth, no mean feat considering the millions of plants that exist on this planet. The studies were also of interest to me because Nakivubu Swamp in Kampala was included.[4] This is the same swamp I visited on my arrival in Uganda in the early '70s, and it is the same swamp where I noticed the sewage canal and the smell. The outflow from the Kampala city municipal sewage-treatment plant is passed by way of this canal into the swamp. From there it flows on into the lake. At present this amounts to an input of five million gallons per day of highly nitrogenous wastewater.

The team found that the plants in the papyrus swamps through which the sewage passes react as would any plant to nutrient-rich fertilizer: they grew bigger and heavier. They also took up more than the average nitrogen and phosphorus and retained higher levels of these nutrients in their tissues. All of which indicates that papyrus swamps would act as a filter.

In much of inland Africa, natural wetlands act as physical catchments to trap mud and silt, but it is their ability to act as filters to control pollution and especially to release nitrogen as gas to the atmosphere ("denitrify") that encourages people to use wetlands in the first place. As much as 1.32 tons of nitrate-nitrogen can be denitrified for every acre of wetland each year.[5] This is an amazing level of no-cost water treatment.

The removal of phosphorus by the same wetlands is more difficult. Some phosphorus is combined with iron, aluminum, and calcium compounds. It is in this way sequestered and trapped in the microbial layer surrounding the roots (the "biofilm") as well as in the oxygen-poor peat, silt, and mud.

A small amount of phosphorus is also taken up directly into the stems and rhizomes of the plants and other living organisms in the wetland ecosystem, where it is used for growth. But as a rough guide in planning, the more total phosphorus that needs to be removed from the wastewater, the larger the vegetative component will need to be.

As mentioned before, natural wetland filters can be made more effective if they are harvested. This is equivalent to changing the paper or cartridge in any sort of filter. Harvesting in this case means cutting and removing, not just burning, because burning the stems within the swamp would just speed up the recycling. The best-case scenario is for the cut stems to be removed to a place on land some distance from the lake, where they can then be mulched or safely burned to provide ash as a fertilizer for cultivated plots. Another option is to chop them up and incorporate them in building material or pelleted fuel.

But even if a wetland is not harvested, it still does a good job since the older parts of the plant deposited as peat and the biofilm that sloughs off can lock in enormous amounts of nutrients over the years.

All of this is true of man-made filter swamps as well. Some constructed wetlands, for example, have operated as N and P filters for over 20 years before having to be renewed.[6]

Filter Swamps—Gone but Not Forgotten

During the recent well-publicized drought on the lake from 2000 to 2009 that left the papyrus swamps high and dry, the fear persisted that come 2011, at the end of the 11-year long-range weather cycle, when the rains finally did come there would be a great erosional flush of nutrients off the land directly into the lake. Nutrients would also be released from the dead swamp vegetation, and that would be washed in along with sewage—all of which happened.

The sad thing is that it could have been prevented by a more rigorous energy and water conservation effort along with a lake-wide action plan carried out in a truly multilateral way. As a result of this neglect, today the lake is considered "eutrophic," the polite word that means "over-rich in nutrients," or polluted.

One effect of such enrichment is the upsurge in growth of algae, or "blooms," which results in an excess of organic matter and a strong depletion of oxygen in the water (which was discussed earlier). This is the same effect seen in a fish tank when a fish hobbyist overloads the tank with fish food. The fish die of suffocation in the tank as in nature. In Lake Victoria, the flush from the land in 2011 produced an increase in algae and aquatic weeds (water hyacinth), which thrived on the new nutrient inflow. This is the same effect seen in the Sea of Galilee when the Huleh Swamps were cleared years ago, but now it is a change that can be followed from space. Thus, several years ago during a period of unusually heavy rains, the influx of runoff and nutrient-rich sediment into Lake Victoria was spotted by a NASA satellite equipped with an MRI spectroradiometer.[7] The satellite detected a change in color of the water in one bay of the lake, which changed initially from its normal blue to brown, followed by a dramatic increase in green from algae and water weeds. The NASA report was interpreted as a flush of nutrients that was confirmed on the ground by a fresh outbreak of water hyacinth and algae.

Over the last five years a general decline in fisheries on the lake by more than 50% has been ascribed to overfishing, but after the rains in 2011, reports appeared in newspapers, on TV and radio of a further decrease in fishing due to a large increase in the growth of water weeds.[8] This comes as bad news for the 60,000 fishermen who depend on the lake for their livelihoods. The problem is made worse because the water in this lake is also a major drinking water supply for millions of people. In 2004, algal blooms on the eastern (Kenyan) side of the lake resulted in a temporary shutdown of the drinking water supply to Kisumu, a town of one million inhabitants.[9]

Until proper sewage treatment is installed lake-wide on Lake Victoria, the low-cost solution to this massive problem is to encourage the growth and well-being of papyrus swamps. This can be done by maintaining high water levels and harvesting papyrus stems and water weeds for use as soil amendments and green fertilizer at a distance from the lake. This will also help curb the algal blooms and bring nutrient levels down. It has been estimated that if the wastewater entering Lake Victoria was more equitably distributed over a larger portion of the swamps, and harvesting and removal were carried out, up to 70% of the nitrogen and 76% of the phosphorus coming into the lake from effluents could be removed.[10]

Tourism and Multiuse—a Lesson from the Ancient Egyptians

Despite their positive role as virtually cost-free filters, the papyrus swamps of the lake are not well conserved. A recent aerial photographic survey along the shores of Lake Victoria by Owino and Ryan showed losses in the swamp cover in some areas of 34–50% between 1969 and 2000. This is due to the attractiveness of swampland to farmers. Because of its rich organic content and its closeness to water, the land is often deemed available for farming and settlement whether or not it is protected by law. Once cleared of papyrus, the land is immediately put under cultivation by farmers who know how to deal with peat, and they put it to good use. However, they could also be conservation-minded by helping to replant a certain portion of the lakeside in papyrus once the water again rises, but this doesn't happen and the loss continues.

Owino and Ryan predicted that at the current rate of loss, the swamps immediately bordering Lake Victoria will disappear by 2020. In that case, people in East Africa will begin suffering from the same fate Egyptians suffer today. What's the solution? One way to conserve the swamps is to manage them as part of a multiuse program. In that way, users become stakeholders and manage them much like the owners of papyrus plantations did in ancient times in Egypt.

Ilya Maclean of the University of Exeter in England, with a team of colleagues from the University of East Anglia, carried out an in-depth study of the value of papyrus swamps in East Africa in the region around the lake. Using satellite imagery and fieldwork, they looked at over 30,000 small and large papyrus swamps in Uganda alone. Maclean concluded that the most profitable solution to swamp conservation in the region, and probably many other places in Africa, lay in the traditional multiuse system already practiced by many rural households in Uganda.

This involves the harvest of papyrus stems for thatching, wall and ceiling screens, fences and floor mats, and for making handicrafts such as baskets, hats, fish traps, winnowing trays, and table mats. The multiuse of a neighborhood swamp is not restricted to crafts, but includes clearing small patches for subsistence farming, small-scale brickmaking, and fishing in and near the swamp. Maclean's work provides further guidelines. He calculated that the average household could harvest about 1,500 papyrus culms per year from local swamps, and as long as the density of people did not exceed one to two households per acre, the swamp would survive.

He also found that the average direct return would usually be in excess of $4,200 per acre of swamp, which is enough to support a Ugandan household on a sustainable basis (where the per capita income in 2003 averaged $1,440). Typically, a family lives on higher ground nearby, shares the swamp with other families, and the swamp income is not the only source of household income. In any case, it far exceeds the value derived from wholesale swamp clearance by local or national developers, since the income from that kind of development usually goes elsewhere and very little of it comes back to local rural people. Maclean's work supports the impression about wetlands that is gaining ground around the world—that they are valuable resources in more ways than one.

In discussions with African developers, government officials, and aid agencies, the idea often pops up that swamp conservation can be achieved by promoting ecotourism—tourism that brings responsible people to natural areas. This is tourism that not only conserves the environment but improves the welfare of the local people. Ecotourism has great appeal to planners because it holds out the promise of money made, ecosystems conserved, and everyone gaining in a win-win situation. But in practice this successful scenario is only true in cases where a national program is already in place to coordinate the effort and guarantee that the benefits will come down to local levels.

A good example of that is in Botswana, where tourism is a significant income producer and directly benefits people living in the Okavango Swamp. In areas around Lake Victoria, however, tourism has little or no local effect. Lakeside households receive little, if any, of the money spent by tourists on services and handicrafts. In order to be successful, it also helps to have programs in place that provide infrastructure, such as that used in the estuarine swamps in the Sunderbans National Park in India, where nature walkways and a network of bird-watching towers have been provided.

In the case of Lake Victoria, one productive effort is the Lake Victoria Environmental Management Plan that treats the lake as a common natural resource between Uganda, Tanzania, and Kenya, and a valuable one at that. The World Bank invested $80 million in the original plan. A second phase of the plan has been announced that will amount to $135 million, with 50% of the funds to be spent through the national governments on socio-economic development.

With infrastructure and promotional plans in place, ecotourism activities might succeed if the featured programs encourage villagers to participate in sustainable-use activities such as mat-making and handicrafts for sale by cooperatives. Papyrus papermaking, as is done in Cairo, might be one of the activities taken up in this way. But all this is for the future. Right now, encouraging traditional multiuse by rural households in a sustainable fashion seems to be the best path toward papyrus conservation in this part of Africa.

Protection and Conservation

Another way of protecting wetlands is to declare them internationally recognized wetlands, or Ramsar sites, as was done in Uganda. This allows volunteer agencies to become involved in conducting conservation education activities and helping local people develop community-based management plans, as well as empowering local fisheries associations to promote sustainable fisheries and tourism. All of which would probably fit well within the Lake Victoria Environmental Management Plan.

One of the Ramsar sites on Lake Victoria is at Mabamba Bay, an extensive swamp in which the globally threatened shoebill (*Balaeniceps rex*) can be found. The site also supports an average of close to 190,000 birds of many species and is part of the wetland system that hosts approximately 38% of the global population of the blue swallow (*Hirundo atrocaerulea*), as well as the Papyrus Gonolek (the *mnana*), the globally threatened Papyrus Yellow Warbler, and other birds of global conservation concern.

Any conservation effort, whether village-based or national-level, would be helped if the lake level were not allowed to drop as much as it does. High water levels help isolate and protect the swamps. Thus, whatever power generation is installed in Uganda should be of the type that requires the most efficient re-use of water. A good start will be the Bujagali hydropower project in Uganda on the Victoria Nile, a power plant that has been installed seven kilometers downstream that reuses the water passing through the two upstream plants. This may well serve as a model. It is expected to generate an additional 250 MW that will allow Uganda to substantially retire expensive thermal generation equipment. Because it is a run-of-the-river facility, it will not require any large storage basin or extensive flooding of surrounding regions.

∽

In the beginning of 2010, one year earlier than predicted, torrential rains fell in the Lake Victoria Basin; suddenly the level started rising and the swamps and fisheries recovered to some degree. The battle for control of the lake's resources was over—for now. If anything, it showed that Tanzania and Kenya have little or no recourse and virtually no control over a common resource. Any pressure they did bring to bear politically fell on deaf ears. The national interest for electricity in Uganda superseded regional and environmental interests.

And what of the future, when a general drying of the climate is expected? In years to come, the lake will probably go through cycles that will perhaps be even more drastic. Hopefully by then new sources of energy in Uganda will preclude the disastrous recent past, and the swamps surrounding the lake will be sustained to strong enough levels to prevent the extreme runoff into the lake when the flood comes and prevent the nearly equally disastrous water hyacinths and algal blooms.

The time seems ripe to put into practice a long-term conservation effort to protect the aquatic ecosystems of the lake while all three countries are once again in a cooperative frame of mind. And it's just as well that they are ready to put the bitter past behind them, because a far more serious war threatens as the upstream countries of the Nile Basin pit themselves against Egypt and Northern Sudan over the use of water on the Nile.

In the East African marketplaces, the shopper can often find a light cloth wrap, a *khanga*, useful for many things and typically emblazoned with Swahili proverbs. One says "*Wapiganapo tembo manyasi huumia*," or "When elephants fight, the reeds get hurt," which is appropriate to the times and the coming war along the Nile.

16

War Along the Nile

"What is Egypt going to do—bomb us all?"[1]
—Isaac Musumba, Uganda State
Minister for Regional Affairs

We left our white stork some time back, flying south from the Levant down the Jordan Valley to Egypt and the Sudd. As the bird continues on its way to southern Africa, following the thermals high above the land, it passes over the geological rift that forms the Y, the place where the Red Sea and the Gulf of Aden join the Great Rift Valley. This rift is slowly and surely tearing apart a large portion of the continent. When after millions of years it deepens enough, the sea will rush in, creating a new gulf as Somalia breaks away from Africa. Until then it is a place of geologic tension. It is also a place where humans and their humanoid predecessors existed for 10 million years. More recently it is the site of a 21st-century phenomenon, the Water War, the place where the fight has begun over the question "Who owns the Nile?"—a question that greatly affects the fate of papyrus.

ᐁ

African countries are beginning to realize that in the Nile Basin they are sitting on a gold mine. Just as ancient Egypt was the granary of ancient Rome, Africa is rapidly becoming the breadbasket of southern Europe, China, and the Mideast. A number of countries and transnationals are involved; chief among them are Arab and Chinese investment organizations, and European companies and their African counterparts—all in search of investments in natural resources that are lacking in their own countries. This follows from the recent surge in global food prices. Countries like the United Arab Emirates, South Korea, USA, Japan, Saudi Arabia, China, and United Kingdom are shopping for vast tracts of arable land close to water. The Nile River Basin is ideal for this.

And it's not just agricultural production, but also the domestic need for green fuel that has developed throughout the world. As Jonathan Clayton tells us in an article in *The Sunday Times*, "Demand for green energy is set to soar. From next year, European Union legislation will require that all transportation fuels contain a 10% biofuel component. Last week China reiterated its plan to source 15% of its diesel and petrol from renewable sources by 2020." In Ethiopia, British Sun Biofuels has acquired over 7,400 acres to grow *Jatropha*, a plant used for the production of bio-diesel; Sekab, a Swedish company, is planning to invest up to $400 million in producing bio-fuels from sugarcane on 2 million acres in Tanzania; Egypt plans to grow wheat and corn on 2 million acres in Uganda; and Qatar has begun negotiations with Kenya for a long lease on 100,000 acres.

These enormous investments totaling billions of dollars are aimed at the land, which is cheap for leasing or buying and comes with a ready labor pool and water that is found in the Nile Basin in boundless supply. It's all there for the asking. Or is it?

The first time any country dips a bucket into the Nile River, they are subjected to scrutiny by Egypt and Sudan, who claim the exclusive use of the Nile water under agreements drawn up in 1929 and again in 1959. This is the same law that set the Agreed Curve and regulated what level of water could be legally taken from Lake Victoria.

How did it happen that the East Africans gave away the rights to all this water? The short answer is that they didn't.

In 1929 and in 1959, Egypt and Sudan agreed between them that, because they were greatly dependent on the Nile, they needed to be guaranteed a percentage of the river discharge. With the aid and assistance of the British Government, who at the time "owned" much of the Basin, the percentage was set as 75% for Egypt. Sudan was to be satisfied with only 25%, as it had other water resources. They also agreed that the average annual discharge would be taken as 84 billion cubic meters (26 trillion gallons) and, further, that during the dry season (January 20–July 15) the flow of the Nile would be reserved exclusively for Egypt. This guaranteed them 16.5 and 5.5 trillion gallons of water to use annually (or 55.5 and 18.5 billion cubic meters, respectively), which is often referred to as their "established right" or "historic need." Nothing was said in 1929 or 1959 about extractions by upstream countries at places where the water originates, and that is the present bone of contention.

Years ago it made less difference. Now, with all of the Nile Basin countries anxious to develop a new round of foreign investments that have come their way, they need to begin to lay out irrigation infrastructure and demonstrate dependable water supplies in order to make all this pay off. To do this, they must claim what they call their "equitable share" of the Nile River. In the process, and to the chagrin of Egypt and Northern Sudan, they seem quite willing to ignore the earlier agreements.[2]

Ethiopia, for example, is already well along with project construction that will divert water from the Blue Nile. Ethiopia feels no obligation to mind what the Egyptians say, since Ethiopia (along with countries like Burundi, Rwanda, Eritrea, and the Democratic Republic of the Congo) was never party to the 1929 agreement. And, as reported by Prof. Joseph Kieyah, an economic analyst at the Kenya Institute of Public Policy Analysis, the former British colonies—Kenya, Tanzania, and Uganda—are openly challenging Egypt on the basis that, although Great Britain may have spoken for them years ago, following their independence in the '60s they have all declared the Nile agreements non-binding.

To prove their point, in May 2010 they entered into a new, separate agreement or "Framework" in which they agreed collectively to work toward conserving the Nile River and an equitable use of its water. The key word is "equitable," which means a fair sharing, not the one-sided arrangement of today. Notably, Egypt and Sudan boycotted the meeting and refused to sign the Framework; but the message is clear: the Nile Basin countries are tired of first getting permission from Egypt before using water from the Nile River or Lake Tana or Lake Victoria for development projects, especially since these water sources are all within their own borders. One indication of their attitude is the fact that for the last two years Uganda has stopped reporting to Egypt and Sudan on flow data from Lake Victoria as stipulated in the agreements.

Given that water from the Nile amounts to about 26 trillion gallons as it arrives each year in Egypt, and given the fact that Egypt was allowed to build a long-term storage dam at Aswan, how did it come to this? Decades ago, it appeared that there was so much water, no one bothered. Now we see countries shaking their fists at one another. And we have already had a taste of what happens when Nile Basin countries come up against reality. When Uganda needed water to run its hydropower plants during the last drought, it looked after itself and it left Kenya and Tanzania, two neighbors with whom they have had a long history of cooperation and development, to fend for themselves. It also left 1.5 million acres of papyrus swamps high and dry, putting at risk the last natural barrier between the lake and sewage and soil erosion.

Each day the position seems to strengthen that when it comes to natural resources, it will be every man for himself. Perhaps the former President and Prime Minister of Turkey, Mr. Süleyman Demirel, summarized the prevailing attitude when he said, "We do not ask Syria and Iraq to share their oil. Why should they ask us to share our water?"

In the summer of 2010, Ethiopia opened the gates to allow water from Lake Tana, the source of the Blue Nile, to flow into a 16-mile-long tunnel and fall 900ft onto four turbines that generate 460 MW of electrical power. So far, so good. The use of Nile water to generate power is no problem under the Nile Agreements, as long as the water is directed back into the Nile system once it passes through the turbines. But this project, called the Tana Beles Project, was kept out of the public eye by Ethiopia for a reason. It seems that, without informing anyone, Ethiopia decided that the water exiting the turbines would *not* go back into the Nile. Instead, it would be diverted for use in irrigation, in direct contravention to the agreements—agreements that Ethiopia claims do not apply in its case anyway.

By coincidence, when the tunnel was opened a film crew from the US was in the vicinity. They had arrived to film and report on a story in the Omo Valley about the relocation of thousands because of a dam under construction in a different part of Ethiopia. A side trip was scheduled for the group to go rafting on the Blue Nile but canceled when the water level dropped as the Tana Beles turbines started up.

Far from being a discreet opening of a remote hydropower project in an area normally ignored by the world press, the event was revealed as essentially the first shot fired in the Nile Water War and received worldwide coverage. As it happened, Peter Guber, author of a book on the power of purposeful storytelling, and Richard Bangs, author of *The Lost River*, a book about the Omo and Blue Nile rivers, and co-author of *Mystery of the Nile*, were with the group, who had between them credits like *The Color Purple*, *Rain Man*, the *Lord of the Rings* trilogy, *Gorillas in the Mist*, the *Twilight* series, *Batman*, and even the television hit *Mad Men*.[3]

So much for discretion. The Internet and international news media were soon trading predictions on the Nile Water War and where and when retaliation would happen.

The next move was the announcement that Ethiopia had awarded a contract to build the Grand Ethiopian Renaissance Dam, a gravity dam on the Blue Nile just 25 miles east of the border with Sudan. It will be the biggest dam in Africa and would create a manmade lake twice the size of Lake Tana. At 6,000 MW, the dam will also be the largest hydroelectric power plant in Africa when completed. The plan is to start generating electricity from three of the 15 turbines as early as September 2014.

While the reservoir is filling up, water flow in the Blue Nile may be reduced 25% for three years or more, but that could be much less if the filling period is extended. Though Northern Sudan seems ready to accommodate itself to the problem, the reduced flow is a large potential problem for Egypt where every drop counts. The Ethiopians have countered with the argument that the new dam will be a source of hydroelectric power for the entire region and will manage flood control, thus reducing the risk of flooding and siltation, and extending the life of the dams downstream in Sudan and Egypt.

Where will all this lead?

> *"If the question of Nile waters was sensitive in the centuries before 1900, when Ethiopia and Egypt each had populations of 10 million or less, what will happen over the next twenty years, as their populations each surpass 100 million and the collective population of the Nile River Basin countries reaches 600 million? The Grand Renaissance Dam poses a question as basic as water itself: Who owns the Nile? When the Grand Renaissance Dam closes its gates on the Blue Nile River, whether it is in 2015 or 2025, the time for a final reckoning will have arrived." (Carlson, A. Who Owns the Nile? Egypt, Sudan, and Ethiopia's History-Changing Dam. 2013.)*

ↄ

What would a water war in Africa mean to the fate of papyrus?

If the situation remains as it is now—a series of low-keyed, undercover water-takings, threats instead of bullets, and diplomatic missives in place of bombs—papyrus swamps would still face the same dangers they face every day of the year from industrial pollution and being cleared to make way for agriculture and oil exploration. If the war intensifies, the largest papyrus swamp in the world, the Sudd, would be a pawn, with a good chance it could be drained.

Without any change in the way business is carried out at present, Ethiopia will continue to draw water from the Blue Nile; in desperation Egypt will respond by looking for water elsewhere. The most likely source would be the White Nile and the 1.3 trillion gallons ($5 km^3/yr$) of water to be gained from draining the Sudd.

As we have seen, work on the Jonglei Canal in Southern Sudan stopped in 1983. But even though this area is now in an independent country, the project has never ceased being a prime objective of Egypt. The Sudd may still be up for grabs, since diplomatically it could be used in order to keep the peace, especially since Egypt has in the past threatened war should upper riparians divert the waters of the Nile.[4]

As Fred Pearce, a journalist, author, and environmental consultant, put it, ". . . as the nations of the Nile bicker over its future, nobody is speaking up for the river itself—for the ecosystems that depend on it, or for the physical processes on which its future as a life-giving resource in the world's largest desert depends. The danger is that efforts to stave off water wars may lead to engineers trying to squeeze yet more water from the river—and doing the Nile still more harm. What is at risk here is not only the Nile, but also the largest wetland in Africa and one of the largest tropical wetlands in the world—the wildlife-rich Sudd."[5]

Planners often get off on the wrong foot because they themselves believe the negative images created by developers and the media, to whom swamps are bottlenecks or "mistakes of nature" or "wastelands." Swamps are labeled "places where water is lost," and so must be considered bad news.

Engineers and water managers, on the other hand, more accurately think of swamps as "recharge zones," places where water is naturally put to use or recycled locally to maintain a larger system. This is a point made by the Jonglei Investigation Team in their assessment of the potential for the Jonglei Canal, that ". . . *water evaporated in the Sudd region is not a total loss*; it has its vital local value in the subsistence economy as it has done from time immemorial. It also has potential for future development in the Jonglei area. . . . For those who live in the Jonglei area it is not water lost for, as we have seen, in *the process of seasonal inundation of the floodplain valuable economic assets in pasture and fisheries are created* [emphasis mine]."[6]

The Sudd is a place where water is in motion. Some of it is used by plants to grow, some passes through the system, some is recycled by the local fauna, especially fish, and some seeps into the ground where it recharges the underground aquifer. The annual rate of recharge in the Sudd amounts to about 9ft, compared to 2.3ft in the Everglades, or 3.3ft in wetlands of Niger and Senegal, and 13–66ft in the swamps of the Okavango Delta. So, rather than being "lost," it would be more accurate to think of it as water that is being "stored and filtered for later use."

Another misunderstanding is that swamps "lose" excess water by evaporation. It is true that large papyrus swamps such as the Sudd lose water, but because the papyrus umbels form a dense yet porous canopy over the top of a swamp, it restricts the air flow and traps humidity underneath. The canopy acts like a permeable cover over a swimming pool.

Another factor is the sophisticated C_4 metabolism employed by papyrus, the chief component in one of the most productive plant associations ever known. Most other plants (97%) use the ordinary C_3 metabolic pathway that loses quite a bit of water when fixing CO_2. For example, C_3 grasses growing at 30°C lose approximately 833 molecules of water per CO_2 molecule that is fixed. Papyrus, like the extraordinary 3% of the plant kingdom that are C_4 plants, especially the C_4 grasses, loses only 277 water molecules per CO_2 molecule fixed. This increased efficiency means that water is actually *conserved*.[7]

The result is that in a papyrus swamp, *less water is lost than if the plant were absent*. Or looked at in another way, the rate of loss in papyrus swamps is *less than 75% of that lost from open water*. So, although there is water lost from a papyrus swamp, it is at a very reduced rate. This was confirmed recently using multisensor remote sensing data over a 12-month period in the Sudd, when Rebelo, Senay, and McCartney found a loss of 67.6 in. from open water vs. a loss of only 64.6 in. from flooded vegetation.[8] Once passed into the canal, more water will be lost by seepage and evaporation than if the swamps were left alone.

In practice, the water lost from the Sudd is only about *one third that lost* from Lake Nasser in Egypt, which led Fred Pearce to suggest that one way for Egypt to save water in the future, instead of draining swamps, was to support the building of dams in Ethiopia where, because of the cooler air temperatures, evaporation is even less. This makes hydrological sense and obviates the need for downstream storage. As Pearce tells us: "The shimmering edifice of the High Aswan—monument to hydrological folly—could be dismantled. And then there might be enough water left for nature, as well as for the people of the Nile."

The proposal that Egypt sacrifice the High Dam in order to save the Sudd is an extreme solution that is not likely to happen. A more reasonable plan is the one outlined by Daniel Kendie that combines several earlier ideas with modern perspectives. In general, it involves changing the flow regime of the Blue Nile to avoid evaporation losses. This follows the advice of a recent study of water available for agriculture in the Nile Basin,[9] which pointed to the enormous losses of water by evaporation from dams built in the arid parts of the Basin. The study pointed especially to the Aswan Dam in Egypt and Sudan (annual loss of up to 4 trillion gallons, or 14.3 km³), the Merowe Hydropower Dam in Sudan (400 billion gallons, or 1.3 km³), Toskha Lakes in Egypt (900 billion gallons, or 2–3 km³), and Jebel Aulia Dam, upstream of Khartoum (900 billion gallons, or 2–3 km³).

This last dam was originally constructed in 1937 and became redundant when the Aswan High Dam was built. Several authors have suggested that it be opened up to allow a significant water saving in Egypt, but since then Sudan has installed turbines along the dam for power generation.

Still, the message is clear: by shifting storage from broad shallow reservoirs in arid downstream areas to deep reservoirs in Ethiopia, where lower rates of evaporation prevail, overall losses from reservoir evaporation can be reduced significantly.

A second approach would involve the traditional call for water conservation in Egypt. That, coupled with a program to expand the tapping of deep aquifers (following a model set by Libya) and the use of water recycling and filter swamps in the lower reaches of the Nile, would save enough water to obviate the need for draining the Sudd.

It blows the mind to think that by draining the Sudd, the Jonglei Canal Project would operate in just the opposite way to that of the Transaqua Project, which is intended to deliver water to a dying ecosystem! The revival of Lake Chad and its wetlands is, in a way, the same objective as the reversal of drainage in the Everglades and the re-flooding of the Huleh Swamp in the Jordan Valley—all places where drainage and the drying out of swamps were found to be a mistake. The lesson is inescapable that it would have been better and cheaper to leave these swamps alone and conserve the ecosystems intact, but that is a lesson that apparently takes a while to realize, and not just by the Egyptians.

Recently, in Russia, the people of Moscow suffered through a nightmare summer. Fires, smoke, smog, and ashes blowing into the city from burning peat bogs surrounding the city made life hell. Those Moscow swamps were cleared in the 1900s by Soviet engineers to provide peat for power plants. Now with global warming they are drying faster, becoming easier to ignite, and burning longer. A 30-mile pipeline from the Oka River laid down just to fight the fires was not enough! The government is drawing up plans to re-flood the area.

"Of course," said one Russian official with surprising candidness, regarding the fires, "they would be easier to put out if we had not drained the swamps."[10]

17

It Takes an Army to Save the Sudd

"Will that be the cause of death?" I wondered, as I gazed at the prime suspect in the attempted murder of the largest papyrus swamp that the world has ever seen.

A killer lake of enormous length lay below me, a great narrow sheet of water rising in Aswan and spreading like a long, crooked knife from latitudes 25° to 21°. Seen from the window of an Egypt Air airliner, Lake Nasser looked endless. Stretching as it does across the Tropic of Cancer and beyond, it spans 2,000 square miles and is hard to ignore because it contrasts so sharply with the light pink-brown of the desert soil.

I had the full picture on a recent 150-mile flight along the course of the lake from Aswan to Abu Simbel. On some satellite images it resembles a pool of mercury shimmering in the blinding sunlight, and by all accounts it is not only poised to kill the Sudd, it is also slowly killing the delta and ultimately will do in the Nation of Egypt. It is a serial killer in the making.

For thousands of years Egypt had to cope with the lack of, or too much of, an annual flood. They sought a solution in a series of dams at Aswan, a town near the place where the Nile enters their country. Then at the end of the '60s the High Dam was closed, and over the course of several years the long lake filled. In the years following closure, agriculture in Egypt soared, doubling and tripling production, while electrical power lit up the huts and village streets, and the annual danger of flood or drought became a memory. The waters of the Nile were tamed at last and that was that; the dam was considered a success and old Hapi could take a walk.

Ethiopia strongly objected to the building of the Aswan High Dam. Since Ethiopia contributes 86% of the water contained in the lake by way of the Blue Nile, you would think its objections would bear weight, but they were ignored. Like Uganda's unilateral control of the White Nile on the Lake Plateau, Egypt controls the tap in the lowlands, and once the water crosses the border, it is theirs.

Within a few years, concerns began to surface about the impact of the dam. Many of the concerns were directed toward the fact that below the dam, the flow of the Nile had decreased to a trickle compared to the surging stream of history. The 500,000 gallons-per-second flow seen in the time of Herodotus has been reduced to a mere 33,000 gallons per second in the time of Nasser.

As a result, the salinity in the Mediterranean and water temperatures along the Egyptian shore began to rise and fisheries in the area fell off, both impacts that were traced directly to the decreased flow. Worse, 60 to 180 million tons per year of silt that once fed the farms of the Nile Valley were now held back behind the dam. That caused a loss of land in the delta where erosion normally was balanced by an annual accretion of mud. Subsidence occurred at a faster rate and coastal lagoons widened as marine waves and currents took their toll. Another problem was that farmers in the valley and delta now had to use artificial fertilizers because of the loss of silt. New fertilizers had to be manufactured, using most of the power generated by the dam—a process that depleted electricity, leaving less electricity for local development.

According to several experts, by casting its lot with the High Dam, Egypt was putting itself in a precarious position. If at any time the level of water behind the High Dam lowered significantly, an economic chain reaction would be set in motion. The decrease in agricultural production would cause dislocations of normal life, decreases in export earning, reductions in public services, slowdowns in development, increases in imports, and lower rates of economic growth.[1]

In addition to these environmental and potential economic impacts, the dam had a direct effect on water loss because Aswan is located in an arid region. The intense sunlight and dry weather cause an evaporation of about 12%. Of the 35 trillion gallons stored in the lake (132 km^3), at least 11 billion are lost daily. It now appears that Egypt needs that water, because the chances of getting any more from any other source are getting slimmer every day.

Consider the attitude of upstream countries that are under pressure to use Nile water to satisfy the needs of the new multibillion-dollar investments made by foreign investors. Add to this the global warming predictions that Eastern and Northern Africa should expect less rain, and there is less and less hope, other than draining the Sudd.

Since the '60s, Egypt's population has grown from 40 to 80 million, wiping out the advantage in agricultural production gained by the High Dam, and it now imports over 40% of its total food and 60% of its wheat. Despite the gloomy predictions that water will be scarce, Egypt has put forward big plans to increase irrigated land for food production. According to the 1999 Oosterbaan Report, it already has 8 million acres under irrigation that use its total allocation of 16.5 trillion gallons per year (55.5 km^3/yr) of Nile water under the Nile Agreement. An additional 1 million acres of development is planned in the Toshka Project in the Western Desert and another million in the Al-Salam Canal Project in Sinai.

Where will the extra water come from, if not draining the Sudd? It could be gained from conservation. For example, according to Adly Bishai, founder of the Desert Development Centre in Cairo, Egypt still uses flood irrigation on 70% of its farmland. Flood irrigation depends on spreading a sheet of water over the fields, then allowing the excess water to run back into the river. This technique was effective in preventing salt from building up in ancient times, but today it is seen as a great waste and drives irrigation people to distraction. Flood irrigation is only possible in Egypt because the water costs next to nothing. A recent "Water Issue" of the *National Geographic* compared water cost for one hundred gallons in selected African cities, from which we see that Cape Town pays 42¢, Gaborone 22¢, Nairobi 22¢, Addis Ababa 9¢, and Cairo 3¢. Clearly, some correction is needed. If Egypt were to charge the rate it should, there would be an instant change in the way water is used. It would certainly provide the incentive to install drip irrigation that would cut water use by 25–50%.

On the other hand, when more efficient modern sprinkler or drip systems are used to replace flood irrigation on heavy clay soils, drains have to be installed to prevent salt buildup. That raises the initial cost, but eventually the drains pay for themselves. An FAO 2005 report on Egyptian irrigation quoted annual improved gross production values of $200 or more per acre, and net farm income increases of up to $150 per acre because of drainage.

The Toshka Project that is reclaiming land in the New Valley in the Western Desert is mostly in an area of sandy soils where drip irrigation can be used along with other modern techniques. But not everyone is sold on the Toshka Project. Former Egyptian Minister of Construction and Housing Hasaballah al-Kafrawi described it as a useless waste of money, and he soundly condemned the 315 studies of the project made to date as ". . . a humiliation of the mind."[2] Scaling back on the Toshka Project acreage would save water.

Another approach is for the government to discourage crops that are highly water-dependent, such as a recent decision to reduce rice acreage.[3] This action was taken in response to the Nile Basin countries that have for years called on Egypt to implement downstream water conservation measures in a more serious way. Since rice uses more water than other crops, the water saved could be used to raise more beans and corn. But will such a measure spare the Sudd? Not by a long shot. Any water saved by shifting from rice to other crops will be dwarfed by the needs of the Toshka Project and water wasted in flood irrigation.

It will take much more to resolve the problem of water scarcity. One scheme that does have merit is a program called "smoothing" the Blue Nile. This is a win-win solution that intends to fix the problems that have vexed all three of the primary users of the Blue Nile: Ethiopia, Northern Sudan, and Egypt.[4] This strategy would address many problems, including losses from seepage and evaporation, as well as the deposit of silt downriver.

The idea is to regulate the flow of the Blue Nile in Ethiopia using a series of four reservoirs that would be constructed in the highlands under a joint program in which all three countries would cooperate. Because the rate of evaporation in Ethiopia is much less than that of reservoirs in the arid zone below, that alone would increase the total amount of water deposited on the door of Egypt. Indeed, if properly managed, Kendie tells us, ". . . water stored in the four reservoirs could be released in May to Egypt when its water requirement is the highest without sustaining the great loss by evaporation now experienced at Aswan. Egypt, however, would no longer benefit from additional water in years of high flood, which would be stored and regulated in the Blue Nile reservoirs. Moreover, lowering the level of Lake Nasser in order to limit the evaporable loss would concomitantly reduce available hydroelectric power at the beginning. But after speedy adjustments are made, Egypt would receive additional water for irrigation and electricity from Ethiopia." (Daniel Kendie, 1999. *Egypt and the Hydropolitics of the Blue Nile River.*)

As to whether the three countries would cooperate, Ambassador David Shinn, an Adjunct Professor at George Washington University and former US Ambassador to Ethiopia, notes that Nile Basin countries have already taken important steps to minimize conflict by creating several organizations to resolve problems cooperatively. Most important is the Nile Basin Initiative (NBI), a regional partnership. Also, the World Bank coordinates the International Consortium for Cooperation on the Nile (ICCON), which promotes financing for cooperative water resource development. A Blue Nile cooperative effort that would bring Egypt, Sudan, and Ethiopia together in order to create a reliable Blue Nile flow is no longer a farfetched idea, and would generate enough flow to satisfy the long-term needs of Egypt and Sudan. If so, the Sudd drainage becomes less of a priority.

☙

Water savings are also possible in Egypt by recycling wastewater, and the Al-Salam Canal Project is a good example. Here the intent is to reclaim

1 million acres of desert in the Sinai on both sides of the Suez Canal. The project uses a mix of fresh Nile water from the Damietta branch and wastewater from drains in the delta. The combined stream flows through a 162-mile canal that passes under the Suez Canal to reach desert land further to the east.

When the idea for this canal was conceived years ago, the Nile as it passed through the delta was still considered a moderately clean river, though it did have localized pollution problems. Nowadays, according to Dr. Abdel-Satar of the Egyptian National Institute of Oceanography and Fisheries, it is in danger of becoming "a waste collecting system."

For those families in the delta dependent on wells, by 2005 the situation had gotten so bad that, as an FAO report informs us, ". . . local communities in the northern Nile Delta could no longer use groundwater for their domestic requirements since it is naturally highly saline." Unluckily, they are now reliant on canal water. Although towns and villages are generally equipped with water purification plants that can remove sediments and pollutants, these plants do not often remove everything they're supposed to. The report said that many household users simply draw canal water and then let it stand for purification. Not a wise or sufficient thing to do with this kind of water, because the user is still susceptible to water-borne diseases and toxic pollutants.

Even water intended for recycling suffers in the delta, since many drains and irrigation canals cutting through rural and urban settlements have turned visibly black, indicating that the water has gone septic, a condition confirmed by the alarming levels of biological oxygen demand (BOD, an excellent measure of pollution) and incidences of poor health. Still, as the FAO report indicates, farmers in the delta are happy to use drainage water for irrigation. They value the nutrients introduced by sewage elements in the water; however, they are concerned about the possibility of industrial toxins since they have no way of identifying whether those are present or not.

They definitely have cause for concern. Scientists from the National Research Center in Cairo (Hafez et al., 2008) recently carried out a study on the water in the Al-Salam irrigation scheme and found it was characterized by high amounts of dissolved salts, heavy metals, and organic compounds, all indications that the water was "not suitable for irrigation and drinking purposes and needs treatment."

Obviously, pre-treatment of water intended for irrigation in the Al-Salam Canal Project should be a priority, and the potential is there for recycling wastewater. One study in 2004 by Mostafa et al. estimated that wastewater from all major urban centers in Egypt amounted to 1.5 trillion gallons (5 km³). Add to that the drainage from irrigation in the delta, which amounts to 2 trillion gallons (6.7 km³), and the total far exceeds the 1.3 trillion gallons (5km³/yr) to be gained from draining the Sudd.

∽

Every year without fail, at least two or three news items appear in the media announcing the discovery of a large untapped underground reservoir in the North African desert. Almost certainly the stories refer to a geologic entity called the Nubian Sandstone Formation, which we are told is the world's largest fossil water aquifer system. It spans an area of almost 500 million acres. A multi-layered Quaternary basin located deep underground in the eastern end of the Sahara Desert, it crosses the political boundaries of Chad, Sudan, Libya, and most of Egypt, and contains the equivalent of 3,750 years of Nile River flow.

Anyone hearing this for the first time must wonder why any of these countries would have the gall to complain about water supply! Their future seems secure in that regard, and might prompt a response such as: "In any case, they have no need to drain any wetlands and can afford to leave natural plant and animal resources as they are."

A fine sentiment, and one I agree with—but there are problems. First of all, this is old news. Large-scale development of the Nubian Sandstone aquifer in Egypt has been under consideration since 1960. Second, the biggest constraint is money. It's expensive to drill down and tap water 1,500–9,000ft below the surface. Typically, one well can cost almost a half million dollars and the cost goes up each year.

Across the border in Libya, where seemingly unlimited amounts of money are available and this aquifer is the only natural source of water, it is tapped in a big way. The Libyans have invested $34 billion to provide water for agricultural needs and a population of only 6 million. On Google Earth, the satellite images of the southern part of Libya show a number of large circular outlines of huge automatic irrigation projects, which in turn indicates the extent of water used for agriculture. Libya has also built enormous reservoirs to hold water for the domestic use of urban populations.

Egypt, with 400 wells in the southwestern part of the Western Desert, has already invested $610 million in the East Owainat Project where 250,000 acres are being reclaimed using this fossil water. The Egyptian investment is still only 1.8% of the cost that Libya has set aside, and total extraction of groundwater provides only 8% of its water supply. Perhaps things will change with a recent private investment from Abu Dhabi which provides an investment of $252 million in a deal to grow wheat in Egypt for the Egyptian domestic market using water from the aquifer.

In sum, Egypt expects to take: 16.5 trillion gallons of water each year from the Nile (the "guaranteed" 55.5 km^3 by Agreement); groundwater from shallow reservoirs in the delta and the Nile valley at 2.4 trillion gallons (8 km^3), and 1.2 trillion (4 km^3) from the deep fossil water aquifer; 5.5 trillion gallons (18.5 km^3) from recycled waste water; 450 billion gallons (1.5 km^3) from rain and flood waters; and 520 billion gallons (1.75 km^3) from desalinated water, for a total of 26.5 trillion gallons (89.2 km^3). This is a prediction of what is expected each year until the year 2050.[5]

❧

All of the measures described above will help save the Sudd. But the problem is that water conservation in Egypt doesn't happen overnight; it takes time and money in excess, especially if flood irrigation remains the system of choice for the Egyptian farmer. And it will remain so as long as the price of water in Egypt is kept low, which is something that probably will not change for quite a while because any attempt at setting it at some realistic level will be met by riots.

Another difficulty is the installation of new irrigation methods and drains; these are not willingly taken up by farmers who are dirt-poor to begin with. For most, even the small investment required for drains is a big outlay. As for cutting back on the scope of the new mega projects, politicians cast their lot with the likes of Toshka and the Al-Salam Canal; any backsliding would be seen as a loss of face. Meanwhile, what of the Sudd and the Jonglei Canal?

The canal remains unfinished with only 75 miles to go. All that remains of the 1983 project is a 150-mile weed-covered embankment. And it didn't take long for the oil companies to take advantage even of this, as it presently serves them as a road. What the future will hold is anyone's guess.

The Sudd lies within the territory of the newly established Government of Southern Sudan, which seems quite willing for now to allow the status quo, that is, the continued use of the Sudd and the surrounding seasonal grasslands by the Dinka, Nuer, Shilluk, and other pastoral tribes on a traditional basis, which is fine. But one thing is certain: Egypt has never stopped lusting after the Sudd.[6] Years ago they proposed an even larger plan to drain not only 3,500 sq. miles of Sudd but also about 2 million acres of wetlands in the surrounding Bahr al-Ghazal region to the west of the Nile, and the Machar Marshes to the east.

What could cause them to change their mind and agree with the almost 2 million people living there who feel that the swamps are best left as they are? Or make them sympathize with those who feel that the swamps are a major asset to the region as a recharge basin for water supply? What will it take to convince them that the Sudd is not some "mistake of nature" but actually a great gift to the future generations of Southern Sudanese who may someday depend on it for their lives? Who will save the Sudd? The answer to all these questions is the same: the Egyptian people.

I'm thinking here of the people mentioned by Dr. Salah Hassanein, an Egyptian environmentalist on the board of directors of About Water for Life International, a California-based nonprofit organization dedicated to providing access to clean potable water.[7]

One reason for conservation of the swamps upstream of Egypt is the threat of oil pollution, which is expected from the wells now being drilled in Uganda and Sudan. Pollution in swamps upstream has already been reported in the Sudan by Klaus Stieglitz, vice-chairman of the German NGO Sign of Hope, in 2009. Stieglitz led a fact-finding mission to Sudan's White Nile where he found that "Water flowing off the huge oil installation and accumulating in drilling pits is a major source of contamination which has already reached the sources of drinking water." In one village close to a drilling field, concentrations of salts and contaminants such as cyanides, lead, nickel, cadmium, and arsenic had reached critical levels in the surface water. In addition to endangering the lives of the Nuer, one of Southern Sudan's two main tribes, the pollution also threatens local swamps that support a rich animal diversity including hundreds of thousands of migratory birds and animals.

Oil represents 95% of Southern and Northern Sudan's exports and is both a blessing and a source of tension between Khartoum and the newly independent Southern capital of Juba. Stieglitz urged the facility's operator, a subsidiary of Malaysian oil giant Petronas, to treat the water coming from the operation and prevent it from seeping elsewhere. "To secure public health the government must also improve the quality of drinking water dramatically and at the same time prevent an ecological catastrophe," he added.

Even more catastrophic situations would be caused if the region were cleared of papyrus. A taste of what might happen downstream came recently when a Nile tanker in Aswan south of Cairo leaked 110 tons of diesel fuel into the river, creating a slick 180ft wide by 1.2 miles in length. This caused water managers to block off all water purification stations in the river near Cairo in order to prevent the polluted water from entering the filters.[8] A city of 16.8 million came up against reality. What happens if oil spills upstream occur more frequently? What happens if the upstream river becomes as polluted as the delta is now? Papyrus is one of the few remaining bits of protection against the ravages of a spill on the water supply.

If anything, the BP Deepwater Horizon oil spill in the US has taught us the value of rhizosphere bacteria, the microbial communities associated with wetlands, reed beds, swamps, and backwaters. Today those oil-eating microbes are still at work in Louisiana breaking down oil residues even after the obvious oil slicks, media coverage, volunteers, and oil booms have disappeared. From that experience also comes the advice that the best present philosophy is to just leave the marshes and swamps alone if you expect to have oil spills in a region. In Louisiana, it has been found that cutting or trampling reed beds often does more harm than the oil itself, and indigenous populations of oil-eaters, like papyrus, won't be there to help in the event of a spill if the Sudd swamps are drained.

∽

In 2006, the entire Sudd was designated a Ramsar Wetland of International Importance. As such, it could be developed into a tourist resource even while the residents continued with their traditional lifestyle. The Sudd's potential as a tourist destination rivals that of the Okavango Swamp in Botswana, which is a good example of how such a resource can be used in a sustainable fashion. The Okavango Swamp, along with the other national parks in Botswana, helps bring in a tourism income of millions annually while employing thousands of people.

None of this precludes any future development plans in Southern Sudan that include agricultural or industrial activities, some of which may depend on the groundwater stored in the Sudd. But by then its value as a recharge basin will be recognized—hopefully in time to save it as a national resource.

18

Blood Roses, Papyrus, and the New Scramble for Africa

Lake Naivasha is unique in Kenya, Africa and indeed the world. It is presently faced with some severe problems which threaten its very existence as a lake and a wetland.

—David Harper, 2005, Lake Naivasha
Riparian Assoc. Newsletter

Two thousand machete-wielding men swarmed onto the main road like colonies of angry African bees roused from their hives, determined to kill in defense of their own. Yelling and screaming insults, armed with the traditional all-purpose farm tool of the Kenyan farmer, the razor-sharp *panga*, they were ready to show anyone and everyone that they knew how to use it. A handful of policemen fired into the air, hard pressed to control the mob. Now, some of the mob broke away and chased the opposition.

On one side of the road stretched Lake Naivasha (Map 6, p. 192), where at the water's edge one can see papyrus swamps—the sacred sedge, its umbels rising above the mud and water of the lake where, like the human combatants, it is also fighting for its life. Papyrus is the main component of the wetlands of this lake, and it is dying for lack of water—water that is being drained from the lake to grow roses.

On the land above the road not far from the surging masses are roses in bud, millions of them, red, beautiful, moist, and exotic, grown here by commercial growers who stood to lose a fortune unless the fighting stopped. The resources that feed the roses are also the lifeblood of the wildlife and the papyrus swamps of the lake. Without the lake's water, the roses will die.

To an outsider, there is no way of telling who is who in this mob. The men who are fighting are not wearing distinctive jerseys; if they were, they would be blue for the waters of Lake Victoria and Kisumu, the principal city in western Kenya, the homeland of the Luo, and green for the corn and coffee trees of the Kikuyu, the opposing side, who claim Nairobi as their enclave.

These ethnic clashes came in the wake of a disputed presidential election. First, the Kikuyu were harassed, burned out of their homes, and murdered in Kisumu; then in January 2008, the Kikuyu turned on the Luo. The place they had chosen to do so is significant: a large slum called Karagita on the shores of Lake Naivasha. Some sixty miles northeast of Nairobi, just south of Naivasha town (Map 7, p. 194), it is a place in which 60,000 or more people live. Most work on the flower farms that have taken over the land around the lake.

Overhead, Kenyan military helicopters firing rubber bullets swoop on the crowd, and the wind from the chopper blades sends waves of turbulence out over the papyrus and rattles and shakes the plastic sheeting that shields the roses from the blazing African sun.

What makes this scene so bizarre is that it is being played out in the vicinity of a Rift Valley lake that was once known in colonial days as the ideal vacation site, a playground of the rich and famous, formerly one of the safest places you could go for a weekend in Kenya. Still a popular place for seminars, meetings, and international conferences, 22 people were killed here during the weekend of the riot. Nineteen of them were Luos whom a gang of Kikuyus chased through Karagita and trapped in a shanty that they set on fire. The others were hacked to death with machetes, according to the Associated Press.

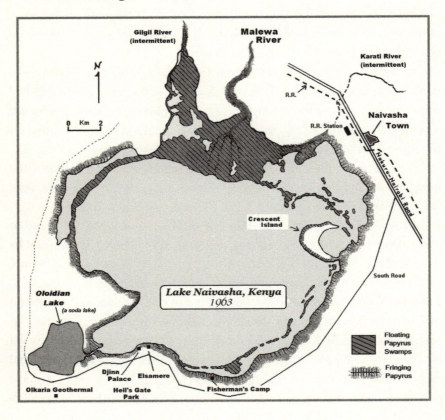

MAP 6: *Lake Naivasha 50 years ago.*

Like the plant symbols of Upper and Lower Nile, papyrus represents the wildlife conservation interests of Kenya while the rose, in place of the lotus, stands for Kenya's economic business interests. Both plants wait now on the sidelines for this awful conflict to resolve itself and for the country to become whole again. It will not be easy. As of March 2008, more than 1,500 people had been killed in Kenya and 600,000 forced to flee their homes. Part of the tension that led to this fighting in Naivasha can be traced back to jobs, conditions in the local slums, and a scarcity of natural resources. Water, be it for roses or papyrus or people, is inextricably bound up in the welfare of all living things in this region: human, plant, and animal.

Even now the conflict simmers under the surface; it is far from over.

෨

Not long after my arrival in Kenya, I found the lake to be an ideal research site, a place where papyrus grew in profusion. Located in central Kenya, it is a place that in the 1920s, '30s, and '40s was a feature of ". . . the hunting grounds of the hedonistic Happy Valley set."

Joy Adamson, the author of *Born Free*, still lived on the shores of the lake, and it was here that some of the scenes in the Adamson films about Elsa the lion were shot.

In the late '70s, Kenya was a different world, a world that belonged to President Jomo Kenyatta. Certainly, I thought, it would be easier to get by here on this magical lake than in the corpse-strewn swamps I'd left behind in Idi Amin's Uganda.

At that time, Lake Naivasha was not a major tourist destination, but it had the potential to become one. Unlike Lake Nakuru, the famous flamingo lake 35 miles to the west, which is a national park, Lake Naivasha was owned by private interests. It had escaped being designated a national park, as many think it should have been, since all the land around the lake was in the hands of white settlers or wealthy Africans or expatriates, all of whom enjoyed the privacy conferred by owning hundreds of acres of exotic landscape. Years later, the lakefront farms began changing hands as the original owners sold to a new crop of buyers: European flower companies and rich African investors, who now had exclusive rights to the lake edge and thus controlled access to the water.

The intensive development of the cut-flower industry followed during the '90s and into the 2000s, so that today over 1,000 tons of vegetables and cut flowers are flown out of Kenya every day, seven days a week. Almost half of these are roses that come mostly from Lake Naivasha.

To support this production, the lake's population of workers shot up from 20,000 to 350,000 within the space of ten years and the town of Naivasha expanded to accommodate them (Map 7). Slums also mushroomed along the road between the town and the main flower farms. A boomtown mentality developed and the crime rate rose, including the tragic murder in 2006 of Joan Root, a conservationist and Oscar-nominated nature filmmaker.

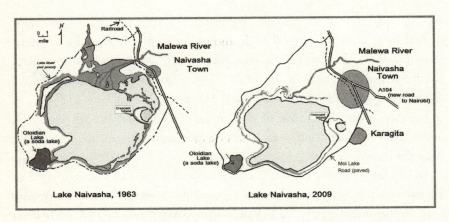

MAP 7: *The general reduction of Lake Naivasha and change in wetlands and the towns. Since 2009, the water level has come back up, but the wetlands are gone.*

Joan noted in her diary the murders of three friends and neighbors, and a police report that the number of armed robberies had risen to eighteen a month. It is here that Joan and her husband Alan Root established a haven for orphaned animals, but in 2006 she was gunned down with an AK-47 in her bedroom, struck by five bullets. As Mark Seal tells us in his *Vanity Fair* story,[1] blonde, beautiful, and fearless, she had been idolized for the pioneering wildlife films she made with her husband. After their agonizing divorce, she devoted herself to an even more dangerous mission: saving her beloved lake from the ecological ravages of Africa's lucrative flower-farming industry. Her murder is believed to have been a contract killing, but the questions of both who fired the shots and who paid for the assassins remain unanswered.

I spent five years on this lake carrying out research on the once-plentiful papyrus swamps that ringed the lake, and I can well imagine the feelings that move people who want to act to save the lake. In Joan's case, her story lives on and has recently attracted worldwide attention. Thanks to Mark Seal's book *Wildflower*, Joan's life will be the subject of a film starring and produced by Julia Roberts. And it will be shot on the lake against a background of the lake and its wildlife, with one exception—the papyrus swamps that were a prominent feature of the lake in Joan's time have mostly disappeared.

The publicity that comes from the movie will show the world what happens when resources become scarce and tempers flare, but it won't save the lake. That task can only be accomplished by the people who live there, who at present are at one another's throats as they scramble for water.

Who are they? The most influential are the flower growers, a consortium of European investors, managers, technicians, rich Kenyan backers, and shareholders. They supply over 33% of the cut flowers in Europe, and the foreign exchange they earn gives them the political power to draw water with few restrictions. They take what they want from the lake and pump what they want from underground, using boreholes that tap into the lake's aquifer. The permit system under which they are regulated has little meaning in the face of their effect on the national economy. A rough estimate of what the growers take from the lake amounts to three to four times the "safe yield," the amount that could be taken from the lake without disturbing the lake balance.[2]

In time, the growers were pitted against the local town of Naivasha that provides domestic water to the burgeoning crowd of workers and service providers. A complicating factor is that the aquifer that recharges the lake is the same one that is contaminated by seepage and runoff from unsewered town houses, slums, and flower gardens.

Water is also demanded in quantity by a local geothermal plant that needs water to cool the very hot water taken from the geothermal zone under the earth. This means more water lost from the lake. Whenever the lake begins to shrink, the geothermal use does not stop. The plant takes its water from the deepest part of the lake and therefore is in the best position to take the very last drop.

Another scrambler is 35 miles distant, the town of Nakuru, the place west of Naivasha that hosts the famous flamingo lake. A major tourist destination, it also supports a local industry that provides vegetables for the capital city, Nairobi. Irrigated agriculture and domestic water requirements make Nakuru a priority user. Consequently, it has permission to draw water out of the Malewa River before it even enters Lake Naivasha.

Lastly are the thousands of newcomers eking out an existence in the slums that have sprung up along the lake edge. By and large, the slum dwellers are bound to be the losers if things continue the way they are going, since they have virtually nothing but their rights. The Kenya Water Act of 2002 requires the government to provide water services to consumers. However, those living in the slum at Karagita have neither the funds nor the technical equipment to tap into the aquifer, or to pump the water of the lake even though it sits a short distance away. When they do acquire the means to exert their rights, they will be a force to be reckoned with.

To make matters worse, a drought set in during the early part of this millennium and the scramble for water coincided with a scramble for land to grow food. Any land not owned by the flower industry was farmed or grazed, so that as the lake retreated so did the destruction of the vegetation. The flower growers cut trenches to reach the receding water of the lake; in the process, the papyrus swamps on the lake were decimated.

In 2010, the rains predicted by long-term weather cycles fell early and the drought was broken. Now the lake is re-flooded along with the former swampland and hopefully papyrus will recover from seed, but the future is far from certain. Perhaps it is prophetic that the town, region, and lake were called "Naivasha," after the Maasai word *Nai'posha*, meaning "rough water," because during any storm the normally placid surface of the lake can change within minutes.

⌒

The violence witnessed by Joan Root a few years ago was an indication of the tension that continued to rise as the lake dried and the earlier drought wore on. Her neighbor on the lake, another conservationist, Lord Enniskillen, told Mark Seal: "The tragedy of her death is that she died trying to alleviate that very poverty which creates the insecurity around here." Some people thought of her as an enemy because she was trying to save the lake and thus keep water from reaching these "blood roses." The anger spilled over following the election, with levels of violence never before witnessed. Surprisingly, during that time, we are told by former head of Kenya Flower Council (KFC) Erastus Mureithi, the country saw a rise in the production of flowers. This was possible because urgent measures were taken to address the situation, such as flying the flowers directly from farms to Eldoret, a town further west with an international airport. Then they were flown to Nairobi for onward transmission to Europe, as opposed to the normal route using the road. Although some workers were displaced by the violence, especially in Naivasha, Mureithi said new ones were hired immediately "to ensure the labor-intensive business of floriculture was not interrupted. The sector has performed admirably in difficult times, under-lining the resilience of the Kenyan people and the economy to survive even at the worst of times." And the major water users continue to draw water in unreasonable amounts.

The rioting that followed the disputed national election is a foretaste of what could happen if the lakeside economy collapsed. One thing that could trigger this would be the European flower market. If it were to bottom out, or shift to another supplier (Turkey and Ethiopia are good possibilities), chaos would reign in Naivasha and Kenya.

What can be done? Putting a halt to new drilling or new water permits is only a short-term solution. The lake is in desperate need of a long-term plan for water use and conservation that can be implemented—and sus-tained—locally. That does not happen at present, so the scramble for water in Naivasha continues.

☙

Lake Naivasha has always been a beautiful place. I first came there on a drive back to Uganda from the Kenya coast when I found that it was almost halfway, an ideal stopping point.

The Lake Hotel where I stayed is a very comfortable place that fronts on the lake. When you wake in the morning, hundreds of birds greet you as you look out over a wide expanse of lawn. More birds await as you walk in the shade of the fever trees. One of the prettiest is the Superb Starling (*Lamprotornis superbus*), a glossy-feathered, iridescent little creature, blue with a white-banded, rusty-red breast. Quite bold, several will land at once on your breakfast tray on the open verandah.

In contrast, strutting around on the lawn is the ugliest bird you'll ever see, the Marabu Stork (*Leptoptilos crumeniferus*), a frequenter of the hotel garbage pit. It is an amazing sight with its scrofulous, fuzzy head and large dirty-looking beak, still filthy from picking over the trash bits.

At the water's edge are sacred ibis and goliath heron that move among the coots, ducks, and pelicans in the shallow water. Jacanas, sure-footed, long-toed birds, run quickly across the floating lily pads. Above them in the trees and soaring out over the lake are fish eagles, their cries echoing in soul-piercing calls that carry across the lake, especially eerie in the morning mist. Late in the afternoon, Mt. Longonot, the volcanic hill in the background above the lake, turns purplish blue-red and stays that way until the sun sets. Just off the shore is Crescent Island, the rim of an extinct volcano and a self-contained game park that was used for filming the lions in the Adamson-inspired films, like *Living Free*. Once the water was high enough to isolate the island, the lions could be let loose to roam since, like many cats, they hate the water.

It is obvious from the start why the Happy Valley crowd loved this place and why settlers and expatriates soon bought up every inch of shoreline, making it a private enclave. The lake was noted for its papyrus swamps, which covered twenty square miles and ringed the fifty-five-square-mile lake. Shortly after I moved to Nairobi from Uganda, I came to the lake almost weekly to take samples and make observations. Tourists from Nairobi would show up on weekends, followed by the occasional expatriate bass fisherman loaded down with sophisticated equipment. Backpackers and campers stayed at Fisherman's Camp, a lovely place in the south. Not far away was the YMCA camp that hosted busloads of Nairobi school kids every weekend.

In all, it was a great place to get away to.

The first European to arrive on the lake was Gustav Fischer, a German explorer who in 1882 was looking for a route from Mombasa to Lake Victoria. With the advent of the railway in the early 1900s, it became a popular weekend spot for European residents. They came out by train on duck-hunting parties from Nairobi to take advantage of the teeming birdlife associated with the papyrus swamps. The small mansions and spacious bungalows that sprang up around the lake were on plots of land often large enough to support herds of game. Many were working farms with dairy herds, breeding cattle, crops of alfalfa and vegetables destined for a local drying plant. Tourists stuck to the eastern shore and the paved road. The peripheral road on the west side was a wide, dusty, potholed track that discouraged road travel. Once the land was bought up, the lake virtually became private property, and the expatriates wanted it to stay that way. During the week, after the tourists had gone, I often found I had the lake to myself. And what a strange and lonely place it was. I worked in the large swamp that once covered the whole northern part, though I also visited swamps in the south, where a white-painted Moorish-style castle, called the Djinn Palace, towers above the shore. It can still be seen from most places on the lake and acts as a marker for navigation as well as a reminder of history.

"Joss," Earl of Erroll, the lady-killer of the film and James Fox's best-selling book *White Mischief*, lived there from 1930 with a string of exotic visitors, such as his lover Diana (Lady Delamere). He was shot in Nairobi in 1941, presumably by a jealous husband. After his death, the Djinn Palace was rented out to Lord Braughton, the man accused (later acquitted) of killing him. Later still, it was bought by Baron Knapitsch, a famous trophy hunter, and today it is owned by Oserian, one of the major flower-growing companies in the area.

Further to the east lived Alan and Joan Root. Then came Jack Block's place; Block was a local hotel magnate who owned the Norfolk Hotel in Nairobi and, previously, the New Stanley Hotel and the Lake Hotel (the last was later owned by Michael Cunningham-Reid). On the west side is Joy Adamson's house, Elsamere, set in a grove of thorn trees with Colobus monkeys scampering about and a spectacular view of the lake. Still further west are the farms of Iain and Oria Douglas-Hamilton, famous for their elephant studies; Mirella Ricciardi, the photographer, and her relatives the Roccos; and the cattle and wildlife ranching family the Hopcrafts.

What did they all have in common? Besides being famous, white, and well-connected, they were ardent conservationists. When they met at the Naivasha Sports Club, they invited people like me to come and talk to them about how the lake could be maintained just as it was, even though forces were already in place to bring about enormous changes. The first indication of this change was the advent of the flower growers, whose farms were already attracting international investors.

And the Africans? Where were they in all this? When Gustav Fischer arrived in 1882, he was met by Maasai warriors in full battle dress, ready to repel him and his party. He promptly turned and fled. After that, the settlers and the British Army arrived, and brought with them their Somali and Swahili house servants. Before long, Maasai, Luo, Kikuyu, Kalengin, and Akamba were working the farms, tending the hotels, and cleaning the houses, while a few rich African businessmen and politicians were buying into the development of the local farms and hotels and, later, the flower business. Some of the African farm workers rose to management level and occasionally some even became landowners. Whenever a settler or expatriate would sell, there was always a willing African buyer, but in general it was a white colonial world and the total number of Africans did not change much. The town of Naivasha remained a sleepy, dusty place for many years.

During all that time, from the '30s well into the '80s, the birdlife and swamps that ringed the lake remained its most interesting feature. What attracted me was the large North Swamp that spanned the delta of the Malewa, the only perennial river entering the lake. This swamp, an almost pure stand of 9,000 acres of easily accessible papyrus, was a magnificent sight. To my eye it was a paradise; for bird watchers it was the jewel of the lake. But the same volcanic soil on which these wetlands thrived was also ideal for the cultivation of export-earning cut flowers and special vegetables for the European market. With a virtually free water supply directly available from the lake or easily pumped from nearby boreholes, a year-round growing season, and an unlimited pool of cheap labor, it was a money-spinner from the start.

Enormous numbers of workers settled near the farms along the road to the east of the lake, now called Moi South Road. Into these areas came thousands from all over, lending truth to the idea that this would be the melting pot of Kenya, the place where all tribes would benefit from the economic miracle and settle down together to enjoy the fruits of *uhuru*, the Swahili word for "freedom." This was not to be. The Maasai were right: "rough water" describes what could—and did—happen as the lake started to change. Further portent was seen in the local volcanic geology. With the active fumaroles and steam vents in the south not far from an eerie-looking rock formation aptly called Hell's Gate, the place always seems poised to blow at any minute, either from nature's fury or man's.

✆

The road to Lake Naivasha from Nairobi lies on the main route that goes across Kenya from the coastal city of Mombasa to Uganda. For years the road was dangerously potholed and narrow, its edges cracked and broken in many places. The one section most familiar to me was the part that followed the twists and turns alongside the path of the old railroad, which once wound its way up and down the Rift Valley. The modern tracks follow a more direct route.

Arriving at the rim of the escarpment, before descending I would catch my first glimpse of the lake on the valley floor, glinting dark blue in a brownish-green landscape, and overshadowed in the morning light by Mt. Longonot which loomed to the east.

In the late '70s, this old road was replaced by a new one, a modern highway that went straight along the high ground above the valley rim. Trucks were not allowed on the new road, which made driving easier. My first trip on this clean, dark black surface with its bright white stripes and new route signs was enough to resurrect the joy of driving. And the landscape! After running through a large upland forest reserve, where the foggy, cool, moist air had to be whipped off the windshield by the car's wipers, the road emerged along the sunlit edge of an 8,000ft-high escarpment. The panoramic views of the Rift Valley were astounding. It was easy to be distracted and before I realized it I had arrived at the new turnoff, a road that took me down into Naivasha town which, at 6,000ft (about a mile high, like Denver), was still high enough to leave me breathless after a brisk walk.

Along the road coming down to the lake, I saw the Kinangop Plateau up-close for the first time. This is a grassy tableland that has been populated by Kikuyu settlers. In the early '60s, they were given land titles and working plans for their new acres, but because it was a wet area with tussock grasses interspersed with bogs and marshes, the land had to be drained. This process, started in colonial days and carried forward by the new settlers, is now so complete that today there is very little of the original grassland left other than a small park. The farms here include fields of pyrethrum, the daisy ingredient of natural insecticides, and mixed crops of which the potato dominates. I saw few trees but many, many productive small farms. And at every country bus stop, or "*matatu*" stand (local taxis or minibuses), I saw large sacks or "*debbies*" (4-gallon capacity tin containers) loaded with potatoes and carrots, and open trucks piled high with produce.

Ultimately, the water supply of the lake comes from these areas—the Aberdare Mountains in the north and the Kinangop Plateau in the east, both regions that sit high above the basin. In the '80s and '90s, the foothills of the Aberdares were cleared and cultivated by Kenyans who settled the land and produced food in significant quantities. They also farmed on the plateau where, in 2005, in one district alone farmers produced 1.7 million tons of Irish potatoes.

Rain falling on tussock grasslands, the original natural vegetation, infiltrated the soil and recharged the rivers in a natural fashion. The water seeped into the aquifer that fed the streams, resulting in an even flow distributed over the course of the year. This natural landscape provided water from the land—until the cultivated plots took over. After that, the water was drained away and used for crops in the western highland.

Today these highlands lose a great deal of water through crops and evaporation from exposed soil. As a result, during floods water now comes straight down the denuded slopes. When it enters the streams, hydrologists find, the annual flows are greatly diminished and the water is soil-laden. This is the very soil that will continue to kill the lake now that the swamps have been cleared. The only recourse is to build very expensive sediment traps unless the papyrus swamps are replanted and maintained as filter swamps. As productive as these areas are, they have changed the water cycle for the worse, which is now eroding away the soil and affecting the lake.

When the flower farms arrived in Naivasha, no one was ready for what happened. Neither the town, the settlers, hotel managers, nor flower farms had the services to cope with the phenomenal growth that resulted as the market for Kenya flowers soared. The result was pollution on a massive scale from intensive agriculture, as well as sewage and runoff into the lake. In addition to the problem of pollution, water was being pumped from the aquifer and from the lake faster than it was coming in. It was like inviting a large number of people to a party, then turning off the beer taps. But instead of questioning why the taps were turned off and insisting they be turned on, people scrambled to draw from what was left at last call. Everyone needed water, and everyone had a good argument ready as to why they should be given precedence over others. Even today, years after the deterioration of the lake, few reports or news stories have taken up the question of why the water that was supposed to feed this massive development disappeared. Much of the water that went missing was, and still is, siphoned off before reaching the lake. It is converted into the food that feeds the people in the uplands and supplies the markets in Nairobi and international exports. Thus more and more is consumed in Nairobi and sent to Europe, and less and less is allowed to go on its way into the lake.

In earlier times, there were three rivers—the Malewa, the Gilgil, and the Karati (Map 6, p. 192)—all of which were fed by rainwater flowing down from the Kenya Highlands. With time, irrigated agricultural schemes developed along all these rivers. Lower down in the basin, water was pumped from the aquifers using boreholes, or pumped directly from the rivers. At the same time, the development of farms on the foothills of the Aberdares and the Kinangop went on unabated. The Gilgil and Karati became intermittent, and then stopped, and the flows in the Malewa were diminished. All this was happening well before the flower farms got under way.

Just before heading back to Nairobi, I remember stopping one day at a farm stand in Naivasha where I bought three cabbages and put them on the back seat of my car. Driving off, I happened to look back at them in my rearview mirror and realized they filled the whole back seat. What I was looking at was an example of what the flower growers saw in the great potential of the Naivasha soil, but instead of cabbages they had their eyes on cut flowers, especially roses. The prices were high enough to evoke dollar signs before their eyes. They went to bed at night dreaming of the profits that would come about when they brought together the volcanic soil of the lakeshore, the abundant supply of fresh water, and roses that could be shipped by air to satisfy an enormous market that peaked on St. Valentine's Day; and while they dreamed, the lake dried.

Popular thinking was that the multi-million-dollar market would change Kenya the way outsourcing has changed Asian countries. Environmentalists both locally and internationally were outraged at the impact that was evident from the start. Unfortunately, their recommendations had only a minor effect, and the government seemed powerless—or unwilling—to stop the onslaught. Perhaps this was because the people working on the farms, the owners and managers of the flower farms, as well as businessmen and workers throughout the country did not think of what was happening as an onslaught. After all, this was no different from the coffee and tea farming that had gone on for a hundred years in Kenya. To most Kenyans, the farming and marketing of flowers was as natural a business as any other agroindustry. Coffee growing had even been romanticized by Karen Blixen in her famous book *Out of Africa*.

The coffee industry in Kenya uses a wet method that requires a great deal of water, with the growers applying a variety of chemicals, resulting in coffee farming being the number one major polluter of surface water in the country.[3] Pollution is not an obvious concern because the coffee farms are located in rural areas where more than 77% of smallholders who produce the crop are located. Coffee and tea growing are part of everyday life. Flower growing on Lake Naivasha was just another industry, though more obvious. It would be hard for Kenyan environmentalists to make a case, but the number of Greens in Kenya has grown steadily over the last forty years. There are now Schools of Environmental Science in the colleges and universities, concepts of conservation and ecology are now taught in the grade schools, and this new generation benefits from the earlier efforts by animal conservationists in Kenya, who showed them how they might succeed. Burning large piles of ivory at public bonfires to show that the illegal trade would not be tolerated, making movies like *Born Free* and *Serengeti Will Not Die*, and writing books like *Among the Elephants* were examples of how to attract attention and promote solutions. Wangari Maathai's

2004 Nobel Peace Prize for her contribution to sustainable development in Kenya proved to everyone that much could be achieved in this area. It also helped the environmentalists' cause that Lake Naivasha is the *only* freshwater lake in Kenya, and thus had a distinct fauna and flora. All the other lakes are soda or saline with a balance of salts and natron that make them unpalatable.

Lake Naivasha was fresh, visible, and vulnerable, and the environmentalists were ready to fight. They retaliated early against those who placed commercial interests first by making the lake a Ramsar Wetland of International Importance in 1995. This is a move that if followed with action allows for the conservation and wise use of wetlands and their resources. But, although elsewhere it is effective as a technique to slow the misuse of wetland resources, in the case of Lake Naivasha it had little effect. Perhaps because Lake Naivasha is not a national park, it cannot be easily legislated or regulated. The Naivasha Ramsar site consists only of the lake and a buffer zone that includes the swamp fringe surrounding the lake; it *doesn't include* the land or the flower farms. But this doesn't absolve the flower farms from their negative impacts. Unlike the Kenyan coffee and tea plantations which affect river water outside of protected areas, the flower farms border on an internationally designated wetland. This made it doubly important that the flower farms take precautions, as their impacts are felt directly by the fauna and flora of the lake.

This arrangement whereby they were allowed to continue farming around the periphery of the lake was made in order to accommodate the fact that the lake is entirely surrounded by private land. It was left to the community to voluntarily look after its lakeside interests, which apparently did not happen.

Tension increased between the different players in the environmental scenario during this period. One person who stepped in and took matters into her own hands was Joan Root, one of the leading lakeside conservationists whose murder signified the end of the expatriates' splendid isolation. They—and the rule of law—were no longer any match for the Yukon gold-rush atmosphere created by the flower-growing industry.

The next startling event was the disappearance of the papyrus swamps. By 2008, over 90% were gone. Among the swamps lost was the large one of 9,000 acres in the north, shown on Map 6 (p. 192). Its disappearance was clearly evident on satellite photos and the latest maps (Map 7, p. 194). This was shocking news, because this swamp had been the subject of research for over thirty years, five of which included my own work. In recent years it provided a habitat that attracted more and more attention from African biologists. But now all of that is history, and in its place a complication presents itself.

With the papyrus swamps around the lake gone, there are no longer any barriers to the influx of sediment and pollutants. Any rainfall will bring increasing loads of nutrients directly into the lake, which is already at its breaking point.

By the beginning of 2010, after the swamps were gone, the drought ended, the El Nino rains arrived, and instead of the lake snapping back to its normal self, 700 fish died due to lack of oxygen caused by fertilizer runoff and algal blooms.

This fish kill outraged local residents, who believed that the flower farms had dumped some chemical into the lake. Subsequent examination of the fish and dissolved oxygen in the water proved conclusively that eutrophication was the cause of the fish deaths. Dr. Stephen Mbithi, a marine expert, said that the vast majority of fish had died with open mouths, and that the larger fish had died first, followed by smaller fish. This indicates suffocation and a lack of oxygen due to algal growth. It also indicates that sewage had been flushed into the lake and that now the lake was well and truly polluted. Ultimately the culprits were the towns, the irrigated schemes upriver, the flower farms, and agriculture in general.

During the past fifteen years there have been several efforts made to protect the lake and the swamps and to educate the people living within its 1,235-square-mile catchment. This work is coordinated by the Lake Naivasha Riparian Association (LNRA), an association of local landowners who own land abutting the lake. Started in 1925, it was reorganized in recent years to include among its membership hotel owners, tour operators, the Kenya Power Company, ranch owners, flower growers, small farmers, domestic plot owners, cooperatives, and the Naivasha Municipal Council itself.

One of the most important actions of the association was the development of a management plan for the lake. Since all the major lakeside landowners belong to the LNRA, it was the ideal group to guide the plan, which was meant to control human activities in the area and stem any decline of the quality and quantity of the lake's waters. Adopted in July 1996, the plan was updated in early 1999. It commits members to monitor all activities on the riparian land (land exposed in times of dry weather), to protect the papyrus belt, and to observe a 100-meter "buffer zone." Shortly thereafter, the plan was declared not legal, and in its place the government turned to self-regulation to conserve the lake. The flower farms were told to execute their own conservation plan through a Water Users Association.[4]

Would the flower farms ever be able to rise to the occasion and clean up their industry as well as help in restoring the lake? Will there ever be a White Knight who will rescue the situation? Until now this was considered too far-fetched. It would never happen. But it seems there may be some relief in sight—which is fortuitous, because the water level of the lake is currently higher than it has ever been, and perhaps this is the best time to institute changes before the next drying cycle takes the lake down to new lows.

Among the rescuers, Kenya has a model flower farm that can show everyone the way of the future. It is no ordinary farm, but one that is well on its way to becoming an international model of how to run a flower farm in a sustainable way. The farm, called Oserian, is unique. It was formed in 1969 as a family concern producing vegetables; it later evolved into a cut-flower farm in 1982.[5] The owner, Mr. Hans Zwager, and his wife and family have devoted themselves to doing things the right way. They rank today among the top flower farms on the lake in terms of production, yet they rank over the top environmentally.

The farm is located on an estate that includes an 18,000-acre wildlife sanctuary and a 3,000-acre wildlife corridor that allows game to safely pass from the lake south to the man-made water holes of Hell's Gate National Park. The 620-acre flower farm run by Peter Zwager represents less than 5% of the total estate and yet, because it is run so efficiently, it has a smaller carbon footprint than comparable greenhouses producing flowers in Holland. By using a combination of plant nutrition with bio-control agents designed to prevent and combat a range of diseases that affect flowers, Oserian has become one of the world's largest Integrated Pest Management Flower Farms. With one 2½-acre greenhouse devoted to producing, each week, more than three million *Phytoseiulus persimilis*—parasitic mites that attack spider mites—it saves millions each year on chemicals alone. They use natural ventilation and steam release to prevent mold buildup and thus also save on fungicides.

By far the most astonishing advance at Oserian was its move to tap into the local geothermal vents, the geological formation that gives Hell's Gate Park its name. The geothermal turbines make the estate energy self-sufficient, while the carbon dioxide from the same well is used to drive productivity in the greenhouses to higher levels. The steam from their geothermal plant also helps control the relative humidity and temperature in the greenhouses; this in turn reduces and regulates water requirements so the plants receive only what they require from drip systems. The roses are grown hydroponically using an inert substrate made from pumice stone mined and crushed locally on the estate. This same system allows them to control the pH, nutrients, and nutrient strength of the water in which the flowers grow, water which is then collected and recycled, along with any estate waste runoff, through a filter swamp. All of this is supplemented with a rainwater collection system. In sum, they take a minimum amount of water through metered boreholes, the ideal green industry. To top it off, they have planted 300,000 trees to make the area a better place to live![6]

And the work force? Oserian is Fair Trade Certified, which means that the farm must continuously improve conditions for the workers—whether it's their pay or how they live. The 4,800 farm workers plus dependents live near the farm in free or subsidized housing, with health and primary education provided along with nurseries for day care. They pay the highest floricultural wages in Kenya and help with local village water projects and schools.

In the final analysis, it must be said that Oserian and a few other sustainable farms locally are in the minority in the Lake Naivasha area. The majority of growers do not farm sustainably, so although Oserian has shown everyone the way, it's now up to the government to act.

It would also help if the towns (Naivasha and Karagita) would close ranks with the Riparian Owners Association, the Growers Group, and responsible sustainable development groups like Imarisha in order to help the poor and rural communities to obtain water, sewerage, and garbage recycling services within the lake area.

Another encouraging effort is the plan to construct a filter swamp across the delta of the Gilgil River. Because the Gilgil flow is intermittent, a series of levees, dikes, and barrages can be put in place. The idea is to create a filter swamp and keep it flooded year-round to allow papyrus to grow there. These newly restored papyrus swamps will be confined to flotation devices made of recycled plastic water bottles; this way the swamps will continue to float even as the water levels decrease. The swamps would never again be stranded where they could be subjected to cutting and burning. The restoration program has already begun under the guidance of Ed Morrison and David Harper, researchers who have worked on the lake for many years.[7] They also propose that the papyrus restoration program be supplemented by projects that rehabilitate the catchment and restore degraded habitats along the rivers and around the lake edge. The cost of the program would be partly borne by the flower farms.

There is no reason why papyrus filter swamps could not be set up to filter individual farm wastewater. Managed by individual flower growers, the size of the filter swamp would be proportional to the company's operation. Swamps so created could provide the basis for a sustainable local craft industry, as well as birdwatcher sites and ecotourism. Cultivating, harvesting, and promoting such a system would be an easy task for business interests that handle millions of dollars in export sales, and are capable of surviving and even expanding in the face of civil unrest, droughts, and disasters that would normally level other agribusinesses.

A major effort by the growers in this regard would show the international environmental community that the roses from Kenya are not simply the "blood roses" of the sensationalist press, but the product of an integrated and coordinated system that involves local people and cleans up its own environment.

Thirty years after the fact, as I thought of the damage that came about when the swamps were cleared, I also thought of the thousands of hungry Africans who live there and are always in search of land. I realized then that whatever solution is found must be resolved in favor of these people. It does no good to conserve and restore a natural resource if people starve to death in the process. The current scramble for land in Africa is an example of how big business goes about the kind of development that brushes aside such scruples.

Today the restoration of the Everglades is seen by the World Bank as a paradigm for sustainable development and a worldwide guide for resolving global water conflicts. For others it is also a restoration blueprint for America. One of the objects of this book is to illustrate the importance of papyrus, and to show that papyrus is really worth conserving as a resource for the future. The plant that involved us in one of the oldest human-plant relationships in recorded history now depends on us for its vitality. This is a trust we cannot ignore.

∾

There is a haunting coincidence between the cutting and clearing of swamps today in the rest of Africa and the clearance of papyrus in ancient Egypt. A thousand years ago during the Islamic Era, arable land in Egypt was as much at a premium as it is today. When farmers cleared the swamps, they did so because of the demands of their Arab conquerors. To the people who amassed great wealth from Egyptian agriculture and lived in palaces in the emerging city of Cairo, the swamps were simply distractions. Papyrus lost value with the introduction and substitution of other materials, and then succumbed when agricultural pressure came to bear. The North Swamp of Lake Naivasha in Kenya disappeared for the same reasons—the increasing value of cash crops and the demand for local market commodities. In the case of North Swamp, the water supply was used for agriculture, which was deemed more valuable than the biota of the lake. In Lake Victoria, the swamps are pitted against the value of water needed to generate energy. It obviously comes down to the perceived value of a natural resource and actual value, which is often only apparent in the long term.

In the Huleh Valley, a national investment of $25 million in 1993 made a world of difference in the integration of papyrus swamps with ongoing development and a way of life. In Africa, national economic resources at that level are often not available, and when they are, they are more properly earmarked for general development. In order not to detract from needed general development, or from resources that are scarce already, the cost of stopping and reversing pollution in Lake Naivasha must be borne by the major agricultural and industrial users. That is not likely to happen immediately. Even with a flower export market worth hundreds of millions of dollars annually, it will be difficult to institute a "user pays" attitude. Thus, scarce financial capital combined with the reluctance of those involved leaves the conservation of these common resources, such as the swamps of Lake Victoria and the wetlands in the Okavango, Congo Basin, and Southern Sudan, in the hands of regional environmental initiatives and tourist development agencies. The situation will stay that way until the perceived value of papyrus swamps comes closer to reality, and when the swamps can pay their way once more. Would such a thing ever happen? It did in the Huleh Valley, where papyrus now thrives and does its duty filtering the water. There the water table has risen, alleviating local agricultural concerns, the plant and animal species have blossomed, and birdlife in enormous numbers has returned. Diversion of peat water and local sewage into treatment plants and subsequent use for irrigation are expected to reduce the flow of nitrates by at least 40% annually. The same may yet happen in Cairo, once enough filter swamps are in place. Elsewhere . . . there is hope.

19

The Zambezi, the Victorians, and Papyrus

Initially the Victorian explorers were searching for the source of the Nile, a task taken on by John Speke first with Richard Burton, later with James Grant. By the time Samuel and Florence Baker made their trip to the upper reaches of the Rift Valley, West and East Africa were already considered "done."

Attention shifted to the area east of the Congo and south of Lake Victoria, a region that today comprises Malawi, Zambia, Mozambique, and parts of Tanzania (Map 8, p. 213), the cradle of the Congo, Nile, and Zambezi Rivers.

Typically, this area was reached by caravan from the island of Zanzibar on the coast, going due west along paths established by slave traders, who were still active in the region. Tales of exotic mountains, tribes that defied imagination, savannas with unending herds of game, river valleys and water in profusion, including a cluster of large and small lakes still unknown to the outside world, drew the explorers here. By far the greatest attraction was the fact that somewhere among these lakes or rivers was the ultimate source of three major rivers. Could it be that there was a *common* source? That possibility added heat to the already fevered Victorian imaginations.

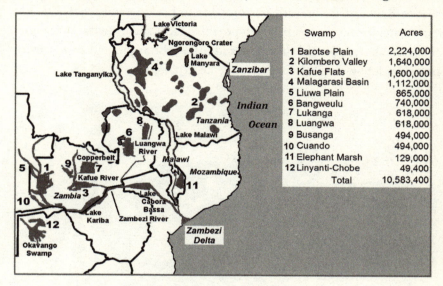

	Swamp	Acres
1	Barotse Plain	2,224,000
2	Kilombero Valley	1,640,000
3	Kafue Flats	1,600,000
4	Malagarasi Basin	1,112,000
5	Liuwa Plain	865,000
6	Bangweulu	740,000
7	Lukanga	618,000
8	Luangwa	618,000
9	Busanga	494,000
10	Cuando	494,000
11	Elephant Marsh	129,000
12	Linyanti-Chobe	49,400
	Total	10,583,400

MAP 8: *Major swamps of the Zambezi region.*

The arrival of Livingstone in the region caused much interest and excitement back in England. A scientist and bush doctor, he was also a man born of the working class and an explorer who discovered a waterfall and named it after his queen, yet who, on the other hand, advocated the reform of Empire. A cherished example of the missionary activist, he advocated the expansion of commercial interests yet crusaded against slavery. To the Victorians he was Everyman's hero, and his motto summed up everything he and they stood for: "Christianity, Commerce, and Civilization."

When he landed in Zanzibar in 1866, he was getting on in years. It was already thought that he would not have many more African treks to follow. From Zanzibar he traveled west and north, exploring and sending back reports. Just to be on the move was a bracing experience for him. His party was smaller than most expeditions, and by necessity he sought out and relied on the help of Arabs at every turn, people who were obviously connected to the slave trade. Though criticized for this association, it allowed him to report in full on the actions of the slavers while simultane-ously providing details of geography and natural science.

He sent his letters and reports back to the coast by runner, thence by boat to Zanzibar for onward transmission to London and the world. The reports made exciting reading and provided facts and eyewitness accounts of cruelty that supported the ideals and fueled the arguments of a growing anti-slave lobby. And so, for five years he explored.

Dr. Livingstone and porters crossing a papyrus swamp.

His goal was to examine the drainage of a chain of lakes that included Lakes Malawi, Mweru, and Bangweulu (Maps 5 and 8, pp. 141 and 213), all three of which he described for the first time. They were considered important pieces in the puzzle. Unluckily, the southern ends of the last two lakes are located in excessively swampy places, places where papyrus swamps abound. In the case of Lake Bangweulu, the papyrus swamp is even larger than the lake itself. Livingstone's worst moments seem to be his passage through these swamps, which like many things in Africa by his reckoning were always "inviting mischief." Also, he never seems to have mastered the art of walking in a papyrus swamp. As he records on 26 September, 1867, "Two and a half hours brought us to the large river we saw yesterday; it is more than a mile wide and full of papyrus and other aquatic plants and very difficult to ford, as the papyrus roots are hard to the bare feet, and we often plunged into holes up to the waist."

Then suddenly his reports stopped arriving in London and it was feared he had taken ill or worse. An American newspaper, the *New York Herald*, offered the services of Henry Stanley, by then a well-known explorer with firsthand knowledge of Africa. He rose to the challenge and found Livingstone alive, but grown old and weakened by fever, dysentery, and poor diet.

After their momentous meeting in Ujiji in 1871, Stanley stayed on for four months while Livingstone recovered, and together they explored the rivers and lakes of the region. They were especially interested in the Ruzizi, a papyrus-lined river that connects Lake Kivu to Lake Tanganyika (Map 5, p. 141). Several explorers before them had said or suggested that Lake Tanganyika drained into Lake Kivu by way of this river. The assumption was that Lake Kivu then drained into Lakes Edward and Albert, and from there into the Albert Nile. If true, it meant that Lake Tanganyika (the longest lake in the world and one of the deepest, second only to Lake Baikal in Siberia) was merely an extension of the Nile! All that was needed to confirm this was to witness the northerly direction of flow of the Ruzizi. But the minute Livingstone and Stanley arrived on the river, it was obvious to them that it flowed *south*, indicating that Lakes Kivu and Tanganyika were part of the Congo drainage system (Map 5, p. 141). This incident accounted for the famous picture of Stanley and Livingstone leaning together over the gunwale of their boat as they closely examined the water of the Ruzizi (p. 216), a scene that in one form or another made the front pages in many of the world's newspapers in the 1870s. Coincidentally, it provided the world with its first great view of what papyrus swamps really look like. The tall stems, graceful umbels, abundant birdlife—it was all there, and it showed this illustrious pair as if they were drifting through a swamp in ancient times. All that was lacking was a set of royal throw-sticks and a pharaoh or some other noble to show them how to really take advantage of a papyrus swamp.

In his diary, Livingstone chafed at the way other explorers made hasty decisions, too often based on little information. He singled out as an example a statement by Samuel Baker—our Sam—who said that "Every drop from the passing shower to the roaring mountain torrent must fall into Albert Lake, a giant at its birth." This attitude of Baker and his smug certainty that Lake Albert was so important as a catch basin brought from the good doctor the comment: "How soothing to be positive." Yet until his death Livingstone himself was convinced that the Lualaba River was the ultimate headwater of the Nile. In fact, it was subsequently shown to be the source of the Congo (Map 5, p. 141), but by then it mattered little as Livingstone was resting peacefully in Westminster Cathedral.

Livingstone and Stanley in a papyrus swamp at the mouth of the Ruzizi River, 1871.

Once replenished by supplies from Stanley, Livingstone went on his way and Stanley returned to the coast. Livingstone's last trek took him in the direction of the swamps of Lake Bangweulu, a course that some say led to his death. Deeper and deeper he waded into this world of water.

> *March 1873—It is impossible to describe the amount of water near the Lake. Rivulets without number. They are so deep as to damp all ardour. . . . The water on the plain is four, five, and seven feet deep. There are rushes, ferns, papyrus, and two lotuses, in abundance. . . . The water in the country is prodigiously large: plains extending further than the eye can reach have four or five feet of clear water,*

*and the Lake and adjacent lands for twenty or thirty miles are level.
. . . The amount of water spread out over the country constantly
excites my wonder; it is prodigious. . . . (Dr. David Livingstone,
1874,* The Last Journals.*)*

Horace Waller, the compiler of Livingstone's journals, commented in
1874: "As we have said, a man of less endurance in all probability would
have perished in the first week of the terrible approach to the Lake. . . .
It tried every constitution, saturated every man with fever poison. . . ."
Soon enough it caught up with this frail, gray-haired, emaciated old hero.
Exhausted, unsteady on his feet, litter-bound and fever-stricken, he died
in May 1873 at Chitambo. His heart was buried in Africa and his mummified body sent home for a state funeral. He died as he lived, constantly
moving on to new and exciting adventures. The Ancient Egyptians would
perhaps say that he had already reached Heaven, as he had died inside a
papyrus swamp—a Field of Reeds.

Livingstone close to death inside a papyrus swamp.

20

An Unwanted Legacy

By all accounts, the wetlands in the Zambezi region that Livingstone struggled through are still there. A mosaic of seasonally wet grasslands interspersed with seasonally flooded forests and scattered small permanent papyrus swamps is encountered along the Kafue Flats and the Kafue River (Map 8, p. 213). This is a major tributary that heads south, flowing through the Copperbelt before it joins the Zambezi.

One interesting thing about the region is the constancy of species in these wetlands. The botanist, range manager, or ecologist traveling the length of Africa soon becomes used to seeing the same wetland plants. It makes little difference whether you are in the swamps of East and Central Africa or the Sudd, the reed grass (Phragmites), bulrush (Typha), and papyrus (Cyperus) prevail. Sometimes the three are on their own or sometimes in combination with other Africa-wide species such as the water-tolerant grasses Echinochloa, Oryza, Miscanthidium, and Leersia, as well the floating so-called hippo grass, Vossia, common in deep water.

In the Zambezi Basin these shallow, seasonally saturated, grassy wet-lands are called "*dambos*," a local term meaning a very wet depression. Although Livingstone thought they were endless, dambos make up only 20% of the plateau regions of Central and Southern Africa. Even so, their presence is impressive by any standard.

While most dambos are waterlogged for at least a portion of the year, quite a few dry out at the surface during the four- to six-month dry season. However, the sponge-like center stays moist, and that sustains the aquatic grasses and reeds that are typical of this monotonous landscape. The only relief from these acres of reed beds is the shade that comes from trees and bushes that grow up on termite mounds or the upper drier slopes of the dambos away from the bottomland. Unfortunately, the shade provided by these trees and bushes also serves as a habitat for the tsetse fly, against which the local herders and farmers have to defend themselves.

The wetlands and aquatic environments in the region, as impressive as they are today, are no longer the wild, unsullied ecosystems of 150 years ago. The changes that have occurred are due mostly to man's activities. About 10% of the dambos are farmed during the dry season when the edges dry out enough to be cultivated. In the wet season the same areas are fished, while year-round 40% of the seasonal grassland margins are grazed, and 30% have been converted to national parks and are reserved for eco-tourism.[1]

Within limits, this sort of multiuse of the land is sustainable and is con-sidered a desirable goal. It is only when activities get out of hand that the trouble begins. Large-scale clearance of dambos, excessive poaching, and overgrazing or overfishing, for example, will upset the balance. Another large difference between the time of Livingstone and today is the discovery of extensive deposits of copper and cobalt, the mining of which has created the pollution that now threatens the region. Almost 40% of the people of Zambia depend on the Kafue River for their well-being and are thus affected.

Mineral deposits have made Zambia one of the most industrialized countries in Africa. However, any advantage this may have given the country was negated when world copper prices collapsed in 1975, damaging the Zambian economy. As a result, a very high percentage of the population still lives below the poverty line. In recent years the copper mines, now privatized, have benefited from a rebound in copper prices. That and a maize bumper crop have helped turn the economy around. Foreign investment has also helped. China has invested close to $3 billion in the Zambian economy, according to recent government figures.

The Dambos: Overworked and Underpaid

As Livingstone found, the Zambezi Basin is blessed with a significant array of swamps and dambos (Map 8, p. 213). Although these ecosystems function here in the same way as wetlands in many other places in Africa, in this region they have been tasked with double duty. Not only have they had to work hard at recharging the water table and trapping silt and sewage, but for the last 80 years they have also had to clear heavy metals from mine wastewater.

The heavy metals referred to are iron, cobalt, copper, manganese, molybdenum, and zinc, all metals required in trace quantities by living organisms, but which in excessive levels can be damaging. Others, such as vanadium, tungsten, cadmium, mercury, plutonium, and lead, are of no use to the human body, and their accumulation over time can cause serious illness.

Mine waste contains elevated concentrations of these metals because mine wastewater is acidic. It gets that way because ores often occur in sulfide form; exposure of the sulfide ores to oxygen and water during the process of mining leads to the formation of trace amounts of sulfuric acid, enough to leach out heavy metals.

While the mines are in operation, the water is pumped and drained from the work areas. But once mines are abandoned, the water table returns to normal and acid mine waste is left to seep out unhindered into the local water bodies. Thus the intense mining and ore-processing activities in the Copperbelt produced quantities of wastewater that were often discharged into the dambos, where the trapping of metals, especially cobalt and copper, has gone on for years.

Since the process of trapping heavy metals is dependent on the pH of the water, the best retention happens when wastewaters have been neutralized, a practice that was often neglected. Consequently, for the wetlands the job has been all uphill; and although they succeeded in trapping insoluble compounds into their oxygen-poor peat, mud, and sediments, they were overwhelmed in the process. As a result, contamination can now be detected 400–500 miles downstream in the Kafue River before it joins the Zambezi.[2]

The Copperbelt wetlands have been receiving wastewater from mining activities for many years, during which time wetland plants were left to die and be recycled in the peat. Thus massive accumulation of toxic metals has been buried in the swamp sediment.

Looked at another way, one could say that the wetlands provided a respite during the past 80 years, during which period appropriate environmental rules and regulations should have been put in place and enforced by the responsible agencies. Mining companies should have installed water-quality monitoring systems in order to manage toxic sediments and prevent their buildup into untended heaps. Proper maintenance of mine-waste dumps to neutralize acid waste and prevent toxic runoffs should have been part of normal mine operation. Instead, mining and smelting have saddled Zambia's Copperbelt with a huge environmental legacy.[3]

In 2006, according to a survey published by the Blacksmith Institute, an organization monitoring pollution in the developing world, Kabwe, about 80 miles north of the capital Lusaka and home to 300,000 people, was designated Africa's most polluted city. It also has the dubious distinction of being ranked as the world's fourth most polluted site.

Today, all of the interventions needed to make the river basin a more wholesome place to live will be expensive and difficult to install. Meanwhile, as pointed out in a recent review of the region, "the Zambian Copperbelt is burdened by an economic and environmental paradox. On one hand, development and growth of the mining industry is crucial in addressing Zambia's social and economic plight. On the other hand, all natural drainage routes of mine effluent inevitably enter the Kafue River, often passing through natural wetlands, which form the headwaters of this system."[4]

Since the alternatives to dambos are few, Zambia must face up to another problem: the wetlands that have previously acted as filters could still harbor dangers. The metals could again become mobile if the dambos in this region were drained for cultivation, or if they were to become acidified for any reason. Any action of this sort would flush metals out of the system into a local river where they could become a major source of pollution years after they were released from the mines.

Solutions

Fortunately, the dambos in the Copperbelt have been well studied, first by a team from Oxford University, including Constantin von der Heyden and Mark New of the Centre for Water Research and the School of Geography in Oxford, and more recently by a team from the Palacký and Charles Universities in the Czech Republic, headed by Dr. Ondra Sracek.[5]

It is obvious from their work that, for economic reasons, the dambos within the Zambezi Basin must continue to act as filter swamps for years to come, in which case mines would be better off using managed or constructed wetlands in combination with the dambos in order to obtain adequate water treatment. Also, before it is discharged, mine wastewater should be neutralized as a mandatory measure. Although wetlands often contain carbonate-rich groundwater with a high capacity for pH buffering and thus some neutralization will occur naturally, their efficiency as filters is greatly increased if mine wastes are neutralized beforehand.

Though older dambos are no longer as effective as they used to be, von der Heyden and New showed that older, saturated dambos can successfully be rejuvenated by giving them a rest. Also, as mentioned earlier, the filtration by wetlands can be made even more effective if the plant matter is harvested to remove the nutrients and heavy metals from the system.

Papyrus to the Rescue

The ultimate solution in the Copperbelt is perhaps to modify existing wetlands or construct new ones that would allow the deposited metals to be filtered out and disposed of. This is standard practice in conventional sewage-treatment systems. Your local cesspool man is a good example: he pumps out your backyard septic tank, hauls the sludge away for drying ("dewatering"), and disposes of it as mulch.

The problem in the Copperbelt is that many of the wetlands concerned are dominated by rooted plants, such as reed grasses and cattails. That vegetation would have to be cleared away in order to get at the sediments underneath, in which the metals are trapped. This would mean destroying the wetland. One way around this is to harvest the top part of the reeds for forage or mulch and let the base re-grow. But clearing tons of heavy metal from sediments is a major obstacle to overcome, and harvesting alone will not do it.

One attractive scheme that might work in the Zambezi wetlands comes from a recent study by Tom Headley and Chris Tanner, scientists working at the National Institute of Water and Atmospheric Research in Hamilton, New Zealand. They set out to design a low-maintenance system to remove heavy metals from stormwater before it drains into local water bodies. The method they selected is a four-part system composed of: (1) a settling basin where coarse material settles to the bottom, following which the water flows into (2) a basin with a floating mat of wetland vegetation, where fine particles and heavy metals are removed; the water then flows on to a third basin that contains (3) a small pond surrounded by a rooted wetland, where removal of nutrients and more metal takes place, after which the water flows down (4) a cascade to aerate it before it is released.

The beauty of their system is that the floating wetland plants in the second basin can be moved aside to allow the metal-containing sediments in the sludge to be pumped out.

How would that work in Zambia? First of all, a floating wetland that grows in quantity in the Zambezi River Basin and that has proved itself a strong remover of heavy metals is already at hand: papyrus. If several Copperbelt dambos were restructured to allow deep water to be retained and papyrus was encouraged to cover the surface, a perennial floating system would be created that might be more useful as a filter swamp than the classic dambo. Papyrus has the advantage in that the floating matrix of the swamp and the roots produces peat as well as a fine, light sediment that falls to the bottom of the swamp as sludge. This can be pumped out and carted away, dewatered, and disposed of. Also, the stems of papyrus, which we know can take up copper and cobalt in quantity, can be harvested and, instead of being used as mulch or fodder, can be mechanically chopped up or pulped to produce building materials, such as softboard.

This would remove the metals from the food cycle and would produce a cheap, useful byproduct. A rigid fiberboard was manufactured from dried papyrus stems and successfully sold in Uganda and Rwanda in the '70s and '80s, but both production units succumbed to competition from cheap imports.[6] With some sort of tariff protection in Zambia, it just might work.

Such a papyrus-based system designed specifically for the Copperbelt would be an economic alternative to the conventional sludge and sediment removal system used by industry, and it would generate a sustainable and productive wildlife habitat, a haven for migratory and indigenous birds and animals, all things that I'm sure Mother Nature—and the people who live in the region—would approve of.

☙

Among the many things buried in Zambia, besides Dr. Livingstone's heart and tons of heavy metals, are perhaps the remains of a living fossil, an animal called "*Emela-Ntouka*" that was said to have been slaughtered in 1933 by Waushi tribesmen along the shores of the Luapula River, which connects Lake Bangweulu to Lake Mweru (Map 5, p. 141).

Past history and observations today tell us that the African swamps are places of natural refuge. We are also told that they harbor great numbers of higher and lower plant and animal species, but, as in so many other ecosystems throughout the world, there is still much work to be done in finding and identifying species yet undescribed. The importance of such work is paramount, but it must also be conceded that in the swamps there is a special case for continuing work on species of the fantastic variety—that is, monsters, fictitious or real.

These creatures serve a purpose, as they have down through history: providing a scare factor that is of practical use. For example, what better addition to the existing papyrus swamp flora than the prehistoric elephant *Moeritherium*, that smooth-skinned, four-foot-long denizen of the swamps of Faiyum, the place in Egypt where papyrus swamps were common enough. With its flexible upper lip and snout, it spent most of its time half-submerged in the primeval Egyptian swamps, perhaps resting—much like the sitatunga does today—entirely submerged in a papyrus swamp with only its nostrils above water.

Knowing that such a creature was capable of making your next step your last step if by chance you trod on it, and if it rose up in response with its razor-sharp, hippo-like tusks pointed at you while it charged with the speed and force of a Volkswagen, you might believe that it is as useful a conservation measure as any fence or ranger patrol.

The Moeritherium is wishful thinking, as it is known to us only through some fossil teeth. On the other hand, cryptozoologists tell us that the Emela-Ntouka lives today. And not only is it living and hiding in the swamps of Lake Bangweulu, it is brownish-gray in color with a heavy tail and a body of the shape and appearance of a rhinoceros, having one long horn on its snout. It is about the size of the largest living terrestrial animal, the African Bush Elephant.

At 13,000–20,000 lbs, whether real or imaginary, we are looking at a formidable scare factor.

Could any branch of science be more appropriate to the study of swamp monsters than cryptozoology? More important, this "study of hidden animals" is now in a bid to be recognized as a branch of zoology that includes looking for *living* examples of animals that are considered extinct (such as dinosaurs), or animals whose existence lacks physical support but which appear in myths, legends, and first, second, or thirdhand reports. It is a discipline determined to be taken seriously. By conducting their work with scientific rigor, an open mind, and an interdisciplinary approach, cryptozoologists intend to prove themselves by bringing home the "real" thing, or "cryptid."

This pivotal cryptozoological event actually came to pass in 1938 when a Coelacanth was discovered off the eastern coast of South Africa. A fish considered to be the "missing link" between fish and tetrapods, they were believed to have gone extinct 65 million years ago. So there is a case for the existence of undiscovered, unlikely, or fantastic creatures. And further, many of the scientists involved in cryptid research have credentials. They also have sound reputations built on real fieldwork. But in order to succeed, they must have a modicum of boldness and flair, otherwise it would be impossible to defend their work, which is often based on folk tales with only a few tiny grains of truth.

The biologist and explorer Dr. Roy P. Mackal, who has gathered details while on two expeditions in the Congo region, is a good example of a crytozoologist. In his 1987 book *A Living Dinosaur*, Mackal noted that the live sightings of the Emela-Ntouka did not report a neck frill, which he would have expected on a ceratopsian. Furthermore, the Ceratopsia are absent from Africa's fossil record. On the basis of this kind of evidence, the cryptozoologist and author Loren Coleman suggested that the Emela-Ntouka is a new species of semi-aquatic rhinoceros.

The intriguing thing about African aquatic cryptids is that there are so many of them and they live in papyrus swamps. Further west and north within the Congo wetlands and swamp forests, for example, we have reports of: the *Mokele-mbembe*, a living sauropod dinosaur 16 to 32ft long that lives in the Likouala swamp region; a giant turtle in Lake Tele whose shell is 12 to 15ft in diameter; and the *Mbielu-mbielu-mbielu* or *Nguma-monene*, snake-like animals 130 to 195ft long with a serrated ridge running down their backs like that of a crocodile.

Any of these would serve as the ideal protector of the local papyrus swamps. We find proof of this in the words of the world-famous zoologist and biologist Ivan T. Sanderson, who in 1931, while paddling up a river in the heart of Africa, recalled the experience: "I don't know what we saw, but the animal, the monster, burned itself into my retinas. It looked like something that ought to have been dead millions of years ago. As a scientist, I should have been happy, of course, but this encounter was so frightening, so nasty that I never want to see it again."

The modern factor of pollution may change the cryptid game considerably. Instead of strange creatures still around from an ancient past, these would be mutated creatures of the future. After all, the idea has been around for some time that out of the swamp slime from pollution will come a new cryptofauna, a concept that forms the basis for the fictional *Teenage Mutant Ninja Turtles* from the storm sewers of New York City by way of Mirage Studios in 1984.

The same concept livened up the world of Charles Dickens 160 years ago, at a time when people were just beginning to be concerned about what else might arise from the mess that mankind was making of the aquatic world. In 1855 the famous scientist Prof. Michael Farraday, writing in the *Times*, described the filth of the Thames, which had become a national humiliation. He called it a fermenting sewer, while Dickens noted that the mire and mud in the city was deep enough to believe that Creation had just begun. From this, he thought, it would "be wonderful to meet a Megalosaurus, forty feet long or so, waddling like an elephantine lizard up Holborn Hill" (*Bleak House, 1853*).

From Dickens's time until today, the Thames is a marvel of successful clean-up, and proves that it is possible to redeem even an extremely polluted aquatic ecosystem and still maintain a growing human population. Though it required large sums of money and many years of constant dedication, and though storm events still bring inflows of untreated sewage, the Thames estuary has been transformed. It now supports normal fisheries, the passage of migratory salmon, and a massive yield of freshwater resources for public use.

From this we can see that there is hope for the Kafue River. With the help of sewage-treatment facilities and filter swamps of papyrus—with or without monster fauna—the Zambezi could survive.

❧

The delta of the Zambezi River for many years was cut off from public view because of a civil war that lasted 16 years and killed over 900,000 people. The area of the delta consists of a 5,800-square-mile region where the river divides into many branches with reed-fringed banks, sandbars, and permanent and seasonally flooded low-lying wetlands, including about a quarter of a million acres of papyrus swamps.

In addition to the effects of the war, the delta suffered from the impacts of two large dams built at Kariba and Cahora Bassa (Map 8, p. 213). It is today only about half as broad as it was before the construction of these dams. The Kariba Dam, built in the '50s, required Operation Noah in 1960 to capture and rescue 6,000 large animals and numerous small ones threatened by the lake's rising waters. Further downstream, the Cahora Bassa Dam was filled in 1974, after which time the dam trapped sediment and brought about a constant flow. This disrupted the natural cycle of wet-dry periods and resulted in a reduction in the size of the floodplain and a reduction in the number of channels in the delta, as well as a loss of local fisheries and depletion of birdlife.

The loss of sediment deposition in the delta resulted in coastal erosion, a 40% loss of mangroves, and a decline in prawn catch by 60% between 1978 and 1995. Some of these changes parallel those of the Nile Delta when the Aswan Dam was closed; the difference is that the water allowed through the Aswan Dam is used up in irrigation, so that only a small amount reaches the Nile Delta and this is not enough to stop salt water intrusion. In the Zambezi Delta, the water still flows as before but the flow is now a steady stream, except during heavy rain when the dams are in danger of overtopping. Floodgate releases during flood events are an enormous ongoing problem. Both of the dams on the Zambezi cause havoc to the residents and the animals and plants when water is released in quantity to the floodplain. For example, rising levels in Lake Kariba in March 2010 led to the opening of the floodgates, requiring the evacuation of 130,000 people and causing concerns that flooding might spread to nearby areas.

Though it has never been an important long-distance transport route, the lower Zambezi is deep enough to handle barges, and it is navigable from its mouth in the delta up to the Cahora Bassa Dam. Now with coal mining going forward in the central provinces by companies headquartered in Brazil and Australia, Mozambique expects to start producing over 20 million tons of coal per year in the next five years. The short-term transport solution by rail to the port of Beira on the coast south of the delta will be superseded by river transport, which makes it imperative that the Zambezi River be made navigable.[7] An initial investment of $200 million will begin the process which will presumably widen and deepen the main channel. With that, the delta will change again.

There is already concern in the country about environment issues, and awareness growing of the long-term cost of impacts. Recently, the two parties who earlier waged the Civil War faced off in Parliament, but this time it was a fight over environmental matters, as the largest opposition party, the former rebel movement RENAMO, accused the government of "putting the lives of thousands of people at risk" by authorizing an aluminum smelter to release emissions without passing through filters while their fume-treatment facilities were being rebuilt.[8]

❦

The ecology of the delta was studied in 2001 by a team headed by Richard Beilfuss, Vice-President of the International Crane Foundation and Adjunct Professor at the University of Wisconsin and the Universidade

Eduardo Mondlane in Mozambique. Beilfuss et al. noted that in an earlier study in 1910, "vast expanses of papyrus marsh" had been found and marked on maps as Mozambican "Sudd." But they found little evidence of any papyrus in this area in aerial photos taken in 1960 at the time Lake Kariba was being filled. Today, after a subsequent reduction in delta swamps because of the dams, the papyrus swamps make up only about 200,000 acres.

It is obvious that in recent times the Zambezi River in Mozambique and the delta wetlands have had a respite; but how long that will last, no one knows. Thankfully, the water-quality problems that exist upstream in Zambia do not exist yet in the delta. In Lake Kariba, heavy metal accumulation in the sediments and pollution from sewage are evident; but downstream in Lake Cahora Bassa, the water quality still seems quite good.

As industry begins to grow in Mozambique, especially mining and smelting of aluminum, it is expected that the Zambezi below the Cahora Bassa Dam will begin to change and the wetlands of the delta will suffer, unless the lessons learned in the Copperbelt are applied here as well. The task ahead will be to draw up and implement a plan for the river and the delta, both of which are unusual and varied enough to be managed as tourist resources—much like the Okavango Swamp in Botswana, a swamp that brings in millions in foreign exchange while employing thousands of people, and is a place where papyrus thrives and helps keep the place vibrant and alive.

21

The Okavango, Miracle of the Kalahari

What does a papyrus swamp look like from space? We know of one—the Okavango Swamp in Botswana—that looks like a giant print of a bird's foot. Papyrus grows along the major channels that cut through the swamp; these channels lined with papyrus are distinctly seen in satellite images in contrast to the arid terrain of the Kalahari Desert, which surrounds the swamp. Gradually the watercourses peter out at the "toenails" as they grade into the reed-choked wetlands that make up much of the Okavango seasonal swamps. Since the watercourses radiate out from an apex, the effect is that of looking at a green footprint left by an enormous six-toed bird (Map 9, p. 231).

Why such an unusual topography? Is there any significance in the outline, like the lines the Nazca Indians in South America cut into the face of rock formations, which depict earthly and mystic shapes, designs difficult to see unless you are a great distance above the earth, presumably because this is the way the gods see them? Or is it an extraterrestrial reaffirmation of the international symbol for peace—a sign made up of the semaphores for N and D (possibly standing for nuclear disarmament?) and coincidently the Celtic symbol for peace, which happens to be a circle with the imprint of a chicken or raven's foot inside?[1]

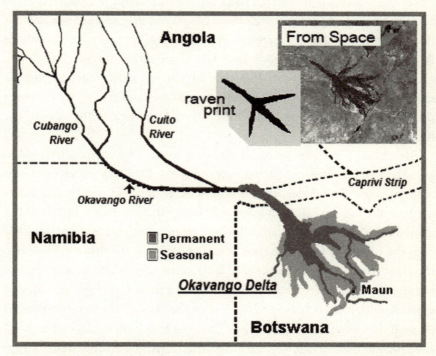

MAP 9: *The Okavango Delta (based on NASA, FAO Aquastat 2005, and OKACOM).*

Mystical musings aside, in the case of the Okavango there is no mystery. The toes are splayed out along two fault lines, geologic features common to the rift system that extends from the eastern Rift Valley into this part of Botswana. As in the case of the northern geological rift where the Red Sea and the Gulf of Aden join the Great Rift Valley, many millions of years from now this part of Botswana that lies between the faults will be split apart as the continent divides. Meanwhile it is geologically a very active area that is slowly sinking.

The Okavango River originates in the tropical highlands of Angola. From there it flows southward through parts of Namibia on its way into the Kalahari, where it ends in a large alluvial fan referred to as the Okavango Delta. Water flows into the region because of the gently sloped, slowly sinking terrain, but as it flows across the delta it disappears because it evaporates or is soaked up by the substrate. Since little or no water leaves the system, it is referred to as an "inland" delta. Kennedy Warne, co-founder and editor of *New Zealand Geographic* magazine, described the flood as a miracle that ". . . happens in slow motion . . . this part of southern Africa is so flat that the floodwaters take three months to reach the delta and four more to traverse its 150-mile length. Yet by the time its force is spent, the flood has increased the Okavango's wetland area by two or three times, creating an oasis up to half the size of Lake Erie at the edge of the Kalahari Desert."

Almost 6,100 square miles in size and covered by seasonally flooded grassland and permanent papyrus swamps, the Okavango Delta is about as large as the Everglades, and similar to other deltas in that the river disgorges onto a delta plain that is roughly triangular in outline, but there the similarity ends. The Okavango Delta is unusual in many ways; not only does the water not flow into the sea and evaporates into thin air, but when the floodwater arrives it noticeably lacks suspended mud, the one quality common to so many tropical rivers. As a result there is no layer of alluvium as in other deltas, such as the Nile before the Aswan Dam. Since there is no mud deposited, there are also no levees or bars built up, as on the Mississippi, and the soils are not the fabled black fertile stuff that made Egypt a world power in ancient times—instead, they are a weak slurry of sand and organic matter. In the Okavango Delta there are hundreds of islands composed of this sand and organic material that support shrubs and trees.

Land subsidence within this delta happens more rapidly in some places than others, and it is to such places that the water flows and helps produce a soil with the aid of tree roots. Thus we have dust and sand from the Kalahari mixed with deposits induced by the aquatic vegetation as a basic soil generated within the system. This is mixed with organic matter derived from termite mounds, which rise above the level of the floodplain. As a result, the delta somehow keeps pace with the sinking terrain. The soils produced, however, are not very fertile, and throughout much of the delta there are few areas suitable for large-scale commercial irrigation.

Prof. Terence McCarthy, from the School of Geosciences at the University of the Witwatersrand in Johannesburg, has carried out numerous studies of the Okavango Delta that describe this process of salt-trapping by trees and the soil-building activity of the termites. The combined effort of trees and termites keeps the water in the swamps fresh and helps expand the islands. In addition, papyrus grows aggressively across the channels and in the process produces peat that is recycled by the local fauna and flora. According to Prof. McCarthy, this compensates for the subsidence so that the delta remains an alluvial fan of remarkably uniform gradient.

This also means that there was never a scramble to stake out claims on fertile land. Nature was left in control. Niles Eldredge, the famed paleontologist and curator and chairman of the Department of Invertebrates at New York City's American Museum of Natural History, points out that the Okavango is today the closest thing remaining on earth to a true Eden, the place where the story of mankind began, a place of primordial settled existence where the game was as thick then as it is today.

In his book *Life in the Balance*, Dr. Eldredge gives us a great description of what it feels like on first entering the Okavango swamps. "For one thing, in the eastern reaches at least, the main watercourses are lined with tall reeds, peppered with small stands of papyrus. Even standing in the boat, you cannot see beyond the thick wall of grasses and papyrus, except in places where the watercourse widens, or where there has been a recent fire. As you go northward, the papyrus increases in frequency, until it is the dominant and, ultimately, the only plant lining the waterways. This plant, with its long, tough green stem and frizzy top knot, has given us the very word 'paper'."

A host of indigenous and migratory birds make the delta their home. More than 500 species live there, including the African fish eagle, flamingoes, sacred ibis, and the slatey egret, a threatened species that breeds here. Many species of fish thrive in the water, like tiger fish, sharp-toothed catfish, barbel, and bream.

The Okavango is also a place where salt taken out by trees is left behind in brine pools and salt crusts. The combination of fresh water and salt acts as a powerful magnet during the dry season as large herds of elephant, buffalo, and thousands of antelope looking for forage arrive in the swamps, and they in turn attract predators such as the unusual lions here that have learned to swim from island to island.

The marsh-dwelling antelopes found here include the lechwe (*Kobus leche*), an animal similar to but larger than the sitatunga. Like the sitatunga, they do not do well on dry land, and so keep on the move following seasonal changes in the swamps. Their legs are covered in a water-repelling substance that allows them to run quite fast in knee-deep water. Unlike the sitatunga, the lechwe have smaller hooves and are not confined to papyrus swamps; they can take advantage of other types of swamps, where they are regularly seen grazing shoulder-deep in the water.

The fauna and flora of the Okavango have become a prime tourist attraction. The result, as pointed out by Warne in his 2004 article in *National Geographic*, is that "Botswana has strong economic as well as political reasons for wanting to keep the delta pristine: Okavango tourism is second only to diamond mining as a foreign-exchange earner. The delta is a golden egg, but Botswana neither feeds nor owns the goose."

He is referring to the fact that the Okavango River originates in Angola and passes through Namibia before arriving in the delta. In Botswana the river feeds the swamp habitat and supports the abundant and exotic bird life along with elephants, lions, hippos, and crocodiles. Botswana sees it as an important asset to biodiversity; Namibia and Angola see it as water. Since water can be equated with development and progress, it is hard for Namibia and Angola to resist using that water to irrigate fields and provide for domestic needs, no matter what happens to the animals and plants downstream.

The Okavango wetlands, like those of so many other areas in Africa, now stand in danger because of water diversion. Apparently they must suffer, but the questions are by how much and in what ways. Immediately threatened is the basis of a large tourist industry. In 1997 it was declared one of the world's two largest Ramsar sites (the other is the Sudd in Southern Sudan). Also about that time, Namibia announced plans to pipe water from the incoming Okavango River to its capital city, Windhoek, and other central regions. Plans were also forthcoming from Angola and Botswana.

River inflow during the November–April rainy season brings to the delta 353 billion cubic feet of water that disappears into the sand or is lost to evaporation. All three countries have needs that depend on the same water from the same river. Of these, Botswana itself has the most ambitious plans, including dredging and building levees to increase and regularize flows and create reservoirs, as well as various canals and pipelines. All are intended to improve livestock management, provide for water supplies, and commercial irrigation, along with supplying water for a nearby diamond mine.

The potentially adverse effects of such plans are under consideration by the tripartite Okavango River Basin Commission (OKACOM), established in the mid-1990s with Angola, Botswana, and Namibia as members. Officially, they meet once a year and affirm that government officials have an interest and a willingness to collaborate with district and village councils on a range of small-scale projects. This allows the water users in the basin to move away from a model of strict water rights to one of basin-wide "benefit-sharing." Most recently the group discussed creating a trans-frontier wildlife park for tourists, along with other methods of sharing tourist-related revenue. The discussion on the Okavango encourages conventional water projects as well as alternative projects that use surface and groundwater for sustainable development, such as communal ranching, wildlife management, and ecotourism.

Does all this sound like a water war? Not really. The discussions are, thankfully, not full of the angry statements so common to the Nile Basin talks. In an interview with Anthony Turton, a specialist consultant on water, energy, and socio-economic development in southern Africa, on the subject of a pipeline that Namibia hopes to build to divert water from the Okavango River, Turton said that Namibia needs the water to promote development and give its country greater water security. He also reiterated that the pattern of water flow through the Okavango is well understood. "The river experiences two infusions, or pulses, every year and the engineers know that water cannot be taken from the river before these pulses have been allowed to progress through the length of the water course.

"The Okavango is misquoted," he continued, "as being a river in conflict. . . . There is a river basin commission that is functioning extremely well, but for the uninformed person, they tend to misinterpret the posturing of the different commissioners who make certain statements, without understanding the underlying dynamics. There is a high level of cooperation in that river basin."

◌

It is uncanny how like Egypt Botswana is. Lying as it does inside a desert, it depends on 94% of its water coming from outside, compared to Egypt's dependency of 97%. Both have large deltas, both import a great deal of their food, and both depend on industry (diamond mines in Botswana and oil and gas in Egypt) and tourism for their foreign exchange. The largest difference is the lack of silt that in ancient times made Egypt a world power with standing armies supported by the food production that came from the silt. In the Okavango Basin, according to a 2006 benchmark paper by Prof. Donald Kgathi et al. from the Okavango Research Institute, there is not much erosion from the Angolan Highlands; the natural vegetation composed of shrubs, grass, and trees has been preserved. This happens because of the low population density in the region, in turn due to the widespread occurrence of tsetse fly (*Glossina spp*). Also, the basin is situated far from heavily populated areas. The water in the river is thus relatively pristine, though phosphates are beginning to rise as more farmers turn to chemical fertilizers to help the impoverished soil.

Without nutrients or silt coming in, how then does the wetland vegetation survive? Keith Thompson, my former colleague in Uganda whom you met in the beginning of this book, felt that the Okavango Swamp already contains the chemical elements that the swamp needs to survive. Nitrogen, potassium, and phosphorus largely contained within the plants themselves are recycled into the peat. In fact, the papyrus that thrives at the apex of the Okavango Delta enjoys a high growth rate because the microbes associated with it can fix more than enough nitrogen for its needs. The same plants also trap what little nutrients or silt might come along. In the future, when land in the Angolan Highlands comes under cultivation and the silt in the river rises along with higher phosphorus content, the Okavango papyrus mats will act as a buffer.

Up to a point this is good, but as Warne points out, the managers, safari guides, and boatmen who work the swamps every day are appalled at the way papyrus responds to the increases in phosphorus. What they see is the unbelievable expansion of growth that we saw in the Lake Victoria swamps when sewage is passed into the papyrus swamps. This increase in phosphorus allows papyrus to spread out over channels at the head of the swamp, thus blocking paths previously cleared and making it more difficult to get around in the swamp. In the past, hippos cleared these channels, but with the increase in tourist traffic and decline in hippo numbers, channel clearance now becomes an ongoing problem.

Unlike the delta in Egypt, the wetlands of the Okavango were never cleared, although the margins were farmed for thousands of years. The farmers confined themselves to the seasonally flooded grasslands called *"molapo"* along the edges of the delta. The molapo were cultivated and cattle grazed on them using methods of traditional subsistence farming that are still common along the western and southeastern fringes of the delta. This kind of farming is risky, since the extent of the flood varies considerably each year and the farming effort must be coordinated to coincide with the start of flood recession and the start of the rainy season. If the fields are not flooded and kept watered, only meager yields can be expected.

Still, this is the kind of low-impact, low-investment farming system that should be encouraged and improved on, perhaps with the aid of small-scale irrigation using modern water-saving methods. As Prof. Kgathi says, "While conservation of the natural environment is critical, the pressing development needs must be recognized. The reduction of poverty within the basin should be addressed in order to alleviate adverse effects on the environment."

Improved molapo-type farming could help, but is instead in decline because of the attractions of urban life and the quick money to be made from the tourism sector. For example, Prof. Kgathi noted that 60% of the people in the delta are engaged in some form of services or work that relates to tourism, but it is often conventional high-end tourism: big-game hunting, fishing excursions, and up-market photographic safaris—the kind of tourism that pulls in millions in foreign exchange but generally fails to promote rural development because it marginalizes the poor. The best kind of eco-tourism that would conserve wetlands must be the kind tied to programs and projects like the Green Zone Cooperatives in Mozambique or the Campfire Program in Zimbabwe. The Campfire Program ensures local participation in decision making and sharing of all revenues earned through the program by producer communities. It fully subscribes to the axiom that no development program can succeed in rural or communal areas if it disregards the beliefs and attitudes held by the people it is intended to benefit.[2]

Of the 125,000 or so people affected, about half live in the Maun region, the urban center in the southeast. The others live on the margins of the seasonal wetlands, where they make use of the wildlife, fish, papyrus, reeds, thatching grass, trees, veldt products (tubers, etc.), small-scale cattle ranching, and molapo cultivation. They sound very much like modern-day counterparts of the ancient marsh men of Egypt.

The Okavango sits a continent apart from the Nile, yet the impression is inescapable that here is what the Nile Delta might have looked like 6,000 years ago. As Dr. Eldredge noted, it is an Eden preserved with its multitude of game animals and birds. It is also a place where marsh men pole boatloads of tourists along channels that are lined with walls of green, like the royal bird hunters of old plying the papyrus swamps in which the sacred sedge towered over all.

In ancient times, the 1,100,000 acres of papyrus swamps of the Nile Delta provided a vast natural resource that generated millions of dollars; today the 300,000 acres of papyrus in the Okavango adds a fascinating twist to the other famous attractions in Botswana, all of which have created a tourist haven. The income from tourism in 2010, according to the government of Botswana, was estimated to be $1.3 billion and to generate 54,000 jobs—small in comparison to the income from diamonds, but important for diversification. Botswana now ranks 42nd in the world in terms of long-term growth expected in the tourism sector, much of it due to the Okavango River and the swamps.

Through the years, thousands of studies have been conducted of the Okavango, and numerous seminars and conferences have been held. The Okavango Research Institute (ORI), located in Maun, a constituent part of the University of Botswana, is a marvel at coordinating this research.

One of their undertakings is a joint project with the Kalahari Conservation Society and the International Union of Conservation of Nature (IUCN)—the Biokavango Project, which will build local capacity for sustainable use and help the tourism sector to directly contribute to sustainable small-scale, multi-use rural development (including fisheries, agriculture, and hunting). This interest in community-based natural resource management and eco-tourism—that is, "tourism that conserves the environment and improves the well-being of local people"—is more in line with what is needed.

If Botswana succeeds in involving the entire community in sustaining their own lives as well as the biodiversity of the Okavango Swamp, and does this in the context of shared resources with neighboring countries, it will set a great example by providing a much-needed model for the development of the Sudd as well as for the Nile Delta, and perhaps other river basins in Africa like the Zambezi and the Congo.

22

Papyrus Blooms Again in the Holy Land

. . . As the afternoon glow of impending dusk settles over the valley, a raft of white pelicans begins to peel away from Lake Agmon. Taking flight in clusters of several dozen at a time, they glide against the backdrop of the darkening sky, undulating in broadening flocks, transforming into a trail of white confetti caught in the breeze. . . .

—Rene Ebersole, 2009. *Crossroads.*
AudubonMagazine.com

I wondered what the Huleh Swamp looked like thirty years after my first trip there. Things had changed since the 1970s. A reserve had been set up and the birds had returned. What effect did this have on the Jordan River and the Sea of Galilee, I wondered, and what had happened to the remnant papyrus swamp left after they had drained the original swamp? The chance to go back came during a recent vacation trip to Jordan and Egypt in 2010. This allowed me to take a side trip to the Huleh Valley to see it again firsthand.

I drove there the day after landing at Tel Aviv and staying overnight at a small inn near the well-advertised Huleh Nature Reserve. The next morning, after parking my car in the spacious parking lot, I walked through a neat picnic area and past a modern snack bar, recalling the earlier disdain of my fellow bus passengers when they balked at the sight of a rusty cyclone fence.

My goal was the Visitor's Center. Along the way, I was happy to see that the fence had been replaced by graveled paths, well-trimmed lawns, and for me the ultimate luxury: a solidly built walkway that went out through a papyrus swamp all the way to the water's edge.

The papyrus, bright green and flourishing, with each tall stem topped by an umbel, seemed as healthy as ever.

When I'd left the Huleh Valley in the 1970s, the deep smoking caverns of burning peat were an eyesore. Whether flooded by winter rains or turned into black dust in the summer, they were a reminder of what could go wrong. Today, the 865-acre enclave of papyrus in the Huleh Valley has become famous (Map 10, p. 242). It was Israel's first nature reserve. Along the way, the Society for the Protection of Nature had come into being and the reserve was declared a Ramsar site, a Wetland of International Importance.

Waiting for me at the Visitor's Center was Dr. Didi Kaplan, a robust, outdoorsy woman dedicated to ecology and the management of natural resources, and scientist in charge at the reserve. She sat me down at an outside table with several of her colleagues from the Israel Nature and Parks Authority. They were interested in my views about using papyrus as a filter swamp in Africa. In the Huleh Valley, they had spent a great deal of time and money diverting sewage from the swamp, and as clean-water ecologists, they didn't take well to my suggestion that they might profit from doing research in the area of sewage treatment.

They were hardly impressed even after I pointed out the results in Uganda in the Nakivubu Swamp on Lake Victoria, which suggested that sewage might actually increase the growth rate of papyrus. I persisted in pointing out to them that they were ideally set up to carry out controlled experiments on papyrus, as they had access to analytical laboratories. "This is a great opportunity to find out how efficient papyrus is as a filter swamp," I pleaded with them. "Think of the international implications." But the idea of bringing sewage back into the reserve was hard to accept.

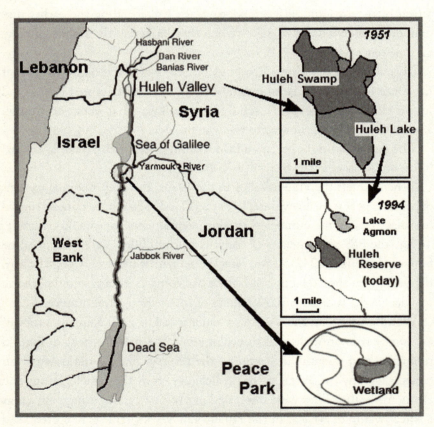

MAP 10: *Jordan River, the Huleh Swamp, Lake Agmon, the new Reserve on the Jordan, and the Peace Park on the Yarmouk River.*

We ended with my suggestion that they might try the process in a confined part of the reserve where they could control the outflow and the seepage. They agreed to think about it, but no commitments were made.

It was a weekday and the reserve was not overly crowded, but still hundreds of visitors streamed through. And I was told the weekend crowds were even more impressive. Park authorities estimated that at least a quarter million visitors come through the Huleh Valley annually, which means a large part of that number would come through the reserve, and part would also visit Lake Agmon, where I was going next.

As we sat in the picnic area lunching on some frozen chicken dinners left behind by one of the tour groups, we watched the buses going and coming. I was reluctant to leave; it was a pleasant surprise to see a papyrus swamp being treated as a tourist hot spot. There were even signs warning tourists not to pick the umbels, a sign that papyrus was considered a protected plant!

Once I made my pitch for using papyrus in an experimental filter swamp, I was free to go. But before I left, I was given a guided tour of the now-precious papyrus swamp and the impressive walkway through the swamp. This was built about 3ft above the water—and still the papyrus towered above us. Compared to my earlier expeditions in the Ugandan swamps in the '70s, and Sam and Flooey's trudge throught the Sudd, this was a piece of cake.

Later that day I drove on to Agmon Lake, a few kilometers north of the reserve. This is the lake that was created by scooping out a large hole in the peat of the original papyrus swamp. Here, papyrus is also in evidence, along with nutsedge and other marsh plants that are particularly favored as bird food. Dr. Doron Markel, a water scientist working on the Sea of Galilee and Agmon Lake, was waiting for me. A tall, fit, no-nonsense fellow, he was used to fielding hot questions like "Israel is running out of water. Why?"

We discussed the original swamp drainage and the changes in water chemistry that followed and brought about the reclamation effort in the '90s. Doron told me that the publicity resulting from draining the original papyrus swamp brought criticism down on the water planners, but it wasn't until the negative impact started showing up that they decided to do something about it. Eutrophication in the Sea of Galilee was worsening, heavy floods in 1968 and 1981 swept nutrients into the water, and in 1971 and 1991 there were fish kills.

As we have seen on Lake Victoria and Lake Naivasha, nothing attracts the public's attention more than a fish kill—a modern, man-made version of the Biblical plagues. The white, bloated bodies of fish washing up on shore brings instant media coverage and public outrage; yet, like the human corpses in Lake Victoria during Idi Amin's time, by the time one sees the evidence, the harm is already done.

In the Sea of Galilee, the nutrients and sewage in the water had already stimulated the growth of algae, which in turn had sucked up all the available oxygen and left the fish gasping for air. Because of these worsening conditions, and under the prompting of a small band of courageous Israeli environmentalists, in 1993 the state invested $25 million in a program to protect and improve the Huleh Reserve and reclaim a further 250 acres for Lake Agmon. It was the biggest environmental project ever started in Israel. A network of 90 kms of canals was constructed, pumping stations and regulators were installed, a deep partition was driven down to prevent seepage, and a pipeline was built that would divert sewage effluent. As a result, the river's course was partially restored, Lake Agmon replaced Huleh Lake, and tourist facilities were built to accommodate the birdwatchers.

Doron explained that under the present scheme some water from the Huleh Reserve is directed into Lake Agmon where it mixes with fresh water from the Jordan before it is sent downstream to the Sea of Galilee. This arrangement gives the water technicians a chance to regulate water quality and the depth and amount of flow throughout the system.

The new Huleh Reserve and Agmon Lake amount to only 7% of the original swamp. Could this pint-sized David take on the Goliath of old? Could it reverse the damage caused by draining 15,500 acres of virgin papyrus swamp? The answer seems to be yes. In recent years, the water table has risen, alleviating local agricultural concerns, and the reserve has blossomed. Within the first two years, 74 plant species have spontaneously colonized the new wetlands, and papyrus has been reintroduced from seedlings. It flourished and once again became the dominant plant in the new swamp that evolved. This demonstrated that papyrus has a high potential for successful re-establishment, though it also indicated that papyrus swamps require a period of time to recover. It doesn't happen overnight.

When wetlands are brought back, the results can be spectacular, especially for birdlife. Over 500 million birds now pass through the valley twice a year, going and coming. Fortunately, in this case there were groups ready to monitor and record what happened. The Huleh Bird-Watching Centre, part of a network in Israel that operates under the wing of the Ornithological Centre of the Society for the Protection of Nature, is very active in the region. The Centre was founded to provide local environmental awareness and protection of birds through research, conservation, education, and ecotourism. Their website (www. birds.org.il) keeps track of bird news in the Huleh Valley and the three main habitats that have developed there: the Huleh Reserve itself with its extensive marshy habitats, Lake Agmon with its open water and marshes, and the reed-fringed fishponds in the area that provide a range of micro-habitats.

A wintering population of Common Cranes (*Grus grus*) has grown enormously, from a few hundred in the 1970s to more than 25,000 birds. Also overwintering are East European and Russian populations of ducks, with over 20,000 mallards, 10,000 shovelers, 31,500 Common Teals, as well as other duck species, hundreds of Black and White Storks, Glossy Ibis, thousands of herons, and Great White and Little Egrets. Great Cormorants and hundreds of Pygmy Cormorants are now very common during the winter, along with about forty species of waders, including rarities such as the Sociable Plover.

Another species, once scarce in Israel but for which Huleh has become an important wintering area in recent years, is the Citrine Wagtail. It is also one of the key wintering places in Israel for localized breeding birds, such as Armenian and Great Black-headed Gulls.

So many visitors come to see the cranes and other such birds that the scene assumes a hectic, almost bizarre appearance. Rene Ebersole, writing for *Audubon* in November 2009, observed ". . . all types of tourists: a group of uniformed army officers—guns slung over their shoulders—pedaling colorful four-wheel carts; schoolchildren riding in the tractor blind, pointing and laughing each time a crane honks or fans its wings; serious birders lined up behind a spotting scope for a glimpse of three greater flamingos out on Lake Agmon."

It gets even wilder as the reserve staff sets out food. Years ago, in order to stop the cranes from raiding nearby farms, the staff decided to provide food, which became one obvious factor as to why the flock has stayed on and has grown. Once the cranes feed, they fly back to the shallow water to roost in the shade of papyrus and other wetland plants. All the while, tourists and birdwatchers are hauled back and forth in a mobile bird blind, which holds about a hundred people. Pulled by a tractor, it is drawn up close to the birds that are constantly crying out and creating a deafening uproar. I played the scene back on a portable tape recorder and could hardly hear myself think. In the background, our guide, armed with a megaphone, was trying to compete with the shrieks of children, the chugging of the tractor, and the noise of 25,000 hungry cranes.

The start of the northward departure of birds in mid-February corresponds with the massive spring passage in May, so there is never any significant decrease in bird numbers in the region (Map 11, p. 247). Many of these species' entire population passes through the valley, such as the White Stork (*Ciconia ciconia*), the Levant Sparrowhawk (*Accipiter brevipus*), the entire population of European White Pelican (*Pelecanus onocrotalus*), and Lesser Spotted Eagle (*Aquila pomarina*).

About 100 breeding species now occur here, including rare species such as Golden Oriole, Pygmy Cormorant, and Mustached Warbler. The Clamorous Reed Warbler, Black Francolin, and White-breasted and Pied Kingfishers are resident in the valley. The area's heronries, including Night Heron and Little Egrets, with smaller numbers of Little Bittern and Squacco Heron, are among the largest in Eurasia.

Because of this enormous increase in birdlife, there is great interest in tracking migration patterns here. Dr. Yossi Leshem, a well-known Israeli ornithologist who lectures in the Department of Zoology at Tel Aviv University and is the former director general of the Society for the Protection of Nature in Israel (SPNI), has established a world-renowned bird-tracking center at Latrun, a former British fortress halfway between Tel Aviv and Jerusalem. Using a jury-rigged Soviet-era radar set purchased from Russia, he tracks the flocks of birds. The migrating birds need shafts of warm air, created by hilly regions, to gain altitude and then glide. In addition to thermals, many birds follow the narrow land bridges between continents, found only in the Mideast and Panama.

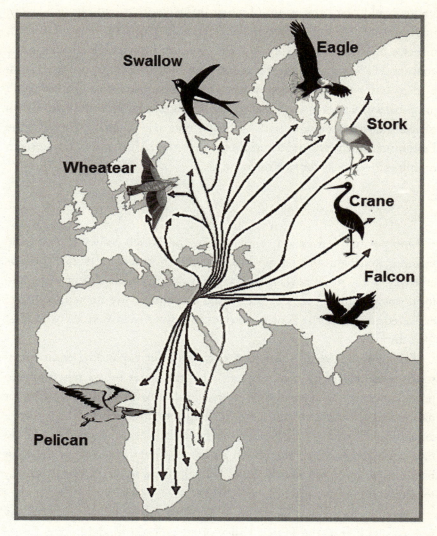

MAP II: *Bird migration routes passing through the Huleh Valley (courtesy Y. Leshem).*

Dr. Leshem's center is ideally positioned to monitor the birdlife, as it sits right in the middle of many of the flocks' flight patterns. He is also the man in the middle when it comes to a recent problem that surfaced regarding avian flu. A *USA Today* story reported on the concern in Israel that these enormous flocks of migratory birds passing through Huleh

Valley could carry the strain of avian influenza that had ravaged flocks in Asia and killed sixty-two people. According to Dr. Manfred Green, director of Israel's Center for Disease Control, the virus is already in the country. He is worried that it could mutate from a strain transmitted from bird to bird—and occasionally from bird to human—to one that could jump between humans and threaten millions of people worldwide. Israeli officials have taken precautions and have intensified coordination with the Palestinian Authority and its neighbors in Jordan. Meanwhile, Dr. Leshem monitors the flocks for sick birds.

One positive indication of change in the Huleh Valley is that local farming, tourism, and nature protection authorities are working cooperatively. More good news is the fact that the diversion of peat water and local sewage into treatment plants and subsequent use for irrigation are expected to reduce the flow of nitrates into the Sea of Galilee by at least 40% annually.

The new reserve also provides a rationale for expanding commercial tourist resources within the region. This translates into a movement to provide even more habitat for seasonal birds. "At present, the forces for nature and tourism in the area are working very positively for the future— extending the area of marsh and creating undisturbed open water and field habitats—and ensuring the Huleh Valley continues to be one of the most bird-rich places in the Middle East" (Huleh Birdwatching Centre, Society for Protection of Nature in Israel, 2013).

I met Dr. Lesham at his office in Tel Aviv, where he told me that any way you look at it, the Huleh Valley offers a bright model for the future of papyrus. The Huleh Reserve and Lake Agmon, together with a larger buffer zone (selected agricultural fields and fishponds), comprise an area of over 15,000 acres which has now been placed on the tentative list of World Heritage sites. Although the buffer zone is mostly in private hands, the total area is close to the original acreage of the Huleh Swamp before it was drained. The Huleh Valley Natural Heritage site will hopefully be upgraded to a fully designated site at some future date.

Interest has also been piqued in using the restoration of papyrus and other wetland plants to create even more more bird sanctuaries along the Jordan River. Acceptance of the idea comes at a time when tourism has become an important economic driver in the Mideast. Jordan's King Abdullah II believes that "Other regions in the world testify to how tourism can promote peace and stability. In fact it is a two-way street, for without peace and stability there wouldn't be tourism."

The king told a press conference that the ". . . region is entering a new millennium, ready to face the challenges of peace." What better way to start than the action taken in 2007 by the mayors of the Jordan Valley Regional Council (Israel), Beit Shean Valley Regional Council (Israel), and Muaz Bin Jabal Municipality (Jordan). They signed a Memorandum of Understanding to create a Peace Park on the Jordan River, a place that will restore pride of place to the river valley and create new opportunities for the local populations. The Peace Park would involve the creation of a protected area on both sides of the river to provide greater opportunities for biodiversity protection, cooperative management, joint research programs, education, and collaboration on nature-based tourism.

Although a border zone is understandably necessary, both Jordan and Israel have already created the precedent of opening the border fence for controlled, guided tourism at several locations. Plans for the Peace Park include the re-flooding of a dry lakebed and creating a bird sanctuary at the juncture of the Jordan and Yarmouk Rivers just south of the Sea of Galilee (Map 10, p. 242). Planning and design have already begun under the guidance of Professors Alan Plattus and Andrew Harwell, who led a team of local architects and members of the Yale University Schools of Architecture and Forestry to the Jordan River site in 2008.

This is a positive regional effort being launched by the Friends of Earth Middle East, a joint effort involving Palestine, Jordan, and Israel, which has garnered all sorts of awards (Green Globe, 2010, and the Skoll Award, 2009). The three co-directors of the project, Gidon Bromberg, Nader Al-Khateeb, and Munqeth Mehyar, were honored by *Time* magazine with Environmental Heroes awards in 2008. The new Peace Park wetland so created will serve as an additional habitat for the 500 million migratory birds and will supplement the Huleh Valley phenomenon.

The potential to develop the area for ecotourism is outstanding due to the natural beauty of the area, where nature trails can be developed discreetly hidden on a side of the riverbank, enabling hikers, bikers, and bird watchers to explore the park and the protected area on both sides of the river. Hopefully one of the plants introduced into this new wetland will be papyrus. Although papyrus is no longer found growing naturally in the wetland flora of the region, Pliny the Elder reported that it grew in Syria in 77 A.D., and there is good evidence that it also grew in Jordan in *wadis*, where Bedouin used it for crafts up until the 1900s.

As the Huleh Swamp Reserve has proven, papyrus would be a logical choice for bird-friendly wetlands along the Lower Jordan River Valley, as well as something that would be instrumental to the restoration of an entire region's population of fish, potable water, and a reduction in pollution. In addition, it would create a birdwatchers' paradise and would certainly be a great tourist attraction because of its early association with the ancient world. A plant so involved in the history of the world perhaps deserves the chance to become one of the world's Green Peacemakers, a position formerly occupied by the olive branch.

23

The Rift Valley, a Safe Haven
for Birds

When it comes time for the great winter migration, the bird world divides itself into flappers and gliders. The passerines, for example, fall into the former group, small, numerous, and full of beans, literally, as they emerge from a spree of binge eating and take off into the airways in a mad dash to get to their winter grounds in Africa. They fly at night to avoid predators and use the cool night temperatures to conserve energy. Flying as direct as possible over deserts, water, and all sorts of terrain, they quickly put the mileage behind them as they scramble to reach their place in the sun.

The gliders, such as our White Stork, fly thin, hoping to eat along the way. Since they must travel during the day over land where thermals are generated, you can watch them start in the late morning as they glide back and forth, wings outstretched, searching for the updrafts that will carry them in a spiral of warm air until they reach heights where they are almost invisible to the naked eye.

When the warm air of the thermal disperses, they glide on until they find another one that lifts them again. In this way they conserve energy, but pay for it because they have to follow a longer, more restricted route—and they must get very hungry on the wing.

If we were following banded White Stork No. 981981, who overwintered in Mozambique in 1969,[1] we'd be flying for about nine hours each day once the sun is high enough in the sky, soaring on thermals above the great canyon of the Rift Valley, an enormous corridor flanked by escarpments that runs the length of Africa from the Red Sea almost to the South African coast.

Our stork—let's call her Lisa—is bound for Mozambique, so she has to fly south beyond the East African Great Lakes, then across Tanzania, Zambia, and Malawi, where she veers east following the Zambezi River. Here she passes over the long series of lakes, ponds, and wetlands interconnected on the valley floor by rivers with papyrus swamps large and small sprinkled along the way. One of her first stops in Africa might have been at the edge of a papyrus swamp in one of the Rift Valley lakes in Ethiopia, and one of her last stops, 2,400 miles later, might have been in a papyrus swamp on the eastern edge of the Zambezi Delta, just short of the Indian Ocean.

South of Lake Victoria, soaring over Tanzania she will find perennial watercourses and floodplains in which swamps are common enough (Map 8, p. 213), with vast papyrus swamps in the Malagarasi Basin to the west, and the Kilombero Valley to the east. Even in the famous Ngorongoro Crater inside the Serengeti Park she will find two swamps dominated by papyrus, the Gorigor and Mandusi. Papyrus is also common along many of the Tanzanian rivers in and out of the game parks, including the Mara, Pangani, Wami, Ruvu, Rufiki, Kafufu, and Ruaha.

Perhaps Lisa will decide to spend the night there; if so, she will settle in a tree or shallow water for at least 14–16 hours of rest. She is safer roosting in plantlife in Africa than on pylons or electric poles elsewhere. Electrocution is a major cause of death of the White Stork. A team from the German Agency of Nature Conservation found birds with broken wings, broken legs, broken beaks, swollen legs, or in otherwise bad condition stuck in mud after landing with both feet on a live wire, or colliding with high-tension wires.

After arriving in the Zambezi Delta in Mozambique and staying through the winter, she will turn around, leave southern Africa and, if she can avoid being electrocuted, pierced by an African arrow, or shot at in Syria or Lebanon where the hunting pressure is the greatest, she will return to Europe in the early spring.

Safely back on her nest after a long hazardous journey, Lisa may recall that she had flown over millions of acres in order to search out the verdant plant cover near water where dinner waited. The river edges and lakeside reed swamps teem with treats that would appeal to her, but her favorite of all would be a fishpond, if she could find one. In Europe, where White Storks are coveted and cosseted, she might be allowed to eat her fill from a fish farm, but in Africa the local fish farmers are not as forgiving. More often than not she will have to make do with a buffet from nature: a varied selection of frogs, small fish, large insects, worms, and snakes that are abundant among the aquatic grasses, bulrushes, reeds, and papyrus of the African swamps.

The Great Rift Valley that she traversed is one of the earth's most remarkable geological features. It is also one of the longest rift valleys on earth and spans two continents. It stretches over 4,400 miles from the Taurus Mountains in Turkey to the Zambezi River Delta in Mozambique and includes almost two dozen countries: Turkey, Syria, Lebanon, Israel, Palestine, Saudi Arabia, Yemen, Egypt, Sudan, Republic of South Sudan, Djibouti, Eritrea, Ethiopia, Uganda, Rwanda, Kenya, the Democratic Republic of Congo, the United Republic of Tanzania, Malawi, Zambia, Botswana, and Mozambique.

The valley is globally important as a flyway for billions of migratory birds. Twice a year, five hundred million birds of 280 species follow this route of passage, some traveling more than 5,000 miles annually from their northern breeding grounds in Europe and Asia.[2] Once in the valley, they find there the steep cliffs and high daily temperatures that produce ideal conditions for the generation of thermals, the hot air currents that raptors and large soaring birds need for their long journeys.

About 80,000 Eurasian Cranes (almost the entire world population) winter within the valley. The entire world population of Lesser Spotted

Eagles, the entire Palearctic populations of Levant Sparrowhawks and White Pelicans, and significant world populations of White Storks, Cranes, and Honey Buzzards pass through a portion of the Great Rift Valley.

It is also home to enormous biodiversity as well as an extraordinary array of cultures, so much so that Kenya has proposed it as a World Heritage site. This effort is a natural outgrowth of the fact that the valley is topographically distinct, something well shown in the 2010 BBC movie *The Great Rift: Africa's Wild Heart*, a film narrated by Hugh Quarshie in three episodes built around the themes of fire, water, and grass. The film describes the highest mountains and deepest lakes of Africa, all found in the valley, along with the ash layers from active volcanoes that encourage the grasslands and provide the forage needed by the massive herds of game.

The Rift Valley is also thought to be the "cradle of humanity," the place where our human ancestors stepped out of the forest, and the place of origin of three of Africa's main rivers, with water flowing north from Lake Tana in Ethiopia and from Lakes Victoria, Albert, George, and Edward in East Africa into the Nile, or southeast along the Zambezi and southwest into the Congo. In all cases the headwaters are filtered and protected at their origins by papyrus swamps.

With so many illustrious geophysical credentials and unique biological phenomena, it is easy to overlook another feature of the valley, one that has enormous impact on birdlife and the survival of animal and plant species— the interface between saline and fresh water. In no other place on earth do we find so many closed lakes. These are shallow waterbodies with one or more influent rivers but no exits; consequently, they have high mineral contents that result from the evaporation of water that leaves salt behind.

Water flows into Lakes Turkana, Natron, Nakuru, Manyara, Eyasi, Elmentaita, Magadi, Bogoria, Chad, Naivasha, and the Okavango Delta as well as many small lakes in Ethiopia and elsewhere, and it stays there.

In the case of Lakes Chad and Naivasha and the Okavango Delta, salinity is kept low because salts are taken out by seepage; but in most other cases the water becomes saline or alkaline or soda. As a result, there is a division between species, something that is hinted at on the cover of the BBC Rift Valley DVD. Here we see two male hippos, mouths wide open as they clash against a background typical of the *Rift Valley*, the lush green hills of an active volcano, Ol Donyo Lengai, the mountain that looms over Lake Manyara, a closed alkaline lake in Tanzania. What is not shown is the fact that the hippos are most likely not in the lake proper, but in the Hippo Pool, a spot on the Simba River just before it passes into the alkaline waters of the lake. Much of the fresh water of the river originates from the small papyrus-fringed Lake Miwaleni a few miles north of Lake Manyara, fed by water coming from a spring via a waterfall.

Since papyrus swamps are confined to those parts of lakes or rivers that are fresh, the plant is an indicator of freshness, which is a vital concern to most birds. Flamingoes, for instance, live on a diet of microscopic algae dredged and filtered from saline and brackish water and are perfectly equipped to survive in the closed lakes of the valley, but *only* if they have access to fresh water for drinking. Likewise, hippos, which normally prefer fresh water, can live in brackish water provided that they have baths in the muddy pools found at the places where rivers enter saline lakes.

Another good example of this kind of interface is the northern end of Lake Turkana where the Omo River empties into the lake. Here again, papyrus swamps on the river indicate to highflying birds the location of fresh water in an otherwise alkaline basin that would be hostile to them. So the papyrus swamps in the Omo Delta are a great place to see a variety of bird species, a place where salt-lovers and freshwater fauna meet to feed and drink. It is also a place enjoyed by predators who gather there as well, perhaps even lusting after the same space occupied by a birdwatcher who occasionally has to concede a seat to a python, jackal, croc, vulture, or a lion or two.

The Omo River, like the Okavango, originates in another country and feeds a lake across an international border; thus negotiations have been in place to prevent Ethiopia from turning off the freshwater spigot to a precious Kenyan natural reource. Meanwhile, the tribal lifestyle of the Turkana region, as well as the enormous tourist and agricultural potential, are all in the balance. Likewise, throughout the Rift Valley papyrus filter swamps and the freshwater sources of many closed basins are at risk where humans want the fresh water for other purposes. A balanced, sustainable approach to avoid disaster seems the only way to deal with such problems. The need here is for an integrated approach where the valley is treated as a system, not in piecemeal fashion.

In this regard, Kenya's interest in designating the whole valley as a Heritage Site is a good start, originating from the fact that the valley bisects a large swath of the nation. They already have the lakes of Kenya listed as Heritage Sites, but the goal now is to broaden the effort to bring together the other countries to form a network in order to protect the many important wetlands critical to birds migrating along the corridor. Bird Life International has identified over one hundred important bird areas within the valley. Many are water bodies that include closed basins and the interface of fresh water crucial to the survival of migrating waterbirds.

Because of the wider, larger goals behind the Greater Rift Valley Program, there are multiple objectives, but one thing to keep in mind is the maxim used in development—that the easiest and most sustainable path to progress is to provide local people with the tools, training, and incentive to take ownership and achieve results.

In the process, wild areas can be locally conserved.

It is also possible to protect wetlands by example. If tourism becomes a money-spinner and if tourists flock to centers of bird migrations the way they do, say, to the wildebeest migration, the Rift Valley countries will take notice. Market forces work in tourism as well as they do in other industries, and they go a long way in protecting the wetlands and water bodies that attract birds, all to the favor of papyrus conservation.

The project attracts a wide range of support because of its globally important nature, including *Flyways*, a project of Music for the Earth that serves as a musical metaphor for the valley. With a range of partners that includes environmental organizations, ornithologists, conservationists, ethnomusicologists, and musicians, it provides music performed by an international ensemble, the Great Rift Valley Orchestra, comprised of musicians from cultures throughout the region and brought together by saxophonist and composer Paul Winter.

The US Forest Service also participates in the Rift Valley program by developing flyway level education activities focused on migratory bird conservation. Introducing environmental activities into schools and youth groups makes conservation a tangible reality for children and inspires future generations of conservationists. The USFS works with Lebanon's Hunting Higher Council and other stakeholders to explore challenges to the sustainable management of hunting activities in Lebanon, and to examine lessons learned in the US on addressing the threats of unsustainable hunting and poaching. It partners with Nature Conservation of Egypt, the Ethiopian Wildlife and Natural History Society, the Society for the Protection of Nature in Lebanon, the Royal Society for the Conservation of Nature in Jordan, the Palestine Wildlife Society, and Bird Life International in supporting the participation of biologists from across the Rift Valley in training programs in California that focus on bird monitoring.

The ongoing effort to make the Greater Rift Valley a World Heritage site is a way to conserve wetlands in this part of the world on a long-term basis. Many objectives of this effort would benefit papyrus swamps. One of the wider, larger goals driving the program is to globally protect swamps using models that work, such as the rehabilitated swamps in the Jordan Valley, which have demonstrated their value as tourist magnets, thus providing a boon to the nation's economy and the people's financial well-being, too. The hundreds of species of migrating birds frequenting the Rift Valley corridor from Europe, Asia, and the Mideast, in numbers greater than five billion, may well entice people from the countries within the valley to work in a cooperative way to promote this trans-boundary region as a place of extraordinary cultural and biological diversity.

24

The Egyptian Solution

Due to the camera angle, it looked like Prof. Dia El-Quosy was standing on water.[1] To the many graduate students and technicians trained by him, this would come as no surprise. He had been with the Lake Manzala Engineered Wetlands Project from its beginning in the '90s and he was highly regarded as the doyen of engineered wetlands in Egypt. If he could tackle the most polluted site in Egypt, armed only with some native plants, walking on water would be easy.

In addition to being project manager, El-Quosy is also Professor Emeritus at the National Water Research Center. He looks a lot like a very serious version of Richard Gere, with his light-gray, wavy hair and clear, windowpane-type eyeglasses. He was explaining to a small audience how the project worked. The wastewater that feeds into the wetland is taken from the infamous Bahr El-Baqar drain near Port Said and pumped into ponds where sediments are allowed to settle. Then the water flows through 60 acres of reed beds. After leaving the reed beds, the water flows into fish ponds and then into Lake Manzala, the largest of the Four Sisters in the northernmost end of the delta.

The project was in full swing by October 2004, and the world of water purification was interested because this was the first major undertaking of this type in Egypt. There had been other engineered wetlands operating in the delta, but nothing like this. People were impressed. Locally, the fishermen had almost given up hope. For thirty years heavy metals have been carried to the delta muds by way of agricultural and industrial drains. They came originally from the effluent of power-based industries that sprang up with the advent of the Aswan High Dam. To make matters worse, a significant portion of the water in the Nile River that used to dilute the incoming wastewater in the lake was diverted in 1997 into the Al-Salam Canal. That canal passes under the Suez Canal and from there goes into the Sinai, where it is used for irrigation.

In addition to the toxic effect of heavy metals, the wastewater entering Lake Manzala contains raw sewage and wastes from agricultural and industrial processing. A 1994 assessment pointed out that many Egyptians could identify fish in the marketplace taken from the lake because of the prevalence of gill diseases, internal parasites, and the unmistakable smell that gave them away. They were afraid to eat them.

In response to these concerns, the idea was broached of a filter swamp in the delta, and a UNDP-funded project was begun under El-Quosy. It eventually cost $12 million but was considered well worth it. The success of the project is due to the cleansing action performed by the reed grass (Phragmites), a plant that is well able to withstand the more concentrated effluents of the Bahr El-Baqar drain, the most notorious source of pollution in Egypt.

Cattail (Typha) and papyrus were also included in the Lake Manzala project, but neither did well because the wastewater from the Bahr El-Baqar is quite saline. All the same, it is amazing the way papyrus keeps showing up in newly constructed wetlands. It has been featured in a small wetland built in Ismailia on the west bank of the Suez Canal, and it is the plant of choice in several filter swamp schemes in Uganda, Tanzania (Zanzibar), Kenya, Ethiopia, Cameroon, and even Thailand. It's almost as if designers of filter wetlands and the general public want the plant to come back and populate the delta immediately, but it will require more time for papyrus to adapt and propagate itself under these new conditions. It would probably do better in constructed wetlands closer to Cairo, where the wastewater is not as salty. The Bahr El-Baqar Drain, for example, increases in salinity by over 100% over its complete length (71 miles from Cairo to Lake Manzala).

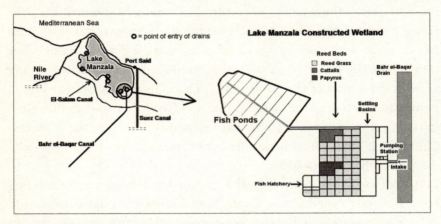

Lake Manzala Constructed Wetlands Program (after El-Din El-Quosy, 2007).

Both the reed grass and cattail are better adapted for saline waste-water, but both are also notorious because of their aggressive and dense growth. They are considered weeds in many places in the world, and it is often recommended by wetland managers that stands of both species be diversified with swamp plants that are more useful as waterfowl food, such as wild millet, smartweeds, rice cutgrass, and wild rice. Outside the delta, in oxidation ponds in the New Valley in the Toshka Project region, Prof. Safwat of the University of Minia is trying out cattail and reed grass species that will bear the brunt of highly saline and toxic wastewater in that region.

Papyrus, on the other hand, although it does not do well in saline waters, is valued for its ability to provide the habitats and niches loved by fish (who will be healthier in this cleaner water) and wading birds. Its capacity to grow in floating mats is also useful in systems where wastewater must pass under the mats and be filtered and cleansed in the process.

After one pass through the reed beds in El-Quosy's project, the water is more oxygenated, has 80% less suspended solids, fewer coliforms, and lower phosphorus, nitrogen, and heavy metal content. As expected, maintenance costs are low, and local livestock handlers harvest the reeds for feed at no cost. It was initially designed to treat 6 million gallons of wastewater per day but is now capable of twice that. As a result, Egypt has a model of how filter swamps could work and how they could help the nation cope. The project is also an important turning point for the rest of Africa, since this is a mirror image of what could be done in many of the other countries of the Nile Basin.

The sequence is clear. Any increase in agriculture that demands more water means that land must be cleared, wetlands must be drained, and hydroelectric power must be developed to provide the energy for fertilizer and industrial development. The resultant pollution is made worse by an increasingly arid environment and reaches a critical point from whence the population suffers.

In other words, they are digging the hole in which they will be buried. How to get out of it? The ladder is provided by a reformed government, with rungs generated by water and soil conservation, renewable energy, sustainable agriculture, and wetlands to cleanse and recycle water.

In a passionate address to the world and especially to his fellow Egyptians, Dr. Hassanein earlier pleaded for the environment to be made a national priority. His immediate goal is to stop the Nile River from becoming a serious hazard to people, and to stop and reverse the present trend of environmental deterioration in Egypt, as well as to help the government enforce the law, and business and industry to minimize the impact on the environment. The goal he had in mind was to save Egypt from the coming environmental tragedy that will materialize if the country stays on its present course. Included in his challenge is the caution to aim for a sustainable future, which would mean turning a receptive ear to the idea that Egypt, as in ancient times, can survive and prosper on the natural resource base that they already have, provided that it is managed in a sustainable way. The water already in the system and that expected from a newly managed Blue Nile will suffice, once it is efficiently recycled and cleansed.

∽

The use of constructed or managed wetlands as filters for wastewater has now caught on in Africa as a practical solution to local sewage problems. Filter swamps come in a variety of shapes and sizes. Cost is a big factor in deciding which type to use. The cheapest is simply a large natural swamp into which wastewater is released. Often the wastewater is spread out to make the cleansing process more efficient. The papyrus swamps on Lake Victoria presently serve in this way.

The next most economical method is to dig out a maze of channels, canals, or ponds to create waste-stabilization ponds or reed fields in which wastewater is allowed to meander. The principle here is to prolong its passage in order to give the pond vegetation or reed beds more time to act. Construction costs are kept to a minimum because mostly hand labor is involved.

The most expensive filter swamps are the constructed wetlands, as in the Lake Manzala case where lined intake canals, pumping stations, and contained gravel beds are laid out and planted with reeds. The system is designed to handle a large regular flow of wastewater. As with solar power, there is an initial capital investment, but operational costs are modest, and the fact that wetland vegetation grows faster and year-round in the tropics makes such a system very attractive.[2]

The Egyptian working model demonstrated that such an approach can be used in the race to save the delta. As Global Climate Change takes its toll, wetland restoration seems the only feasible economic solution, since conventional sewage infrastructure is expensive and the task is enormous.

There is no question that the 60-acre facility at Lake Manzala is doing a great job, but five major wastewater drains enter the lake; the worst one of the lot, the Bahr el-Baqar, delivers 793 million gallons per day (3 mill m³/day), of which El-Quosy's project can only handle a scant 2%. The consequence is that reports are still coming in that all four of the delta lakes are health hazards. But at least now the value of managed wetlands is appreciated, and it is heartening to see reports that Dr. Abdel-Shafy from the Egyptian National Research Center, who used papyrus and reed grass in an engineered wetland in Ismailia, will be conducting workshops and master classes in constructed wetlands directed at water technicians.

There are other conservation efforts in the delta where protected areas have been designated. Lake Burullos has been declared a Ramsar Wetland of International Importance, and the Ashtum El Gamil Protected Area has been created by Prime Ministerial Decree in 1988. This encompasses an area of almost 9,000 acres on Lake Manzala along the sandbar at Bughaz El Gamil near Port Said, the most important connection between the lake and the sea.

Expanding engineered wetlands in the delta will demand that the government take back land already designated for industry and housing. Perhaps wetlands in the future could be expanded by making them part of the national parks in Egypt. According to the National Plan for the Conservation of Biological Diversity, prior to 2017 Egypt plans to increase its 27 protected areas to 40, which will take up 17% of the Republic. Somewhere among those parcels of land, 3,000–4,000 acres of constructed wetlands might be found to rehabilitate the delta.

Prof. El-Quosy told me that his goal is to have 2,000–5,000 acres of reed beds or sedimentation ponds set aside along the coast to resolve the immediate needs of Lake Manzala. He would also like to see many small constructed reed beds on the desert side of all villages and towns in Egypt in order to promote sewage treatment and desert reclamation. This would greatly reduce pollution in the Nile and would encourage small-scale local cultivation of deserts in preference to the unwieldy, inefficient megaschemes favored by past governments.

Where does papyrus fit in? It will be a while before it shows up as a major component in managed wetlands along the coast. This is not for want of a ready market; there is already a demand for it in Cairo and Luxor in the souvenir trade, where cultivated papyrus stems are used to make specialty paper products, calendars, notebooks, etc., as well as finished, framed sheets of paper decorated with colorful hieroglyphics. Papyrus plantations are also popular at theme parks such as the Pharaonic Village that opened in Cairo in 1985. The Village was set up on an island in the Nile that is effectively hidden from the modern downtown skyline with screening trees. It quickly became an Egyptian version of Colonial Williamsburg in that it re-creates ancient times and crafts. Once inside the Village, tourists are taken by barge along papyrus-lined canals to see historic scenes and tableaux acted out by people dressed in period costume, and to marvel at the birdlife attracted back into the urban landscape by the new papyrus swamps.

It was originally set up by Hassan Ragab, the man who brought cuttings of papyrus back to Egypt to start up the souvenir paper industry. In addition to making and selling papyrus paper souvenirs, Ragab's effort had a practical effect—it spawned a host of other papyrus paper factories and institutes that fed into the national effort to keep Egypt among the Top Ten World Travel Destinations. In the recent past, nine million tourists annually generated $7 billion in income, which had enough impact on the government that a plan was advanced to create new job opportunities for many Egyptians.

Tourism, which rose to 14.7 million in 2010, has taken a nosedive after the turmoil of the Arab Spring, but the general feeling is that it will come back, and when it does its future looks as bright and prosperous as ever—and it is a future in which papyrus can pull its weight.

As for the plant itself, it will never again grow as luxuriantly as it did in the swamps of old because the river water has changed. Today the mineral, nutrient, and pollution content are different. This may change with time, but for now papyrus remains a novelty in the land where it once ruled.

Dr. El-Hadidi from Cairo University found a relict population of papyrus growing amongst marsh plants in Wadi Natroum in 1971, and Dr. Serag at Mansoura University discovered a small natural stand in the delta in 2003. Cuttings replanted in a plot in the Nile Delta near Damietta did surprisingly well in Nile water, perhaps because a continuous flow flushed the site, enabling it to survive. But even so, the production of both the cultivated and natural plant is much less than that found in the swamps of Central Africa.

It would help to have papyrus demonstration sites in Cairo, where urban-bound families and the Green Generation would be able to see wetlands in action. Small plots, experimental swamps planted in reed grasses and papyrus, could be featured in places like Al-Azhar Park in Cairo, the Giza Zoo, and private parks such as the Pharaonic Village. Such places would be appreciated by schoolchildren, Cairenes in general, and the new Green Army of the Nile, the ten million Egyptians whom Dr. Hassanein said must be reached through media and educational programs in order to increase environmental awareness and make the environmental vision a reality.

When I read Dr. Hassanein's plea, I realized that one of his goals may already have been reached, since the number of Internet sites and organizations dealing with green issues and the environment in Egypt has grown that much over the past few years. On the Internet today there are also advocacy groups promoting sustainability and environmental protection throughout the Middle East. Future steps will be needed to develop incentives, awards, and assistance programs to reduce pollution and help the nation become more environmentally friendly. In this it helps to promote programs that would protect biodiversity, and obviously those that include protecting the avifauna en route to and from Sudan and Egypt and ecosystems such as the delta wetlands and the Sudd that provide the habitats that allow birds to survive.

With time and experience, Egypt could become a major player in the field of filter swamps, and a source of hope and encouragement for all of Africa.

25

2050, The New Delta

It is late. The travelcraft, a vehicle capable of unlimited travel in, on, or through any medium, was delayed leaving. Some things never change. Our departure was held up for connecting passengers, one of whom had lost a bag. Arriving now in Alexandria after a flight from the States that lasted only one hour, I am amazed to see the new Aerodeck that has replaced the old airport. It is built high on stilts and juts out over the bay, ready to receive our group. As the level of the sea rose, the city went under water and had to be rebuilt. After much of the old delta was flooded, the concrete and steel of the city was recycled into massive dikes and lagoons created to provide the space needed to contain the spacious floating islands on which people now live. Large enough to support villages, towns, and factories, they are built on pontoons and flotation devices made of a light plastic that is manufactured from local vegetation.

We see all this from above as the travelcraft banks before sliding gently to a stop on a cushion of air. We walk out of the craft onto the moving sidewalk that passes us rapidly through an ultra-modern complex. The international customs system, based on electronic information stored on microchips embedded under our skin, allows us to walk directly to the curbside transport where our guide is waiting to show us the New Delta. We are the new generation of ecovisitors, bent on seeing firsthand what has happened to Egypt. We board sleek vehicles that are powered by microfusion plasma reactors and hover just above the ground or water surface. They are ideal all-terrain vehicles that allow us to glide unhindered across the delta terrain.

Here we see polders and dikes planted with reed grasses. The polders provide the platforms on which wind turbines and solar panels are built that power the continuously running pumps, pumps that keep the seawater levels low enough to balance the incoming fresh water. This maintains the New Delta as a floating world with wide plantations of salt grass, reeds, and fish farms stretching as far as the eye can see. Our clear-domed, air-cushioned vehicles allow us an unobstructed view as we scoot along, barely disturbing the water surface, reeds, or raised walking platforms between the fields.

Further along, well away from the brackish water of the coast, we see the beginning of the wide papyrus swamps that have been planted and nourished by effluents from the freshwater collection system, a centralized water carrier that channels all water in Egypt for treatment. Once passed through the reed beds, the water is used in the highly efficient floating farms, hydroponic wonders that use every drop.

Clean water in excess is sent directly from village and town papyrus filter-beds to the eastern and western deserts, which have become the new Edens of this world of plenty. Our visit is short; we have many other places to go. But we are impressed and look forward to seeing the large bird sanctuaries that are maintained throughout the Nile Valley. Cultivation of food, exotic vegetables, and grains for export under the thin plastic roofs of these floating farms has again made Egypt a world granary. In a way, the New Delta is a return to the water-world of archaic times. The ancient marsh men are now the engineers and technicians who keep the system going, and the plastic used on the farms, floating houses, boats, and futuristic buildings is made of plastic that comes from recycled swamp vegetation—papyrus in its new form.[1]

If Hapi were alive and well, he would smile and bow and shake the umbels in his crown to signal good times, and we would be told that we have survived because we listened to the earth spirits and learned to live within the natural system. Now, because we have deserved it, each of us can look forward to an eternal life within our own Field of Reeds.

26

Conclusion

"Paradox. Why, if wetlands are so valuable in their natural state, are they being eliminated at such a rapid rate? The answer to this paradox is that although wetlands serve society in multiple ways, the nature of wetland benefits are such that the owners of wetlands usually cannot capture the benefits for their own use or sale. The flood protection benefits accrue to others downstream. The fish and wildlife that breed and inhabit the wetlands migrate, and are captured or enjoyed by others. The ground water recharge and sediment trapping benefits cannot be commercially exploited. For the owner of a wetland to benefit from his resource, he often has to alter it, convert it, and develop it. That is why, despite their value, wetlands are being eliminated. . . ."

—*A Guide to Living With Florida's Wetlands*, 2013[1]

Today, it is no secret that swamps store water. In the United States, millions of acres have been set aside in the Everglades for just that purpose. But in much of Africa, because surface water has become difficult to find and irrigation needs have skyrocketed, swamps are being drained, thereby destroying wetland systems that are more useful and valuable than even the much-touted rainforest. Wetlands tend to hold back water and recharge water levels in the soil when needed. Africa's water resources have been decreasing as a result of persistent droughts and land-use patterns, and the situation is bound to get worse. Now climate change caused by the major developing and developed nations will magnify these effects. Unfortunately, Sub-Saharan Africa will suffer more than any other part of the world, even though its contribution to global emissions is small.

The wake-up call comes to us in the form of a UN report summarized in a UNEP-GRID press release that warns of the looming future of the African continent. The details are not hard to grasp. The population of Africa is expected to rise from 770 million to 1.75 billion by 2050. By coincidence, the oil resources of the world will peak in that same year, and a food crisis is predicted that will dwarf the most recent one resulting from the last drought in 2012, the warmest year on record, which plunged 100 million people into poverty and hunger.

By 2050, rainfall patterns in Africa will shift. The UN predicts that global warming will cause clouds to concentrate in the central region of the continent, where flooding and massive soil erosion will be the norm along with an increase in water-borne diseases like malaria. Paradoxically, the dry regions of Africa will increase by a whopping 29%. In the driest parts of the continent—the north, west, east, and parts of the south—river flow will decrease, available hydropower will decline, and wetlands will disappear.

In the United States, we are just realizing the importance of wetlands in filtering pollution and flood control. The benefits of wetlands, including papyrus swamps, to the world's ecosystems are enormous.

- Robert Costanza, Professor of Economics at the University of Vermont, estimates that the economic value of flood prevention and other ecological services provided by wetlands is $37,000 per acre per year. This is a sum far greater than any other ecosystem—seven

times higher than that of the next most valuable system, tropical rainforest.
- Wetlands hold 10–20% of the world's carbon, an amount comparable to the carbon content of today's atmosphere.
- Draining tropical swamps releases 100 tons of carbon per acre.
- As pointed out by Michael Grunwald in his bestseller *The Swamp*, it is far easier and cheaper to maintain wetlands than to drain them and then later try to rebuild them once the detrimental effects of that drainage has been wrought.

Despite these benefits, 60% of global wetlands have been destroyed in the past one hundred years; 90% of Europe's wetlands are gone, while 90% of Malaysia's freshwater swamps have been drained for rice. In some parts of East Africa, 50–80% of the papyrus swamps have already disappeared, replaced by cultivation. In Africa, the papyrus swamp is one of the last walls of defense against these changes.

Papyrus is still found at the headwaters of many of the major rivers in Africa, where it protects and nurtures. Years ago it disappeared from Egypt; now it is gone from Lake Chad and many places in West Africa. With the exception of the papyrus growing around the headwaters of the Blue Nile in Ethiopia, papyrus has virtually disappeared from Africa north of the 10th parallel. From 30°N to 10°N, a matter of 1,000 miles, it is gone. The large papyrus swamp in the Sudd is the last bastion, a swamp that is in danger of being drained to provide water for irrigation. Papyrus swamps may yet hold the key to stability in some of the most unstable regions of our planet. For as water becomes a scarcer and scarcer resource, protecting what is available will be key to preventing chaos. The need to restore and preserve what is left is imminent.

◌

In the next to the last scenes of the movie *"The Last King of Scotland,"* the plane carrying a badly wounded young Dr. Garrigan takes off from Entebbe and banks out over Lake Victoria as it turns and heads for home. In the movie commentary, the director Kevin MacDonald calls the lake the "symbol of Africa." Down below, we see a wide shot of a large papyrus swamp on the edge of the lake. Surrounding the tarmac and out in the water of the lake are the same swamps that I saw on the first day I arrived in Africa.

∾

The explosion has yet to happen. In Africa, an ecological time bomb is about to go off, with agricultural, domestic, and sewage pollution along the Nile and in the Central African Lakes. The infiltration of heavy metals from chemical fertilizer use in the delta of the Nile, and industrial pollution along the Zambezi and the Copperbelt, are killing the people, the land, and the water. One of the major flyways for millions of birds in the Rift Valley and the Sudd, the last major natural freshwater fisheries in the world are threatened.

The plant that helped ancient Egyptians grow, expand, and develop into a vibrant society is standing by, ready to help once again. We need to give this plant a chance.

FURTHER READING

PROLOGUE: ANCIENT EGYPT AND PAPYRUS, THE ETERNAL MARRIAGE

Butzer, K. *Early Hydraulic Civilization in Egypt, A study in Cultural Ecology*. Univ. of Chicago Press, E-book. (www.oi.uchicago.edu/research/pubs/catalog/misc/early_hydraulic.html). 1976.

Hassan, F. "The Dynamics of a Riverine Civilization: A Geoarchaeological Perspective on the Nile Valley, Egypt." *World Archaeology*, 29:51-74. 1997.

Herodotus. 440 BC. *The History of Herodotus, Books I & II*. G. Rawlinson, trans. Tudor Publishing Co., N.Y. 1947. Book II (http://classics.mit.edu/Herodotus/history.html).

Kepp, J. "Out of the Deep." Berlin hosts the world premiere exhibition of "Egypt's Sunken Treasures." *The Atlantic Times* (www.atlantic-times.com/archive_detail.php?recordID=552). 2006.

Watterson, B. *Gods of Ancient Egypt*. Sutton Publ., Gloucestershire, UK. 2003.

1: FIRST ENCOUNTER

Baker, S. *The Albert N'Yanza, Great Basin of the Nile*. Macmillan, London. 1866.

Howard-Williams, C. and J. Gaudet. "The Structure and Function of African Swamps." *In* P. Denny, ed.: *The Ecology and Management of African Wetland Vegetation*. Dr. W. Junk, Dordrecht. 1985.

Pliny the Elder. 77 AD. *Natural History: A Selection*. Book XIII:89. J. F. Healy, trans. Penguin Books, London. 1991.

2: NATURE'S BOUNTY

Anon. "The History of Paper." Fact sheet. Confederation of Paper Industries. (www.paper.org.uk). 2008.

Bonneau, D. "Le drymos, marais du Fayoum, d'apres la documentation papyrologique." Vol.1:181-190. *L'Egyptologie en 1979*. CNRS, Paris. 1982.

Brehm, A. *Brehm's Life of Animals*. A.N. Marquis & Co., Chicago. 1895.

Butzer, K. *Environment and Archeology: An ecological approach to prehistory*. Aldine, Chicago. 1971.

Herb, M. *Der Wettkampf in den Marschen*. Nikephoros, Beihefte Band 5. Weidmann, Hildesheim. 2001.

Hurst, H. *The Nile, a General Account of the River and the Utilization of its Water*. Constable, London. 1952.

Jones, D. *Boats*. Univ. of Texas Press, Austin. 1943.

Landström, B. *Sailing Ships from Papyrus Boats to Full-Riggers*. Doubleday & Co., N.Y. 1959.

Landström, B. *Ships of the Pharaohs: 4000 Years of Egyptian Shipbuilding*. Doubleday & Co., N.Y. 1970.

Lewis, N. *Papyrus in Classical Antiquity*. Clarendon Press, Oxford. 1974.

Mahmoud I., I. Mohamaden, S. Abuo Shagar, and G. Allah. Geoelectrical Survey. *JKAU*: Mar. Sci. 20:91-108.

Nowak, R. *Walker's Mammals of the World. 6th Ed*. J. Hopkins University Press, Baltimore. 2009.

Roberts, C. and T. Skeat. *The Birth of the Codex*. Oxford University Press, London. 1983.

Steindorff, G. and K. Seele. *When Egypt Ruled the East*. Univ. Chicago Press, Chicago. 1957.

3: PAPYRUS BOATS, THE PRIDE OF ANCIENT EGYPT

Badawy, A. *A History of Egyptian Architecture. Vol. 1. From Earliest Times to the End of the New Kingdom*. Studio Misr, Giza, Egypt. 1954.

Fahmy, A., M. Fadl, and R. Friedman. "Economy and Ecology of Predynastic Hierakonpolis, Egypt: Archaeobotanical Evidence from a Trash Mound at HK11C." *In* Fahmy et al., eds., *Windows on the African Past. Current Approaches to African Archaeobotany*. Frankfurt: 91-118. 2011.

Hassan, F. "Prehistoric Settlements Along the Main Nile." *In* Williams, M. & H. Faure, eds., *The Sahara and the Nile*, Balkema, Rotterdam. 1980.

Hoffman, A. *Egypt Before the Pharaohs: The Prehistoric Foundations of Egyptian Civilization*. Univ. of Texas Press, Austin. 1991.

Landström, B. *Ships of the Pharaohs*.

Migahid, A. *Report on a Botanical Excursion into the "Sudd" Region*. Cairo Univ. Press, Cairo. 1948.

Postel, S. *Pillar of Sand: Can the Irrigation Miracle Last?* W.W. Norton Co., N.Y. 1999.

Sutcliffe, J. and Y. Parks. "The Hydrology of the Nile." Intern. Assoc. Hydrolog. Sci. (IAHS) Special Publication no. 5. Wallingford, UK (http://iahs.info/bluebooks/SP005/BB_005.pdf). 1999.

Vinson, S. *Egyptian Boats and Ships*. Shire Egyptology, Buckinghamshire, UK. 1994.

Ward, C. "Boat-Building and Its Social Context in Early Egypt." *Antiquity* 80:118-129. 2006.

4: ROPE, THE WORKHORSE OF ANCIENT EGYPT

Hammond, N. and L. Roseman. "The Construction of Xerxes' Bridge over the Hellespont." *Journal of Hellenic Studies* 116:88-107. 1996.

Herodotus. *History*.

Kemp, B. *Ancient Egypt: Anatomy of a Civilization*. Routledge, London. 1989.

Teeter, E. "Techniques & Terminology of Rope-Making in Ancient Egypt." *J. Egyptian Arch.* 73:71-77. 1987.

5: PAPYRUS PAPER, IN ALL THE OFFICES OF THE WORLD

Barnish, S. (Transl.) *Cassiodorus: Variae*. Liverpool University Press, Liverpool. 1992.

Budge, E.A.W. *The Book of the Dead: The Papyrus of Ani: In the British Museum*. Brit. Museum, London. 1895.

Hoffman, A. *Egypt Before the Pharaohs: The Prehistoric Foundations of Egyptian Civilization*. Univ. of Texas Press, Austin. 1991.

Kantor, H. *Plant Ornament: Its Origin and Development in the Ancient Near East*. Ph.D. Thesis, Univ. Chicago, Illinois. 1945.

Kemp, B. *Ancient Egypt: Anatomy of a Civilization*. Routledge, London. 1989.

Lewis, N. *Papyrus*.

Pliny the Elder. *Natural History*. Book XIII:74-82.

Ragab, H. *Le Papyrus*. Dr. Ragab's Papyrus Institute, Cairo. 1980.

Roberts, C. "The Greek Papyri." *In* S.R.K. Glanville, ed., *The Legacy of Egypt*. Clarendon Press, Oxford. 1963.

Roberts, C. and T. Skeat. *Birth of the Codex*.

Theophrastus. *Inquiry into Plants*, Book IV. A. Holt, trans. Heinemann, N.Y. 1916.

Twede, D. "The Origins of Paper Based Packaging." Conf. Historical Analysis & Research in Marketing Proceedings 12:288–300. (http://tinyurl.com/39gqzk5). 2005.

6: THE FLOATING WORLD

Badawy, A. *A History of Egyptian Architecture*. Histories & Mysteries of Man, Ltd., London. 1990.

Brass, M. "Predynastic Egyptian Subsistence Activities." Essay on the *Antiquity of Man* website. (www.antiquityofman.com/Subsistence_activities.html). 1998.

Bush, R. and A. Sabri. "Mining for Fish: Privatization of the Commons along Egypt's Northern Coastline." *Middle East Report Online*. (www.merip.org/mer/mer216/216_bush-sabri.html). 2010.

Dynes, W. "Primacy of Egyptian Art and Architecture." *Dyneslines Blog*. (http://dyneslines.blogspot.com/2004/12/primacy-of-egyptian-art-and.html). 2004.

Erman, A. *Life in Ancient Egypt*. H. Tirard, trans. Macmillan, London. 1885.

Ferguson, J. "Hellenistic Age." *Concise Encyclopedia Britannica*. (www.concise.britannica.com). 2007.

McGrath, C. "Egypt: Fishing in the Sewer." Inter Press News Service. (http://bit.ly/4NLCqe). 2009.

Mullié, W. and P. Meininger. "Waterbird Trapping and Hunting in Lake Manzala." *Biol. Conserv.* 27:23-43. 1983.

Thesiger, W. *The Marsh Arabs.* Penguin, N.Y. 2007.

Tidwell, M. *Bayou Farewell: The Rich Life and Tragic Death of Louisiana's Cajun Coast.* Vintage, N.Y. 2003.

White, J.M. *Everyday Life in Ancient Egypt.* G.P. Putnam's Sons, N.Y. 1971.

Wilkinson, T. *The Rise and Fall of Ancient Egypt.* Random House, N.Y. 2010.

7: THE OTHER MARSH MEN, AN AFRICAN PERSPECTIVE

Roscoe, J. *Twenty-five Years in East Africa.* Cambridge Univ. Press, Cambridge, UK. 1921.

8: SACRED SWAMPS AND TEMPLES OF IMMORTALITY

Bell, L. "The New Kingdom 'Divine' Temple: The Example of Luxor." *In* B. Shafer, ed., *Temples of Ancient Egypt.* Cornell Univ. Press, Ithaca, N.Y. 1997.

Nebet, M. "Styles of House in Ancient Egypt." *Ancient Worlds.* (www.ancientworlds. net). 2006.

Wildung, D. *Egypt, from Prehistory to the Romans.* Taschen, Cologne. 1997.

9: THE FIELD OF REEDS AS A WAY OF LIFE

Burroughs, E. *Tarzan and the Lost Empire.* Metropolitan Books, N.Y. (http:// gutenberg.net.au/Ebooks06/0600911h.html). 1928.

Crabtree, W. "Lake Bangweulu and Its Inhabitants." *J. of the Royal African Soc.* 16:216-226. (An Abstract of von Rosen's Work). 1917.

Livingston, D. *A Popular Account of Dr. Livingstone's Expedition to the Zambesi and Its Tributaries (1858-1864).* John Murray, London. 1894.

Macleod, O. *Chiefs and Cities of Central Africa: Across Lake Chad.* Blackwood & Sons, Edinburgh. 1912.

Sikes, S. *Lake Chad Versus the Sahara Desert: A Great African Lake in Crisis.* Mirage, Newbury, UK. 2003.

von Rosen, E. "The Swamps of Bangweulo and Its Inhabitants." *Roy. Anthro. Inst. Gr. Brit. and Ireland. Man* 14:105-110. 1914.

10: SWAMPS ARE THE FUTURE

Herb, M. and P. Derchain. "The Landscapes of Ancient Egypt." *In* Bollig, M. & O. Bubenzer, eds., *African Landscapes, Interdisciplinary Approaches.* Springer Science & Business Media, Heidelberg. 2009.

Myllylä, S. "Cairo—A Mega-City and Its Water Resources." The 3rd Nordic Conf. on Middle Eastern Studies, Joensuu, Finland, 19-22 June 1995.

Said, M. and A. Radwan. "Effects of the Nile Damming on Alexandria Coastal Waters." Impact of Large Coastal Mediterranean Cities on Marine Ecosystems. Alexandria, Egypt. 10-12 Feb. 2009.

Soliman, A. et al. "Unusually High Rate of Young-Onset Pancreatic Cancer in the East Nile Delta region of Egypt." *Int. J. Gastrointes Can.* 32:143–151. 2002.

Stanley, J. and A. Warne. "The Nile River in Its Destruction Phase." *J. Coastal Res.* 14:794-825. 1998.

11: SARAH STARTS A WAR

Anon. Genesis of Eden. "The Burning of Indonesia." *Dhushara* web site. (www. dhushara.com). 2004.

Anon. Post-Conflict Environmental Assessment Report. UNEP, Nairobi. (http://postconflict.unep.ch/sudanreport/sudan_website/index_photos.php). 2007.

Baker, M. *Out From the Nile: New Rivers, New Civilization in Egypt, Sudan.* (www.larouchepub.com/eiw/public/2006/2006_50-52/2006-50/pdf/48-60_650_nile.pdf). 1997.

Mohamed, Y., H. Savenije, W. Bastiaanssen, and B. van den Hurk. "New Lessons on the Sudd Hydrology Learned from Remote Sensing and Climate Modeling." *Hydrol. Earth Sys. Sci. Discuss.*, 2:1503–1535. 2005.

Roach, J. "Indonesia Peat Fires May Fuel Global Warming." *National Geographic News.* (http://news.nationalgeographic.com). 2004.

Saunders M., M. Jones, and F. Kansiime. "Carbon and Water Cycles in Tropical Papyrus Wetlands." *Wetlands Ecology & Management* 15:489-498. 2007.

Suliman, M. "Civil War in Sudan." Centre for Security Studies, Swiss Peace Foundation, Zurich. (www.ifaanet.org/encop2.htm, and www.africa.upenn.edu/Articles_Gen/cvlw_env_sdn.html). 1994.

12: THE REVENGE OF THE SACRED SEDGE

Anon. (www.jerusalemites.org). 2007.

Bein, A. and A. Horowitz. "Papyrus—A Historic Newcomer to the Hula Valley, Israel?" *Review of Palaeobotany & Palynology* 47:89-95. 1986.

Elewa, H. "Potentialities of Water Resources Pollution of the Nile River Delta, Egypt." *The Open Hydrology Journal* 4:1-13. 2010.

Hambright, K. and T. Zohary. "Lakes Hula and Agmon: Destruction and Creation of Wetland Ecosystems in Northern Israel." *Wetlands Ecology & Management* 6:83-89. 1998.

Moshe, I. "A Geomorphic and Environmental Evaluation of the Huleh Drainage Project, Israel." *Australian Geographical Studies* 40:155-166. 2002.

Tristram, H. *The Land of Israel: A Journal of Travels in Palestine, Undertaken with Special Reference to Its Physical Character.* Society for the Promotion of Christian Knowledge, London. 1865.

13: THE CONGO, ECONOMIC MIRACLE OR PIT OF DESPAIR

Anon. "Production of Castor Oil in India." *Manufacturer & Builder* 26:128. 1894.

Flemming, A. "Malaria: New Drug Lead from Madagascar's Rainforests." *Nat. Reviews Drug Discovery* 6:113. 2007.

Lincoln, F. "Migration of Birds." Circ. 16. *Fish & Wildlife Service*, USDI. 1979.

Rocco, F. *Quinine, Malaria and the Quest for a Cure that Changed the World.* Perennial, N.Y. 2004.

14: A TRAGIC IRONY

Flemming, A. "Groundwater Recharge in Ephemeral Rivers of Southern Africa International Workshop, Cape Town, South Africa." Research in the Support of the EU Water Initiative Sixth Framework Programme (2002–2006): GOCE-CT-2003- 506680-WADE. 2007.

Baumgartner, H. "Swamp Thing: Artificial Wetlands Take Waste Treatment Back to its Roots." (www.memagazine.org/backissues/membersonly/january2000/features/swamp/swamp.html). 2010.

Kitissou, M. "Hydropolitics and Geopolitics: Transforming Conflict and Reshaping Cooperation in Africa." (www.hydroaid.it/FTP/Data_Research/M.%20Kitissou-Hydropolitics_and_geopolitics.pdf). 2004.

Taunt, E. *US Navy Congo River Expedition of 1885.* Dept. of the Navy, Naval Historical Center, Washington, DC. (www.history.navy.mil/library/online/congo_rvr_exp.htm#let). 1886.

15: THE BATTLE FOR LAKE VICTORIA

Kansiime, F., M. Nalubega, J. van Bruggen, and P. Denny. "The Effect of Wastewater Discharge on Biomass Production and Nutrient Content of Cyperus Papyrus and Miscanthidium Violaceum in the Nakivubo Wetland, Kampala, Uganda." *Water Science & Techn.* 48(5):233-240. 2003.

Kayombo, S. and S. Jorgensen. "Lake Victoria, Experience and Lessons Learned" brief, pp 431-447. Lake Basin Mngt Init. GEF IW: LEARN Project (PCU), UNDP, Washington, DC. 2002.

Kull, D. "Connections Between Recent Water Level Drops in Lake Victoria, Dam Operations and Drought." *International Rivers*, an online newsletter. (www.internationalrivers.org/files/060208vic.pdf). 2006.

Mugabe, D. and E. Kisambira. "Lake Victoria Levels at Jinja Dam Raise Eyebrows." *East African Business Week* (Nairobi). 2006.

Okurut, T.O., G.B.J. Rijs, and J.J.A. van Bruggen. "Design and Performance of Experimental Constructed Wetlands in Uganda, Planted with C. Papyrus and P. Mauritianus." *J. Wat. Sci.Tech.* 40:265-271. 1999.

Owino, A. and P. Ryan. "Recent Papyrus Swamp Habitat Loss and Conservation Implications in Western Kenya." *Wetlands Ecology & Management* 15:1-12. 2007.

Riebeek, H. and R. Simmon. "Lake Victoria's Falling Waters." (http://earthobservatory.nasa.gov). 2006.

Stager, J., A. Ruzmaikin, D. Conway, P. Verburg, and P. Mason. "Sunspots, El Niño, and the Levels of Lake Victoria, East Africa." J. *Geophys. Res.* 112:D15106. 2007.

16: WAR ALONG THE NILE

Abdel-Satar, A. "Water Quality Assessment of River Nile from Idfo to Cairo." *Egyptian Journal of Aquatic Research* 31:1687-4285. (http://bit.ly/SqHE50). 2005.

Anon. 2010. *WASH News.* (http://washmena.wordpress.com/tag/nile-river/). 2010.

Carlson, A. "Who Owns the Nile? Egypt, Sudan, and Ethiopia's History-Changing Dam." Origins: *Current Events in Historical Perspective.* (http://origins.osu.edu). Vol. 6, March 2013. Ohio State Univ.

George, S. "Globalisation & War." Address before the International Congress of IPPNW, New Delhi. (www.zcommunications.org/globalisation-and-war-by-susan-george). 2008.

Harvey, J. et al. "Interactions between Surface Water and Ground Water and Effects on Mercury Transport in the North-Central Everglades." Rep 02-4050. (http://sofia.usgs.gov/index.html). 2005.

Kieyah, J. "The 1929 Nile Water Agreement: Legal and Economic Analysis." (http://works.bepress.com/cgi/viewcontent.cgi?article=1000&context=joseph_kieyah). 2004.

El Moghraby, A. and M. el Sammani. "On the Environmental and Socio-economic Impact of the Jonglei Canal Project, Southern Sudan." *Environmental Conservation* 12:41-48. 1985.

17: IT TAKES AN ARMY TO SAVE THE SUDD

Anon. "Rapid Assessment Study, Towards Integrated Planning of Irrigation and Drainage in Egypt." FAO/IPTRID Secretariat, Rome. (www.fao.org/docrep/008/a0021e/a0021e00.htm#Contents). 2005.

El-Shibini, F. and M. El-Kady. "Fruits and Greens Under Irrigated Agriculture in Egypt." *Pub. Nat. Water Research Center*, Ministry of Water Resources & Irrigation, Egypt. 2008.

Hafez, A., M. Khedr, K. El-Katib, H. Alla, and S. Elmanharawy. "El-Salaam Canal Project, Sinai II. Chemical Water Quality Investigations." *Desalination* 227:274-285. 2008.

Mostafa, H., F. El-Gamal, and A. Shalby. "Reuse of Low Quality Water in Egypt." CIHEAM, *Intern. Cent. for Adv. Agron. Studies.* (http://ressources.ciheam.org/om/pdf/b53/00800754.pdf). 2004.

Omara, M. and M. El-Bakrya. "Estimation of Evaporation from the Lake of the Aswan High Dam (Lake Nasser) Based on Measurements over the Lake." *Agricultural Meteorology* 23:293-308. 1981.

Oosterbaan, R. "Impacts of the Irrigation Improvement Project, Egypt." (ILRI), Wageningen, The Netherlands. (www.waterlog.info). 1999.

Ramberg, L., P. Wolski, and M. Krah. "Water Balance and Infiltration in a Seasonal Floodplain in the Okavango Delta, Botswana." *Wetlands* 26:677-690. 2006.

Said, M. and A. Radwan. "Effects of the Nile Damming."

Shinn, D. "Nile Basin Relations: Egypt, Sudan and Ethiopia." *Lectures & Speeches*, Elliott School of International Affairs, George Washington University. Washington, DC. (http://bit.ly/UqF0MB). 2006.

Siegel, S., M. Slaboda, and D.J. Stanley. "Metal Pollution Loading, Manzalah Lagoon, Nile Delta, Egypt: Implications for Aquaculture." *Environ. Geol.* 23:89-98. 1994.

Soliman, A. et al. "Pancreatic Cancer."

18: BLOOD ROSES, PAPYRUS, AND THE NEW SCRAMBLE FOR AFRICA

Barlow, M. *Blue Covenant: The Global Water Crisis and the Coming Battle for the Right to Water.* New Press, N.Y. 2007.

Boar, R. "Responses of a Fringing Cyperus Papyrus L. Swamp to Changes in Water Level." *Aquatic Botany* 84:85-92. 2005.

Epatko, L. "Volcano Stems Kenya's Flower, Vegetable Market." (http://to.pbs.org/duBm7H). 2010.

Fox, J. *White Mischief.* Jonathan Cape, London. 1982.

Gaudet, J. "Papyrus and the Ecology of Lake Naivasha." *Nat. Geog. Soc. Res. Reports.* Vol. 12:267-272. 1980.

Gaudet, J. and J. Melack. "Major Ion Chemistry in a Tropical African Lake Basin." *Freshwat. Biol.* 11:309-333. 1981.

Gitahi, S. "Lake Naivasha: A Case Study on IWRM in Kenya." Network for Water & Sanitation, NETWAS. (www.netwas.org/newsletter/articles/2005/01/7). 2005.

Goldson, J. "A Three Phase Environmental Impact Study of Recent Developments around Lake Naivasha." Lake Naivasha Riparian Owners' Association, Naivasha. 1993.

Harper, D., K. Mavuti, and S. Muchiri. "Ecology and Management of Lake Naivasha, in Relation to Climatic Change, Alien Species Introductions and Agricultural Development." *Envir. Conserv.* 17:328–336. 1990.

Howard-Williams, C. and K. Thompson. "The Conservation and Management of African Wetlands." *In* P. Denny, ed., *The Ecol. & Mgt. of African Wetland Vegetation.* Dr. W. Junk, Pub., Dordrecht. 1985.

Jones, M. and T. Milburn. "Photosynthesis in Papyrus." *Photosynthesis* 12:197-199. 1978.

Kamau, M. "Lake Naivasha Report: Flower Farms Redeemed." *The Standard* (Nairobi). 2010.

McGregor, J. "From Kenya With Love." *McGregor's Blog* at IIED (http://tinyurl.com/l4dwpa7). 2010.

Ministry of Environ. & Min. Resources, CIEN Kenya News Page. (www.estis.net/sites/kenya). 2010.

Mureithi, E. Interview with *AfricaNews.* Feb. 2008. (http://bit.ly/SWWGQU).

Muthuri, F., M. Jones, and S. Imbamba. "Primary Productivity of Papyrus (Cyperus Papyrus) in a Tropical Swamp—Lake Naivasha, Kenya." *Biomass* 18:1-14. 1989.

Muthuri, F. and M. Jones. "Nutrient Distribution in a Papyrus Swamp: Lake Naivasha, Kenya." *Aquatic Botany* 56:35-50. 1997.

Ngonyo, J. Personal interview *in*: "Lake Naivasha—Withering Under the Assault of International Flower Vendors." (www.canadians.org/water/documents/NaivashaReport08.pdf). 2008.

Seal, M. *Wildflower.* Random House, N.Y. 2009.

Singh, T. "Blood Flowers: With Love, From Kenya. Human Sufferings, Ethnic Tensions Add to Political Warfare." *The European Weekly*, New Europe, an online newspaper. (http://bit.ly/c29eDi). 2008.

19: THE ZAMBEZI, THE VICTORIANS, AND PAPYRUS

Stanley, H. *How I Found Livingstone: Travels, Adventures, Discoveries in C. Africa: Incl. an Account of Four Months' Residence with Dr. Livingstone.* Scribner, Armstrong & Co., N.Y. 1872.

Waller, H. *The Last Journals of David Livingstone, in Central Africa, from 1865 to His Death.* John Murray, London. 1874.

20: AN UNWANTED LEGACY

Andrews, M. "Thames Estuary: Pollution and Recovery." *In* Sheehan, Miller, Butler & Bourdeau, eds., *Effects of Pollutants at the Ecosystem* Level. J. Wiley & Sons, N.Y. 1984.

Beilfuss, R., D. Moore, C. Bento, and P. Dutton. "Patterns of Vegetation Change in the Zambezi Delta, Mozambique." Working Paper. (http://bit.ly/Wc7IXV). 2001.

Choongo, K., M. Syakalima, and M. Mwase. "Coefficient of Condition in Relation to Copper Levels in Muscle of Serranochromis Fish and Sediment from the Kafue River, Zambia." *Bull. Environ. Contamination and Toxicol.* 75:645-651. 2007.

Headley, T. and C. Tanner. "Application of Floating Wetlands for Enhanced Stormwater Treatment: A Review." Auckland Regional Council, Tech. Pub. No. HAM2006-123. 2006.

Mackal, R. *A Living Dinosaur? In Search of Mokele-Mbembe.* E.J. Brill, N.Y. 1987.

Magadza, C. "Water Resources Management and Water Quality Monitoring in an African Setting." Guest Forum Readout 27. (www-origin.horiba.com/uploads/media/R027-13-054.pdf). 2003.

Marshall, B. "Predicting Ecology and Fish Yields in African Reservoirs from Preimpoundment Physico-Chemical Data." CIFA Tech. Paper, CIFA/T12. FAO, Rome. 1984.

Nabulo, G., O. Origa, W. Nasinyama, and D. Cole. "Assessment of Zn, Cu, Pb and Ni Contamination in Wetland Soils and Plants in the Lake Victoria Basin." *Intern. J. Env. Sci. &Tech.* 5:65-74. 2008.

von der Heyden, C. and M. New. "Natural Wetland for Mine Effluent Remediation? The Case of the Copperbelt." Global Wetlands Consort., Conf. on Envir. Monitoring of Trop. & Subtrop. Wetlands, Maun, Botswana. 2002.

21: THE OKAVANGO, MIRACLE OF THE KALAHARI

Andersson, J. "Land Cover Change in the Okavango River Basin." M.S. Thesis, Linköping Univ., Sweden. 2006.

Dangerfield, J.M., T.S. McCarthy, and W.N. Ellery. "The Mound-Building Termite *Macrotermes Michaelseni* as an Ecosystem Engineer." *J. of Tropical Ecology*, 14:507-520. 1998.

Du Plessis, B. "Birding Adventure in Botswana." *Great Outdoor Recreation Pages.* (www.gorp.com). 2010.

Eldredge, N. *Life in the Balance.* Princeton Univ. Press, Princeton, NJ. 1998.

Ellery, W., T. McCarthy, and N. Smith. "Vegetation, Hydrology, and Sedimentation

Patterns on the Major Distributary System of the Okavango Fan, Botswana." *Wetlands* 23:357-375. 2003.

Kgathi, D., D. Kniveton, S. Ringrose, C. Vanderpost, A. Turton, J. Lundqvist, and M. Seely. "The Okavango: A River Supporting Its People, Environment and Economic Development." *Jour. Hydrology* 331:3-17. 2006.

Leechor, C. "Developing Tourism in Botswana." Background Study for the World Bank-BIDPA Botswana Export Diversification Study. (http://tinyurl.com/329a8p4). 2005.

McCarthy, T. and J. Metcalfe. "Chemical Sedimentation in the Semi-Arid Environment of the Okavango Delta, Botswana." *Chemical Geology* 89:157-178. 1990.

McCarthy, T., R. Green, and N. Franey. "The Influence of Neo-Tectonics on Water Dispersal in the Northeastern Regions of the Okavango Swamps, Botswana." *J. Afr. Earth Sci.* 17:23-32. 1993.

Oosterbaan, R., L. Kortenhorst, and L. Sprey. "Development of Flood-Recession Cropping in the Molapos of the Okavango Delta, Botswana." Ann. Rep. Intern. Inst. Land Reclam., Wageningen, The Netherlands. (www.waterlog.info/pdf/molapos.pdf). 1986.

Thompson, K. "The Primary Productivity of African Wetlands, with Particular Reference to the Okavango Delta." In *Botswana Society, Symposium on the Okavango Delta and Its Future Utilization.* Gaborone, Botswana. 1976.

Turton, A. "Sea of Sand, Land of Water." MEWREW Occasional Paper No. 6. Water Issues Study Group, SOAS, University of London. (www.awiru.co.za/pdf/trutonanthony10.pdf). 2000.

Warne, K. "Okavango—Africa's Miracle Delta." *Nat. Geogr. Magazine*, Washington, DC. 2004.

22: PAPYRUS BLOOMS AGAIN IN THE HOLY LAND

Al Bawaba. "Jordan's King Says Tourism Could Help Middle East Peace Process." The Al Bawaba Group, *Mideast Information, Media & Technology.* (www.albawaba.com). 2000.

Anon. "Israel's Nature and Natural Parks Protection Agency." (www.parks.org.il/Parks). 2007.

Anon. "The Jordan River Peace Park." Friends of the Earth Middle East (FoEME), EcoPeace (www.foeme.org/projects.php?ind=123). 2010.

Kaplan, D., T. Oron, and M. Gutman. "Development of Macrophytic Vegetation in the Agmon Wetland of Israel by Spontaneous Colonization and Reintroduction." *J. Wetlands Ecol. & Management* 6:143-150. 1998.

Shirihai, H., D. Alon, and I. Shanni. "Huleh—One of the Last Winter Refuges in the Middle East for Birds." (www.hula-birding.com). 2007.

Tal, A. *Pollution in a Promised Land, An Environmental History of Israel.* University of California Press, Berkeley. 2002.

Zohary, T. and K. Hambright. "Lake Hula—Lake Agmon." Jewish Virtual Library, American-Israeli Cooperative Enterprise. (www.jewishvirtuallibrary.org/jsource/Society_&_Culture/geo/Hula.html). 2007.

24: THE EGYPTIAN SOLUTION

Anon. "Lake Manzala Engineered Wetlands." UNDP. (www.undp.org/gef/documents/writeups_doc/iw/Egypt_lakeManzala.doc). 2007.

Abdel-Shafy, H. and A. Dewedar. "Constructed Wetlands for Urban Wastewater Treatment in Egypt." *Sustainable Sanitation Practice* 12:27-32. (www.ecosan.at). 2012.

Cross, H. and L. Fleming. "Control of Phragmites or Common Reed." *Waterfowl Management Handbook* (www.nwrc.usgs.gov/wdb/pub/wmh/13_4_12.pdf). 1989.

Hamed, Y., T. Abdelmoneim, M. El-Kiki, M. Hassan, and R. Berndtsson. "Assessment of Heavy Metals Pollution and Microbial Contamination in Water, Sediments, and Fish of Lake Manzala, Egypt." *Life Science Journal* 10:1. (www.lifesciencesite.com). 2013.

El-Din El-Quosy, D. "The Lake Manzala Engineered Wetland, Port Said, Egypt." (http://iwlearn.net/publications/ll/lake-manzala-engineered-wetland-port-said-egypt-iwc4-presentation). 2009.

El Hadidi, M. "Distribution of Cyperus Papyrus L. and Nymphaea Lotus L. in Inland Waters of Egypt." *Munich Bot. Staatssamml. Mitt.* 10:470-475. 1971.

Oketch, M.A. "The Potential Role of Constructed Wetlands." *OceanDocs* (www.oceandocs.org/bitstream/1834/1470/1/WLCK-41-46.pdf). 2006.

Okurut, T. "A Pilot Study on Municipal Wastewater Treatment Using a Constructed Wetland in Uganda." Ph.D. Thesis, Wageningen Univ., Delft, Netherlands. 2000.

Okurut, T., G.B.J. Rijs, and J.J.A. van Bruggen. "Design and Performance."

Perbangkhem, T. and C. Polprasert. "Biomass Production of Papyrus (Cyperus Papyrus) in Constructed Thailand." *BioResource Technol.* 101:833-5. 2009.

Ragab, H. *Le Papyrus.*

Serag, M. "Ecology and Biomass Production of Cyperus Papyrus L. on the Nile Bank at Damietta, Egypt." *J. Mediterranean Ecology* 4:15-24. 2003.

Stahl, R.A., B. Ramadan, and M. Pimpl. "Bahr El-Baqar Drain System Environ. Studies on Water Quality. Part I: Bilbeis Drain / Bahr El-Baqar Drain." (http://bibliothek.fzk.de/zb/berichte/FZKA7505.pdf). 2009.

26: CONCLUSION

Constanza, R. et al. "The Value of the World's Ecosystem Services and Natural Capital." *Nature* 387:259. 1997.

Green, M. et al. "Long-Term Death Rates, West Nile Virus Epidemic, Israel." *Emerging Infectious Diseases.* CDC serial on the Internet. (www.cdc.gov/ncidod/EID/vol11no11/04-0941.htm). 2005.

Grunwald, M. *The Swamp: The Everglades, Florida, and the Politics of Paradise.* Simon & Schuster, N.Y. 2006.

UNEP-GRID. "Ecosystems and Human Well-Being Desertification Synthesis, A Report of the Millennium Ecosystem Assessment." WRI, Washington, DC. 2005.

ACKNOWLEDGMENTS

Special thanks to those who reviewed earlier drafts, in particular Patrick Denny of London, who also provided photographs of papyrus in the Sudd, and Anne Sandlund for providing so many helpful suggestions on how to write a readable book. I owe a large debt of gratitude to Jacqueline Flynn at Joelle Delbourgo Associates for believing in the book, and Jessica Case at Pegasus for providing encouragement and common-sense advice when it was needed.

I doubt if my research in Africa would ever have amounted to much if I had not gotten a small research grant from the National Geographic Society that was renewed several times and for which I am thankful. I also doubt if this book would have been written without the patience, help, and guidance of my wife Caroline, to whom I am eternally grateful.

Thanks also to my former colleagues in Africa for helping me get my start in the swamps: Keith Thompson and Tomi Petr, formerly with Makerere University, Uganda; Prof. Stephen Njuguna, formerly Dean of the School of Environmental Studies; Prof. Alex Njue, Professor of Botany, Kenyatta University; Dr. Frank Muthuri, Nairobi, Kenya; Prof. Ken Mavuti, Professor of Zoology, University of Nairobi, Kenya; "Mac" Litterick, University of Nairobi; John Melack and Sally McIntyre at the University of California, Santa Barbara; and Mike Jones, Trinity College, Dublin.

Thanks to Dr. Abdel Salam Ragab, Chairman and CEO of the Pharaonic Village, Cairo; Dr. Sayyed Hassan, Director of Papyrus Dept., Egyptian Museum, Cairo; Dr. Magdy Mansour, Director of Conservation, Coptic Museum, Cairo; Hossam El Deeb, Restoration Laboratory, The Library, Alexandria, Egypt; Dr. Ksenija Borojevic, Department of Archaeology, Boston University, Boston; Dr. Jean-Daniel Stanley, Smithsonian Institution, Washington, DC; Sarah Higgins, Lake Naivasha, Kenya; Ed Morrison and David Harper from the Department of Biology, University of Leicester, UK; Dr. Didi Kaplan, Huleh Nature Reserve, Israel; Dr. Doron Markel, Lake Kinneret and Agmon Lake, Israel; Dr. Yossi Leshem, Professor of Ornithology, Tel Aviv University; Robert Brecht, ITC, Netherlands; Corrado Basile, Siracusa, Italy; David Hambright, University of Oklahoma, Norman, Oklahoma; and Dr. Abe Krikorian and Eugene Taylor for their early help in photographing swamps in Africa.

Thanks also to Dr. Ilona Regulski at the Freie Universität, Berlin; Prof. Willy Clarysse, Catholic University, Leuven, Belgium; Dr. Günter Dreyer, German Archaeological Institute, Cairo; and various fellow members of the American Society of Papyrologists for assistance in the interpretation of the history of papyrus in ancient Egypt, in particular Ted Bernhardt, Dr. Thomas Kraus, and Prof. Cornelia Roemer. Thanks to Elaine Evans, Curator of the McLung Museum at the University of Tennessee, for her thoughts on replicas of famous papyri, and Dr. Neal Spencer, Assistant Keeper (Curator) of the Dept. of Ancient Egypt and Sudan, British Museum, for his help and suggestions and access to the Papyrus of Ani and British Museum Study Rooms.

Figures and photo credits: Quite a few images were seen or acquired first on the Commons at Wikimedia (www.wikipedia.org). Thanks to Samuel Manning for permission to use two copyrighted drawings, one of a papyrus boat under sail and another of one under construction, and to Georg Petersen at www.hydroc.de for the aerial photo of Sudd, Steve Johnson at SAREP, Botswana, for one of the Okavango, and Yossi Leshem for use of the bird migration map. Various line drawings were re-fashioned after those of D. Jones, A. Badawy, G. Reeder, M. Herb, A. Erman, O. Macleod, E. von Rosen, W. Budge, N. de Garis Davies, and Wikipedia.

ENDNOTES

1: FIRST ENCOUNTER

1. R. Hecky, 2005. Review of "Conservation, Ecology, and Management of African Fresh Waters" by Crisman, et al., Florida Univ. Press, Gainsville, 2003. *Wetlands* 25:500-501.

2: NATURE'S BOUNTY

1. S. Loiselle et al. reported a net primary production rate of 32,000 kcals per sq. meter per year. ("Tools for Wetland Ecosystem Resource Management in E. Africa: Focus on Lake Victoria Papyrus Wetlands." 97-121. In: *Wetlands & Natural Resource Management*, Ed. Verhoeven, et. al. Springer-Verlag, Berlin.) 2006.
2. Based on a remote sensing survey done over a 12-month period 2007-2008. L-M. Rebelo, G. Senay, and M. McCartney. "Flood Pulsing in the Sudd Wetland: Analysis of Seasonal Variations in Inundation and Evaporation in South Sudan." Earth Interact 16:1-192012. (The areas given in Wikipedia based on older, less reliable data are twice as high as those determined by Rebelo *et al.*)
3. BBC has posted a series of short wonderfully detailed film clips on YouTube showing the ecology of papyrus swamps, especially the weaver birds and boatmakers with their tanqwas on Lake Tana on the Blue Nile (http://tinyurl. com/l8guek7); a shoebill fishing for a lungfish in a papyrus swamp in the Southern Sudan on the White Nile (http://tinyurl.com/jvkppl7); the Nile crocodile in action (http://tinyurl.com/lsl5hwo); and the people and wildlife of the Sudd (http://tinyurl.com/m4jul8c).
4. K. Butzer, *Early Hydraulic Civilization in Egypt* (University of Chicago Press, 1976).
5. T. Hikade, "Stone Tool Production" (*in* W. Wendrich, ed., *UCLA Encyclopedia of Egyptology*, Los Angeles 2010, http://bit.ly/YoOyPh).

6. D. Brewer, *Ancient Egypt: Foundations of a Civilization* (Pearson, Harlow, UK 2005).
7. Six papyrus plants in a grove, papyrus sandals (two occasions), a papyrus boat, papyrus rope, a papyrus float used in hippo hunts, a serekh (reed wall symbol), and the face of a reed temple on Narmer's apron.
8. Prof. Naphtali Lewis was a Distinguished Emeritus Professor at Brooklyn College and an expert on the history of the plant. Referred to by many as the "doyen of papyrologists," his book *Papyrus in Classical Antiquity*, Clarendon Press, Oxford, 1974, is an updated version of his Sorbonne thesis.
9. One such is shown in cross-sectional profile by Mahmoud et al. in 2009.

3: PAPYRUS BOATS, THE PRIDE OF ANCIENT EGYPT

1. An example of an ancient Egyptian boat equipped with an A-frame mast and serial stays is shown in Wilkinson, p. 226, Fig. 410 (*Manners and Customs of the Ancient Egyptians*. 3 vols. J. Murray, London, 1898).
2. See also Wikipedia "Sudd"; and Stephan Weisner, Lund University, Sweden, "Effects of an Organic Sediment on Performance of Young *Phragmites Australis* Clones at Different Water Depth Treatments" (Hydrobiologia 330:189-194, 1996); also J. Sutcliffe, "A Hydrological Study of the Southern Sudd Region of the Upper Nile" (*Hydrological Science Bulletin* 19:237-255, 1974).
3. N. Doyle, "Iconography and the Interpretation of Ancient Egyptian Watercraft" (M.A. Thesis, Texas A&M Univ, College Station, TX, 1998).
4. See enormous number of posts, large and small, used in building early temples and palaces in archaic Egypt described in the work of Ahmed Fahmy, Renee Friedman, and others at Hierakonpolis, 2011.

4: ROPE, THE WORKHORSE OF ANCIENT EGYPT

1. The 2007 web page from *RopeCordNews* (http://www.ropecord.com/new/dl/spring2007.pdf).
2. K. Borojevic and R. Mountain, "The Ropes of Pharaohs: The Source of Cordage from 'Rope Cave' at Mersa/Wadi Gawasis Revisited" (*Journal of Archaeological Research in Egypt* 47:131-141, 2012).
3. N. Lewis, *Papyrus*.
4. Ibid.
5. One famous temple drawing shows a young man stripping the skin from a fresh papyrus stem, perhaps, as suggested by Prof. Quirke, to use as a binder for the bundles being gathered in the swamp by other workers (Fig. 6a in Lewis, 1974; B. Leach and J. Tait, 2000).
6. PBS NOVA (WGBH) online "Explore a Pharaoh's Boat" (http://tinyurl.com/cxjzplx), 2013.

5: PAPYRUS PAPER, IN ALL THE OFFICES OF THE WORLD

1. "The Papyrus of Ani . . . composed of three layers of papyrus supplied by plants

that measured in the stalks about 4½ inches in diameter." (E. Budge, *The Book of the Dead—The Papyrus of Ani*, page 217, 1895).

2. One difference between the modern paper and the paper of ancient times is the degree of overlapping of the wet strips of papyrus stem. As pointed out by Professor Bülow-Jacobsen, former research professor at the University of Copenhagen, ancient papyri show little or no signs of overlapping of strips. Since overlapping is not mentioned in Pliny, it may not be necessary. Bülow-Jacobsen, A. 2009. Writing materials in the ancient world. Chap. 1 *in* The Oxford Handbook of Papyrology. Oxford Univ. Press, Oxford, UK.

3. According to Shepherd, 2008, this is: relative humidity 45-55%; 18-22° C; and light levels at less than 50 lux, with ultraviolet less than 75 microwatts per lume.

4. Parkinson and Quirke, 1995.

5. For a detailed account of the manufacture, history, and preservation of papyrus paper, see the comprehensive review by Bridget Leach, Conservator of Papyrus, British Museum and Prof. J. Tait, Univ. College, London ("Papyrus," Chapter 9 in: *Ancient Egyptian materials and technology*. Cambridge Univ. Press, 2000).

6. Orias website (http://orias.berkeley.edu/spice/textobjects/imports-exports.htm).

7. "An Introduction to the History and Culture of Pharaonic Egypt" (www.reshafim.org.il/ad/egypt).

8. N. Lewis, *Papyrus* (p. 112).

6: THE FLOATING WORLD

1. F. Hassan, "The Dynamics of a Riverine Civilization: A Geoarchaeological Perspective on the Nile Valley, Egypt" (*World Archaeology*, 29:51-74, 1997).

2. N. Lewis, *Papyrus* (pp. 101-102).

3. See Greg Reeder at www.egyptology.com/reeder/muu.

4. See also the Egyptian Monuments website of Sue Bayfield (http://tinyurl.com/dywu7qz).

5. J. Wilkinson, *Manners and Customs of the Ancient Egyptians* (S. Birch, ed., 3 vols. J. Murray, London, 1878).

6. C. Roberts and T. Skeat, *The Birth of the Codex* (Oxford Univ. Press, 1983).

7. R. Bagnell, *Early Christian Books in Egypt* (Princeton Univ. Press, 2009).

7: THE OTHER MARSH MEN, AN AFRICAN PERSPECTIVE

1. D. Kaiza, "Life in the Sudds" (*The East African*, Nairobi, Jan. 2000).

8: SACRED SWAMPS AND TEMPLES OF IMMORTALITY

1. Cleopatra's mother "was African" (BBC online news, 16 March 2009).

2. N. Lewis, *Papyrus*.

3. B. Shafer, "Temples, Priests, and Rituals: An Overview" (*In* B. Shafer, ed., *Temples of Ancient Egypt*, Cornell Univ. Press, Ithaca, N.Y., 1997).

4. L. Bell, "The New Kingdom 'Divine' Temple: The Example of Luxor" (*In* B. Shafer, ed., *Temples of Ancient Egypt*, Cornell Univ. Press, Ithaca, N.Y., 1997).

5. Thoreau, as quoted by R. Giblett, "Henry Thoreau: A 'Patron Saint' of Swamps" (*Postmodern Wetlands: Culture, History and Ecology* (pp. 229-239), Edinburgh University Press, Edinburgh, 1996).

6. "Egyptian Monuments," S. Bayfield website (http://egyptsites.wordpress. com/2009/03/03/merimda-beni-salama).

7. Paula Nielson,"Marsh Arabs of Iraq: Iraqi Heirs of the Ancient Sumerians" (http://middleeasternhistory.suite101.com), 2010.

9: THE FIELD OF REEDS AS A WAY OF LIFE

1. T. Yulsman, "Lake Chad: Shrinking Beauty" (*Discover Magazine* http://blogs. discovermagazine.com/imageo/2013/10/20/lake-chad-shrinking-beauty/), 2013.

2. W. Clarysse, "The great revolt of the Egyptians (205–186 B.C.)" (Berkeley, April 2004, http://tebtunis.berkeley.edu/lecture/revolt.html#rebelmap).

3. C. Oman, *A History of the Art of War: The Middle Ages from the Fourth to the Fourteenth Century* (G.P. Putnam and Sons, London, 1898).

4. Tali Lipkin-Shakhak, "The Forgotten Hero of Entebbe, Dan Shomron: The Lead Actor" (*Ma'ariv*, "Saturday Supplement" magazine, 16 June 2006, http://bit.ly/ T44gfz).

10: SWAMPS ARE THE FUTURE

1. On the large African rivers, these islands are worn down by circular abrasion until they look like large green pizza pies (100yds diam.). They are shown very clearly during a fly-over of the Sudd in *Joanna Lumley's Nile*, 2009 Athena DVD (an RLJ Entertainment Production).

2. Hassan, "Prehistoric Settlements Along the Main Nile" (*The Sahara and the Nile*, M. Williams and H. Faure, eds., Balkema, Rotterdam, 1980).

3. "A Favoured Spot; Egypt Is Making the Most of Its Natural Advantages" (*The Economist*, July 2010).

4. B. Du Plessis, "Birding Adventure in Botswana" (*Great Outdoor Recreation Pages*, http://www.gorp.com), 2010.

5. T. Laylin, "Nile Water Kills 17,000 Egyptian Children Each Year" (http://www. almasryalyoum.com), 2010.

11: SARAH STARTS A WAR

1. *Joanna Lumley's Nile*, 2009 Athena DVD (an RLJ Entertainment Production).

2. M. Suliman, "Civil War in Sudan: The Impact of Ecological degradation" (http:// www.africa.upenn.edu/Articles_Gen/cvlw_env_sdn.html), 1994.

3. P. Howell, M. Lock, and S. Cobb, *The Jonglei Canal, Impact and Opportunity* (Cambridge Univ. Press, 1988).

4. G. El-Qady, M. Metwaly, A. El-Galladi, and K. Ushijima, "Evaluation of Peat Using Geoelectrical Methods, Nile Delta, Egypt" (*Memoirs of the Faculty of Engin.*, Kyushu Univ. 65:1-13), 2005.

5. EPA Water website, http://water.epa.gov/type/wetlands/people.cfm.

12: THE REVENGE OF THE SACRED SEDGE

1.   Discovery News, August 2013 (http://news.discovery.com/history/archaeology/oldest-bog-body-130820.htm).
2.   Tollund Man. Wikipedia.

13: THE CONGO, ECONOMIC MIRACLE OR PIT OF DESPAIR

1.   J. Conrad, *Heart of Darkness*, 1899 (http://www.gutenberg.org/etext/526).
2.   L. Goma, "Experimental Breeding of Anopheles Gambiae Giles in Papyrus Swamps" ("Letters to Nature," *Nature* 187:1137-1138), 1960.

14: A TRAGIC IRONY

1.   M. Kavanagh, "Congo Confident $12 Billion Power Plant Will Proceed by 2015" (*Bloomberg News*, http://tinyurl.com/plkxlfq), 2013.

15: THE BATTLE FOR LAKE VICTORIA

1.   American Institute of Physics website : "The Discovery of Global Warming. Changing Sun, Changing Climate?" (http://www.aip.org/history/climate/solar.htm), 2013.
2.   J. Beck, "Using the sun cycle to predict African rains" (*Geotimes*, http://www.geotimes.org/oct07/article.html?id=nn_rains.html), 2007.
3.   Y. Kiwango and E. Wolanski, "Papyrus Wetlands, Nutrient Balance, Fisheries Collapse, Food Security, and Lake Victoria Level Decline in 2000-2006" (*Wetlands Ecol. and Mgt.* 16:89-96, 2007).
4.   Kansiime, Nalubega, van Bruggen, and Denny, "The Effect of Wastewater Discharge on Biomass Production and Nutrient Content" (*Water Science & Technology* 48:233-240, 2003).
5.   UNEP, 2003 "Phytotechnologies" *Freshwater Management Series No. 7.* (http://www.unep.or.jp/Ietc/Publications/Freshwater/FMS7/13.asp).
6.   D. Jurries, "Biofilters (Bioswales, Vegetative Buffers, & Constructed Wetlands) for Storm Water Discharge Pollution Removal" (Dept. Envir. Quality, State of Oregon, 2003).
7.   NASA, 2012. *The Encyclopedia of the Earth* (http://www.eoearth.org/article/Lake_Victoria).
8.   M. Mwendwa, "Lake Victoria: Pollution Contributes to Fish Decline" (*The Citizen*, http://www.thecitizen.co.tz, July 29, 2012).
9.   L. Sitoki, R. Kurmayer, and E. Rott, "Spatial Variation of Phytoplankton Composition, Biovolume, and Resulting Microcystin Concentrations in the Nyanza Gulf (Lake Victoria, Kenya)" (*Hydrobiologia* 691:109-122, 2012).
10. Kansiime, Nalubega, van Bruggen, and Denny, "Effect of Wastewater."

16: WAR ALONG THE NILE

1.   X. Rice, "Battle for the Nile as Rivals Lay Claim to Africa's Great River" (*The Guardian*, http://www.guardian.co.uk/environment/2010/jun/25/battle-nile-africa-river-resources), 2010.

2. J. Kieyah, "The 1929 Nile Waters Agreement: Legal and Economic Analysis" (Selected Works, http://works.bepress.com/cgi/viewcontent.cgi?article=1000&context=joseph_kieyah), 2007.
3. P. Guber and R. Bangs, "African Water Rights in DeNile" (*Huffington Post*, July 7, 2010).
4. E. Kiggundu, "Egypt Threatens War" (*Ethiopian News & Opinion*, http://ethiopianewsforum.com/viewtopic.php?f=2&t=19488), 2010.
5. F. Pearce, "Does Egypt Own the Nile? A Battle Over Precious Water" (*Yale Environment 360*, http://e360.yale.edu), 2010.
6. Howell, Lock, and Cobb, *The Jonglei Canal*.
7. M. B. Jones and S. W. Humphries, "Impacts of the C4 Sedge *Cyperus papyrus L.* on Carbon and Water Fluxes in an African Wetland" (*Hydrobiologia* 488:107-113, 2002). [Note: This study supports earlier experiments that treat the swamp as a whole, unlike the isolated cut stems used in L. Åse, "A Note on the Water Budget of Lake Naivasha, Kenya," *Geog. Ann.* 69:415-429, 1987.]
8. L-M. Rebelo, G. Senay, and M. McCartney, "Flood Pulsing in the Sudd Wetland: Analysis of Seasonal Variations in Inundation and Evaporation in South Sudan" (*Earth Interact.* 16:1-19, 2012).
9. R. Johnston, "Availability of Water for Agriculture in the Nile Basin" (*In* S. Awulachew, V. Smakhtin, D. Molden, and D. Peden, *The Nile River Basin: Water, Agriculture, Governance and Livelihoods*, eds., Routledge, Abingdon, Oxford, 2012).
10. Andrew Kramer, "Past Errors to Blame for Russia's Peat Fires" (*New York Times*, Aug. 12, 2010).

17: IT TAKES AN ARMY TO SAVE THE SUDD

1. Daniel Kendie, "Egypt and the Hydro-politics of the Blue Nile River" (http://chora.virtualave.net/kendie-nile.htm), 1999.
2. *Egypt News*, March 2008 (http://news.egypt.com) and *1st Edition* program on Dream Satellite Channel.
3. Jeffrey Fleishman and Kate Linthicum, "On the Nile, Egypt Cuts Water Use" (*Los Angeles Times*, Sept. 12, 2010).
4. *The Nile River Basin: Water, Agriculture, Governance, and Livelihoods* (S. Awulachew, V. Smakhtin, D. Molden, and D. Peden, eds. Routledge, Abingdon, Oxford, 2012).
5. M. El-Hawary, "Egypt Forges Strategy to Face Anticipated Water Shortages" (http://www.almasryalyoum.com), 2010.
6. J. K. Lupai, "Jonglei Project in Southern Sudan: For Whose Benefit Is It?" ("The Jonglei Canal Project in Southern Sudan: Why the Hurry and for Whose Benefit Is It?" *Sudan Tribune*, a non-profit website based in Paris, http://tinyurl.com/mja4foa), 2007.
7. Salah Hassanein, "The River Nile, Life of Egypt" (Columbia University Lib. Internet Resources Virtual Library, Middle East, http://www.columbia.edu/cu/lweb/indiv/mideast/cuvlm/water.html), 2010.

8. "Egypt Protects Water Purification Stations along the Nile after Barge Leaks" (http://FoxNews.com, Sept. 2010).

18: BLOOD ROSES, PAPYRUS, AND THE NEW SCRAMBLE FOR AFRICA

1. M. Seal, "A Flowering Evil" (*Vanity Fair* http://www.vanityfair.com/politics/features/2006/08/joanroot200608), 2006.
2. J. Goldson, "A Three Phase Environmental Impact Study of Recent Developments around Lake Naivasha" (Lake Naivasha Riparian Owners' Association, Naivasha, 1993).
3. CIEN—Kenya Newspage, Ministry of Environment and Mineral Resources, 2010.
4. G. Omondi, "State Drops L. Naivasha Water Use Control Plan" ("Business Daily," *Daily Nation*, Nairobi, 2010).
5. C. Hayes, *Oserian: Place of Peace* (Rima Books, Nairobi, Kenya, 1997).
6. C. Woodward, "This Kenyan Boomtown Is Getting Rich On Roses" (*The Telegraph*—Business Insider website, http://www.businessinsider.com/visit-to-a-kenyan-rose-farm-2013-2), 2013.
7. E. Morrison and D. Harper, "Ecohydrological Principles to Underpin the Restoration of Cyperus Papyrus at Lake Naivasha, Kenya" (*J. of Ecohydrology and Hydrobiology* 9:83-97, 2009).

20: AN UNWANTED LEGACY

1. I. Seyam, A. Hoekstra, G. Ngabirano, and H. Savenije, "The Value of Freshwater Wetlands in the Zambezi Basin" (*Conf. of Globalization and Water Res. Mgt: The Changing Value of Water*, AWRA/IWLRI Univ. Dundee, 2001).
2. C. von der Heyden and M. New, "Differentiating Dilution and Retention Processes in Mine Effluent Remediation within a Natural Wetland on the Zambian Copperbelt" (*Applied Geochem.* 20:1241–1257), 2005.
3. N. Sibanda, "Efforts to Halt the Strangulation of Kafue" (http://tinyurl.com/kb7qy87), 2007.
4. C. von der Heyden and M. New, "Differentiating Dilution."
5. O. Sracek, J. Filip, M. Mihaljevic, B. Kribek, V. Majer, and F. Veselovský, "Attenuation of Dissolved Metals in Neutral Mine Drainage in the Zambian Copperbelt" (*Environmental Monitoring and Assessment*, http://www.Springerlink.com/Index/C28mp28p73xnk868.Pdf), 2010.
6. The factory in Uganda was referred to in Lewis, 1989 (p.15) where he refers to a factory in Kampala and another started near Lake Kyoga after the Second World War. The factory in Rwanda (producing a softboard called "Papytex") was still functioning when visited by the author in the 1980s.
7. *TradeMark SA Newsletter* (http://www.trademarksa.net/node/1940), 2010.
8. "Renamo Denounces Mozal" (http://allafrica.com/stories/201011040097.html), 2010.

21: THE OKAVANGO, MIRACLE OF THE KALAHARI

1. Rutledge Etheridge Jr. comment on Celtic poultry rituals (http://tinyurl.com/34kg39u)

2. S. Kasere, "Campfire: Zimbabwe's Tradition of Caring" (*Voices From Africa*, A UN Discussion Website, http://www.un-ngls.org/orf/documents/publications.en/voices.africa/number6/vfa6.12.htm), 2013.

23: THE RIFT VALLEY, A SAFE HAVEN FOR BIRDS

1. W. Van Den Bossche, P. Berthold, M. Kaatz, E. Nowak, and U. Querner, "E. European White Stork Populations" (Germ. Fed. Agency for Nat. Conserv. Bfn-Skripten 66, http://www.BFN.De/fileadmin/mdb/Documents/Storch.pdf), 2002.

2. Information from the Flyways Project website, a project of Music for the Earth (http://flywaysmusic.org/).

24: THE EGYPTIAN SOLUTION

1. "Saving the Nile Delta" (Video, May 2011 UNDP and Gov. Egypt, http://tinyurl.com/mfhgc7n)

2. D. Raymer, "Constructed Wetlands in Kenya" (http://tinyurl.com/cp4osyy), 2009.

25: 2050, THE NEW DELTA

1. A. Khan, "Plastic from Plants? Scientists May Have Found a Way" (*Los Angeles Times*, February 17, 2012).

26: CONCLUSION

1. "Florida State of the Environment—Wetlands: A Guide to Living with Florida's Wetlands" (http://www.dep.state.fl.us/water/wetlands/docs/erp/fsewet.pdf), 2013.

INDEX